MW00872880

EUROPEAN
HISTORY
Foretold

A fascinating account proving God's hand in history. Fulfilled Bible prophecies from the first century until today.

Harold Hemenway

PRESS

Copyright © 2007 by Harold Hemenway

European History Foretold
by Harold Hemenway

Printed in the United States of America

ISBN 978-1-60266-796-9

All rights reserved solely by the author. The author guarantees all
contents are original and do not infringe upon the legal rights of any
other person or work. No part of this book may be reproduced in
any form without the permission of the author. The views expressed
in this book are not necessarily those of the publisher.

Unless otherwise indicated, Bible quotations are taken from the
King James Version of the Bible. Copyright © 1967 by Oxford
University Press, Inc.

www.xulonpress.com

*The reader of this booklet should not construe what is written to
be specific advice or a course of action to be followed with regard
to any needs, problems or goals. The author is not a prophet and
disclaims responsibilitiy for any adverse effects resulting directly
or indirectly from the material presented, suggested procedures,
undetected errors or reader misunderstanding.

Table Of Contents

1

Introduction
Chapter 1

This is "The Revelation of Jesus Christ, which God gave unto him, to shew unto his servants things which must shortly come to pass; and he sent and signified it by his angel unto his servant John: Who bore record of the word of God, and of the testimony of Jesus Christ, and of all things that he saw. Blessed is he that readeth, and they that hear the words of this prophecy, and keep those things which are written therein: for the time is at hand" (Rev. 1:1-3).

John received visions from Jesus Christ in 96 A.D. while exiled on the Isle of Patmos by Emperor Domitian for preaching the Gospel. Irenaeus, who was the disciple of Polycarp, who had been the disciple of John, says in Heresies (180 A.D.) that it was written by John in 96 A.D. in Domitian's reign, and so does Eusebius's Ecclesiastical History. Eusebius also mentions that after John's banishment at Patmos had ended, John went and lived at Ephesus, where he was buried (about 100 A.D.).

Daniel's 70th Week ended in 34 A.D. with Stephen's martyrdom and the outpouring of the Holy Spirit upon the household of Cornelius. For 40 years of testing, the Jews resisted the Gospel (Ps. 95:10). In 66 A.D. they rebelled against Imperial Rome. Jerusalem (including Christians) was surrounded by the legions of Cestius Gallus. The "Abomination of DESOLATION" (Matt. 24:15) is defined in Luke 21:20 as "Jerusalem compassed with ARMIES" that cause "DESOLATION." Then the Roman commander withdrew "for no apparent reason" (Wars 2:19). Jewish Zealots pursued and attacked the army ferociously. This gave a brief opportunity for Christians to obey Messiah's advice and "depart out of the midst of" Jerusalem and "flee to the mountains" and Pella (Luke 21:20-22). Returning Zealots didn't tolerate "deserters." In 69 A.D. Vespacian became emperor and his son Titus returned with his Roman Legions, laid siege to Jerusalem, and Herod's Temple was burned (70 A.D.) where Jews made their last stand. One million Jews perished by famine and sword. Ninety thousand were sold into slavery. Roman legions carried their standards, the EAGLE and the SERPENT (both unclean), into the Temple and sacrificed before them in the traditional Roman manner -- an ox, a sheep and a PIG (unclean) -- hence "ABOMINATION of Desolation" in another sense. Just as Jews of their prince Messiah destroyed his fleshly temple (John 2:19), so the Roman army of Titus the prince leveled the stone temple to the ground because the gold had melted between the cracks. Thus "There shall not be ... one stone (left) upon another" (Matt. 24:2) by this army "flood" (Dan. 9:26).

Meanwhile, Simon Magus (the Sorcerer) of Samaria feigned conversion to Christianity (Acts 8:9-23) and set up a Babylonian Mystery cult. When Justin Martyr wrote his Apology (152 A.D.) the sect of the Simonians appears to have been formidable, for he speaks four times of their founder Simon ... and tells that he CAME TO ROME in the days of Claudius Caesar (45 A.D.) and made such an impression by his magical powers that he was honoured as a god, a statue being erected to him on the Tiber between the two bridges bearing the inscription, "Simoni deo Sancto," Simon the holy god" (Dict. of Christian Biog. 4:682). Hence the Papal claim to being the successor of a "Simon Peter" in Rome when the apostle Peter was never in Rome (Rom. 15:20). But how did Simon Magus acquire the name "Peter"? Genesis 40:5-18 uses the Hebrew words PITHRON and PATHAR which are translated into the English "INTERPRET." Deuteronomy 23:4 mentions Balaam the soothsayer of PETHOR in Babylonia -- a sacred high place of INTERPRETATION. Babylonian priests claimed the sole power to INTERPRET the pagan mysteries. "Ancient history reveals that the pagan deities worshipped by the Babylonians and the Greeks were known as PETERS, not only the gods but the Hierophantal (special gods) in most temples and those priests in particular who were occupied in the celebration of mysteries were styled PATRES" (Bryant's Ancient Mythology 1:354). The truth is that Linus (2 Tim. 4:21) was the first bishop of Rome. He was the son of Caractacus, the British king who was defeated by Claudius in 51 A.D. and taken in chains to Rome with his family. Paul was under house arrest in Rome at the same time and wrote his epistle to Timothy. Paul at this time obeyed Christ's command to "Bear my name before ... kings" (Acts 9:15).

The Book of Revelation was written in code because the pagan Roman Empire ruled Palestine in 96 A.D. and persecuted Christians who taught that Rome would eventually fall. Babylonian Mystery cults also were a threat. By taking Old Testament examples and figuratively applying them to Rome and her cult, Christians understood while Romans remained ignorant. These prophecies "must SHORTLY come to pass" meaning the "HISTORICIST" rather than "futurist" school of prophecy is the primary fulfillment of this pre-written history. John had been promised that he would "tarry till I (Christ) come" (John 21:22) and these visions fulfilled that promise. God's "angel" is Jesus Christ (cp. Gen. 48:16; Ex. 23:20-22, etc.). The word "SIGNIFIED" (semaino) means "to show by signs and symbols." John 21:19 says, "this spake he SIGNIFYING (semaino) by what death he should glorify God." Our Lord did not say to Peter literally, "You will be crucified." Instead he used phrases which would not be intelligible till the fulfillment took place. In the same way, Revelation must be de-coded by using European history and the Bible itself.

"John to the seven churches which are in Asia: Grace be unto you, and peace, from him which is, and which was, and which is to come; and from the seven Spirits which are before his throne; And from Jesus Christ, who is the faithful witness, and the first begotten of the dead, and the prince of the kings of the earth. Unto him that loved us, and washed us from our sins in his own blood, And hath made us kings and priests unto God and his Father; to him be glory and dominion for ever and ever. Amen. Behold, he cometh with clouds; and every eye shall see him, and they also which pierced him: and all kindreds of the earth shall wail because of him. Even so, Amen. I am Alpha and Omega, the beginning and the ending, saith the Lord, which is, and which was, and which is to come, the Almighty" (Rev. 1:4-8).

Our Lord instructed John to send it to seven nearby churches in Asia Minor. Why ASIA Minor? Because "the (Israelite) sojourners of the dispersion (were) scattered throughout Pontus, Galatia, Cappadocia, ASIA, and Bithynia" (1 Pet. 1:1; see also 2 Esdras 13:39-42 & Josephus 11:5:2). They are his Israelite "servants" (1:1). "Thou art my servant, O Israel" (Isa. 49:3). Since the majority of Christians have sprung from the Anglo-Saxon Celtic race, the first reigning election of "kings and priests" will consist largley of Israelite stock. In fact the Greek "ecclesia" (called out ones) comes from the Hebrew "cahal" (called out) found in Genesis 28:3 referring to Abraham's descendants -- "an assembly ("cahal") of people." "Jew and Greek" in the New Testament (Acts 18:4; 19:10; 20:21; 1 Cor. 1:22) corresponds to "house of Judah and house of Israel" in the Old Testament. Greeks were not Gentiles (Acts 14:1-2). Paul says the Ephesians were "aliens" (alienated or separated) "from ... Israel" (Eph. 2:13) meaning they must at one time have belonged to it. The phrase "Him which is, and which was, and which is to come" found in 1:4,8 is a Greek paraphrase of the Hebrew "Yahweh." The King James Version "for ever and ever" of verse 6 is, in Greek, "for the ages of the ages, which refers to the Millenium and post-Millenial ages of the Kingdom of God on the earth. God promised to make physical Israel "kings and priests" in the Promised Land which was a type of the Millenium (Ex. 19:5-6; 1 Pet. 2:9-10). Now these same physical Israelites dwelling in Asia Minor (1 Pet. 1:1-2; 2:9-10; 2 Pet. 3:15; Eph. 2:12-14; Rom. 11:5), through the remission of sins, are made "kings and priests" in the Millenium and after -- better promises.

What do CLOUDS mean? Just as a CLOUD received him as he left the earth (Acts 1:9), so also "He cometh with CLOUDS" referring to a "CLOUD of (resurrected human) WITNESSES" (Heb. 12:1) -- " ten thousands of his SAINTS" (Jude 14-15) as well as a CLOUD (Matt. 24:30) of "all the holy ANGELS with him" (Matt. 25:31). Zechariah 12:10-11 mentions that the Jews who pierced their Messiah will now mourn at his coming because of their previous rejection of him. Jesus Christ as "alpha" created man in his physical image, but man lost paradise in Genesis. Jesus Christ as "omega" will finish that creation in his character-image and restore paradise in Revelation using Israelites.

"I John, who also am your brother, and companion in tribulation, and in the kingdom and patience of Jesus Christ, was in the isle that is called Patmos, for the word of God, and for the testimony of Jesus Christ. I was in the Spirit on the Lord's day, and heard behind me a great voice, as of a trumpet, Saying, I am Alpha and Omega, the first and the last: and, What thou seest, write in a book, and send it unto the seven churches which are in Asia; unto Ephesus, and unto Smyrna, and unto Pergamos, and unto Thyatira, and unto Sardis, and unto Philadelphia, and unto Laodicea. And I turned to see the voice that spake with me. And being turned, I saw seven golden candlesticks; And in the midst of the seven candlesticks one like unto the Son of man, clothed with a garment down to the foot, and girt about the paps with a golden girdle. His head and his hairs were white like wool, as white as snow; and his eyes were as a flame of fire; And his feet like unto fine brass, as if they burned in a furnace; and his voice as the sound of many waters. And he had in his right hand seven stars: and out of his mouth went a sharp two-edged sword: and his countenance was as the sun shineth in his strength. And when I saw him, I fell at his feet as dead. And he laid his right hand upon me, saying unto me, Fear not; I am the first and the last:

I am he that liveth, and was dead; and, behold, I am alive for evermore, Amen; and have the keys of hell and of death" (Rev. 1:9-18).

The "Lord's Day" is the "Day of the Lord" (Acts 17:31; 1 Cor. 5:5; 2 Cor. 1:14; 1 Th. 5:2; Phil. 1:6). In John's first vision, he is apparently looking east while standing in the Court of the Priests. He turns around to see the HIGH PRIEST re-fueling the seven-branched Menorah CANDLESTICK with OLIVE OIL to bring LIGHT to the Temple's HOLY PLACE. This typified the MESSIAH re-fueling the SEVEN CHURCH eras in history by the gift of the HOLY SPIRIT so they can explain the BIBLE to the House of ISRAEL (see Zech. 4:1-6). There would be seven stages in the history of Christianity. The "sharp two-edged SWORD" represents the "WORD of GOD" (Heb. 4:12; Eph. 6:17). CHRIST is the promised HIGH "PRIEST for ever after the order of Melchizedec" (Heb. 5:6) of which the human High Priests were mere types. High Priests wore a "girdle" and a "robe" (Ex. 28:4 & 29:5) paralleling those described here. "EYES as a FLAME of FIRE" (Rev. 1:14; 2:18) is interpreted by Christ himself as one who "SEARCHETH the MINDS and HEARTS" (Rev. 2:23). Penetrating sight. "He is a discerner of the thoughts and intents of the heart" (Heb. 4:12-13). "The eyes of the Lord are in every place, beholding the evil and the good" (Pr. 15:3) just as the rider in chapter nineteen has these same eyes and the same sword. Having "neither BEGINNING of DAYS nor END of LIFE" (Heb. 7:3), he is the ALPHA and OMEGA. "Declaring the END (of history) from the BEGINNING (of time)" (Isa. 46:10) he is the ALPHA and OMEGA. His credentials are that he is the FIRST immortal man born from the dead, the "alpha," and his appearance proves it. Also when all men are made immortal like him, "THEN shall the Son also himself be subject unto Him that put all things under him, that God may be all in all" (1 Cor. 15:28). Therefore He is the "omega" or LAST. He can bring forth "all that are in their graves" (John 5:28). In 1 Corinthians 15:26 we are told "the last enemy that shall be destroyed is death." "Hades, I will be thy destruction" (Hos. 13:14). Jesus is "the resurrection and the life."

"Write the things which thou hast seen, and the things which are, and the things which shall be hereafter; The mystery of the seven stars which thou sawest in my right hand, and the seven golden candlesticks. The seven stars are the angels of the seven churches: and the seven candlesticks which thou sawest are the seven churches" (Rev. 1:19-20).

Who are the STARS? The "STARS" or "angels" are messengers of the seven churches -- the LEADING human TEACHER of each church. The Torah READER (Luke 4:16; Acts 13:15,27; 15:21) or WRITER or MESSENGER (Haggai 1:13) of the Synagogue was known as the "angel" of the Synagogue. The twelve STARS in Joseph's dream represented the LEADERS of the twelve tribes of Israel (Gen. 37:9-10). In Balaam's prophecy, our LORD is a "STAR out of Jacob" (Num. 24:17). The little horn "cast down ... the STARS to the ground, and stamped upon them ... the MIGHTY and the HOLY PEOPLE" -- the Jews and Christians (Dan. 8:9-24). "They that turn many to RIGHTEOUSNESS" are like "the STARS" (Dan.12:3). Our Lord says, "I am ... the bright and morning STAR" (Rev. 22:16). "STARS" therefore represent RIGHTEOUS RULERS.

Church Eras (Ephesus to Thyatira)
Chapter 2
The Ephesus Era Was Called Nazarene
(31-150 A.D.)

Matthew 16:18 says, "Thou art Peter (Gr. "Petros" masculine meaning"stone"), and upon this rock (Gr. "Petra" feminine meaning "massive rock") I will build my church, and the gates of hades ("the grave") shall not prevail against it." And Paul says "the Rock was Christ" (1 Cor.10:4) -- not Peter. Yes, "For other foundation no one can lay but that which has been laid which is Jesus Christ" (1 Cor.3:11). The true church, built on Christ's teaching, would continue to exist through every century down to our day today.

In Judaea, Jewish Christians met together with Jews in synagogues but by about 85 A.D., to make sure of their exclusion, a formal anathema was incorporated in the synagogue liturgy: 'May the Nazarenes and the heretics be suddenly destroyed and removed from the Book of Life.' (p. 21, Chadwick's Early Church). This shows us that Christians actually still considered themselves JEWS long after Christ's death (cp. Rom.2:29).

"Unto the angel of the church of Ephesus write; These things saith he that holdeth the seven stars in his right hand, who walketh in the midst of the seven golden candlesticks; I know thy works, and thy labour, and thy patience, and how thou canst not bear them which are evil: and thou hast tried them which say they are apostles, and are not, and hast found them liars: And hast borne, and hast patience, and for my name's sake hast laboured, and hast not fainted. Nevertheless I have somewhat against thee, because thou hast left thy first love. Remember therefore from whence thou art fallen, and repent, and do the first works; or else I will come unto thee quickly, and will remove thy candlestick out of his place, except thou repent" (Rev. 2:1-5).

Paul visited Ephesus in 56 A.D. and baptised them (Acts 19:1-6). Many Ephesians burned their books on witchcraft because of Paul's witness there (Acts 19:18-20). Just as the city of Ephesus was the first of seven cities on a mail route, so also the Ephesus Era (lit. "Desirable") was the first of seven chronological eras of church history portrayed by the seven-branched Menorah. The first believers were called "Christians" (Acts 11:26) or "Nazarenes" (24:5) who fled from Jerusalem to Pella (Wars 6:5:3) in 69 A.D. They were called "Nazarenes" because Nazareth was where Jesus grew up (Matt.2:23).

"Christianity offered itself to the world, armed with the strength of the MOSAIC LAW ... The divine authority of Moses and the prophets was admitted, and even established, as the FIRMEST BASIS of Christianity.... The history of the church of Jerusalem affords a lively proof ... of the deep impression which the JEWISH RELIGION had made on the minds of its sectaries. The first fifteen bishops of Jerusalem were all circumcised JEWS; and the congregation over which they presided UNITED the LAW OF MOSES with the doctrine of Christ.... The Jewish converts ... who had laid the foundations of the church, soon found themselves overwhelmed by the increasing multitudes that from all the various religions of polytheism enlisted under the banner of Christ: and the Gentiles ... rejected the intolerable weight of Mosaic ceremonies ... The Nazarenes ... elected Marcus for their bishop, a prelate of the race of the gentiles ... At his persuasion the most considerable part of the congregation RENOUNCED the MOSAIC LAW, in the practice of which they had persevered above a century" (Gibbon's Decline And Fall Of The Roman Empire,15:181-182).

"Before the second century was half gone ... the 'Mystery of Iniquity,' had so largely spread over the east and the west ... that a large part of the Christian OBSERVANCES and INSTITUTIONS, even in this century, had the aspect of the PAGAN MYSTERIES" (Mosheim, Ecclesiastical History, Cent.2, Part 2, Ch.4, Paragraph 1).

What was their "first LOVE" (Rev.2:4)? "This is the LOVE of God, that we KEEP his COMMANDMENTS: and his commandments are not grievous" (1 John 5:3). "If ye LOVE me, KEEP my COMMANDMENTS" (John 14:15). "This is LOVE, that we WALK AFTER (in accordance with) his COMMANDMENTS" (2 John 6). "He that hath my COMMANDMENTS, and KEEPETH them, he it is that LOVETH me" (John 14:21). The whole value of affection and friendship is in its practical manifestations.

"But this thou hast, that thou hatest the deeds of the Nicolaitans, which I also hate. He that hath an ear, let him hear what the Spirit saith unto the churches; To him that overcometh will I give to eat of the tree of life, which is in the midst of the paradise of God" (Rev. 2:6-7).

What were "the DEEDS of the NICOLAITANS" (Rev.2:6)? "Nicolaitans" comes from Greek: nikao - subdue and laos - people. They were followers of Nicolas a proselyte of Antioch" (Acts 6:5) who taught that DEEDS of the FLESH do not affect the purity of the soul, and consequently have no bearing on salvation (Hippolytus Refut. 7:24; Irenaeus Against Heresies 1:26:3).

From Eusebius' Life of Constantine, book 3:66, we read, "To speak of your criminality as it deserves demands more time and leisure than I can give.... Why not at once strike, as it were, at the root of so great a mischief by a public manifestation of displeasure? Forasmuch, then, as it is no longer possible to bear with your pernicious errors (of SABBATH-KEEPING -- author), we give warning by this present statute that none of you henceforth presume to assemble yourselves together. We have directed, accordingly, that you be DEPRIVED of all the HOUSES in which you are accustomed to hold your ASSEMBLIES; and forbid the holding of your superstitious and senseless MEETINGS (attending church on SATURDAY-- author), not in public merely, but in any private HOUSE or PLACE whatsoever.... We have commanded... that you be positively DEPRIVED of every GATHERING POINT for your superstitious MEETINGS, I mean all the HOUSES of prayer.... that any other PLACES be CONFISCATED to the public service, and NO FACILITY whatever be left for any future gathering (on God's SABBATH) in order that from this day forward none of your unlawful ASSEMBLIES may presume to appear in any public or private PLACE." With this statute at the Council of Nicaea (325 A.D.) God "REMOVED their lampstand" (Rev.2:5). An alternate interpretation is that Hadrian's edict in 135 A.D. SCATTERED the old church of Jerusalem. In type the actual City of Ephesus has SHIFTED several miles from the place it once occupied also, owing to the sea having receded.

Thus began the 1260-year tribulation by Catholicism (Rev.12:6,14). In 1585 Sir Walter Raleigh explored Roanoke Virginia as a favorable location for an English colony of Protestants. In 1586-1587 (1260 + 325 = 1585), Mary Queen of Scots was convicted and executed for conspiracy. In 1588 the Catholic Spanish Armada was wrecked by a great storm at sea. Thus ended the 1260 years in the wilderness.

But meanwhile Athanasius, A.D. 340 said, "We assemble on SATURDAY, not that we are infected with Judaism, but only to worship Christ, the Lord of the SABBATH." Yes, "The primitive Christians DID KEEP the SABBATH of the Jews; ... therefore the Christians, for a long time together, DID KEEP their conventions upon the SABBATH, in which some portions of the law were read; and this CONTINUED TILL the time of the LAODICEAN COUNCIL (364 A.D.)." (The Whole Work Of Jeremy Taylor, vol.9, p.416). The 29th canon of the Laodicean Council held in 364 A.D. said, "Christians must not JUDAIZE by resting on the SABBATH, but must work on that day, rather, honouring the Lord's Day; and, if they can, resting then as Christians. But if any shall be found to be JUDAIZERS, let them be anathema from Christ." (Nicene and Post-Nicene Fathers, vol.14, p.148) The "little horn" Papacy "will think to change the times and the laws" (Dan. 7:25), the time for the Sabbath law. (364 + 1260 = 1624) In 1623 A.D. the Dutch West India Company sent a vessel to America with 30 families of Walloons (Protestant refugees from S. Netherlands) to the mouth of the Hudson River so they could settle on Manhattan Island. Exactly 1260 years later in 1624 A.D. Albany was established by the Protestant Dutch as a fur-trading settlement. The Pilgrim Separatists also settled New Hampshire and Maine in 1623-24 A.D.

A bishop of Constantinople named Nestorious protested against the virgin Mary being called "Mother of God." So the Emperor called the Council of Ephesus in 431 A.D. to settle this dispute. Nestorious was banished and deposed. The phrase "Mother of God" was formally accepted in 431 A.D. at Ephesus. The "Holy Hill" towering above Ephesus had been dedicated to the "Mother of God" more than a thousand years before Christ. Semiramis taught that when Nimrod her husband died, he was reincarnated as her son, so that she was his wife and mother. Statues of her with an infant in her arms were very popular in Babylon. She was known by different names in different lands. Astarte, Beltis, Cybele, Aphrodite. But in Ephesus she was called Diana -- where the ruins of the Temple of Diana can still be seen.

What does "He that hath an ear, let him HEAR" mean? Isaiah 50:4-5 says, "He waketh mine ear to HEAR as the learned. The Lord God hath OPENED (Lit. "digged") mine ear, and I was not rebellious." A servant for life had his ear "digged" or pierced (Ex. 21:6) and therefore OBEYED.

The Smyrna Era Was Called Ebionite
(31-313 A.D.)

"And unto the angel of the church in Smyrna write; These things saith the first and the last, which was dead, and is alive; I know thy works, and tribulation, and poverty, (but thou art rich) and I know the blasphemy of them which say they are Jews, and are not, but are the synagogue of Satan" (Rev. 2:8-9).

The name "Smyrna" means "MYRRH." MYRRH was used to embalm DEAD bodies. For instance, Nicodemus brought "MYRRH and aloes" to the body of Jesus (John 19:39-40). Therefore Smyrna was a church of MARTYRS.

Smyrna (lit. "Myrrh" or "Incense" or "Bitter") Christians were called "Ebionites (Hebrew ... "POOR men") a name given to the ultra-Jewish party in the early Christian Church.... they ... rejected Paul as an apostate from the MOSAIC LAW, to the customs and ordinances of which, including circumcision, they steadily ADHERED. They kept both the Jewish SABBATH and the Christian Lord's day.... Ebionites (were) ... Jewish Christians of Syria.... His (Jesus') coming did not annul the LAW.... Baptism must be repeated as a means of purification from sin, and proof against disease ... (they were) Essene Ebionites" (p.842, vol.8, Encyc. Brit. 11th ed.).

What is the "Synagogue of SATAN"? It may refer to false Christians as in Revelation 3:9, but here it more likely refers to "JEWS." Many IDUMIANS were forced to become "JEWS" (Ant. 13:9:1) by Hyrcanus in 125 B.C. "EDOM is in modern Jewry" (Jewish Encyc. 5:41). Josephus indicates that only the Essenes were hereditary Jews while the Pharisees and Saduccees were NOT JEWS by birth (Wars 2:8:2). Jesus said to these Jews, "Ye are of your father the DEVIL" (John 8:44) which agrees with Revelation 2:9 where Jesus says, "I know the blasphemy of them who say they are Jews, and are not, but are the synagogue of SATAN." The Pharisees said to Jesus, "We are Abraham's seed, and were never in bondage to any man" (John 8:33). Yet Israel had a long history of bondage in Egypt, Assyria and Babylon. Therefore the Pharisees must have been the other branch of Abraham's seed in Palestine -- EDOMITES.

Here is a description of the martyrdom of Polycarp, bishop of Smyrna: "the Pro-Consul, respecting his dignity and his advanced age -- for he was more than eighty -- and being desirous to save him, urged him, saying, 'Swear, and I will release thee.' 'Reproach Christ.' Polycarp answered, 'Eighty years have I served Him, and He has never wronged me. How can I blaspheme my King who has saved me?' The Pro-Consul, judging his efforts to be unavailing, sent a herald to proclaim: Polycarp hath professed himself a Christian. At that hated name the multitude, both of the Gentiles and the JEWS, unanimously shouted that he should be burned alive. The people immediately gathered fuel from the workshops and the baths, in which employment the JEWS distinguished themselves with their usual malice" (Eusebius Eccl.Hist. ch. 15, p.147).

Gibbon also tells us that the JEWS tried to instigate the Romans into persecuting Christians (Decline and Fall, ch.16).

"Fear none of those things which thou shalt suffer: behold, the devil shall cast some of you into prison, that ye may be tried; and ye shall have tribulation ten days: be thou faithful unto death, and I will give thee a crown of life. He that hath an ear, let him hear what the Spirit saith unto the churches; He that overcometh shall not be hurt of the second death" (Rev. 2:10-11).

How could "the Devil" "cast some of you into prison" (Rev. 2:10) when only the officers of the Roman Empire could throw Christians into prison? Because the Roman Empire is the Devil manifest (Rev. 12:9).

What are the "ten days" of tribulation (2:10)? From 303 to 313 A.D. (Eusebius E.H. 8:15-16), after Diocletan returned victorious from the Persian wars, he persecuted Christians. Hundreds of thousands of Christians died or were banished. On January 13, 313 the "Edict of Toleration" was issued by Licinius. "In 313 A.D. Constantine's Edict of Milan restored confiscated Christian property and gave equal rights for all religions. In that same year Constantine exempted Christian clergy from civil and military service and their property from taxation" (SDABC). Besides lasting ten years, this was also the tenth persecution suffered under ten different emperors' edicts: Nero (64 A.D.), Domitian (95 A.D.), Trajan (107 A.D.), Hadrian (127 A.D.), Marcus Aurelius (165 A.D.), Septimius Severus (202 A.D.), Maximus (235 A.D.), Decius (249 A.D.), Valerianus (257 A.D.) and Diocletian (303 A.D.).

"Our faith" is what "overcometh the world" (1 John 5:4). How do we get that faith? "Faith cometh by hearing, and hearing by the word of God" (Rom. 10:17). Bible study therefore gives us faith to overcome the world. Being fully convinced of the truth of the Bible gives a Christian power to "deny ungodliness and worldly lusts, and to live soberly, righteously, and godly in the present world" (Tit. 2:12).

The Pergamos Era Was Called Paulician
(313 - 1100 A.D.)

"And to the angel of the church in Pergamos write; These things saith he which hath the sharp sword with two edges; I know thy works, and where thou dwellest, even where Satan's seat is: and thou holdest fast my name, and hast not denied my faith, even in those days wherein Antipas was my faithful martyr, who was slain among you, where Satan dwelleth" (Rev. 2:12-13).

By 337 A.D., about half the inhabitants of the Roman Empire professed to be Christians -- many doing so just to keep their positions because Christianity was now the State Religion. Christians were no longer thrown to wild beasts in the Colosseum, or burned alive in the Circus of Nero, no longer commanded to offer incense to the gods or worship a serpent. Pergamos means "Married to Power." The high priest of the old Babylonish religion was the original Pontifex Maximus. The king of ancient Babylon had been both king and High Priest, or Pontifex Maximus. When Belshazzar was slain (Dan. 5:30), and the Chaldeans were defeated by Darius the Mede, the Babylonian priests were expelled from Babylon. Some fled to Tibet where the ancient Babylonian religion is preserved intact. But the most important moved to, and settled their Central College in, Pergamos -- "Satan's seat" (Rev. 2:13) where the worship of Aesculapius the serpent child of the "incarnate sun" continued. When one of the kings of Pergamos, named Attalus III, died in 133 B.C., he bequeathed all his dominions to the Roman Empire. Thus Julius Caesar took the title of Pontifex Maximus (Supreme Pontiff) -- the living representative of the Babylonian Sun god -- descendant of the gods. From henceforth he was divine. The Emperor Gratian was the first "Christian" emperor to refuse the insignia of Pontifex Maximus. It was incongruous, he thought, that a Christian emperor should bear a pagan title. But this title he discarded was soon taken up and conferred on Damasus, the Pope of Rome. Notice that Satan's throne has three transfers. Babylon to Pergamos; Pergamos to Pagan Rome; Pagan Rome to Papal Rome, then Christ will return and destroy it. David's throne, the "throne of the Eternal" (1 Chr. 29:23), also has three transfers (Ez. 21:27). Jerusalem to Ireland; Ireland to Scotland; Scotland to England or Great Britain, then Christ will return to sit upon it.

"Antipas" is a Greek contraction for "Antipater" (against Pope) who was a pastor of Pergamos who was martyred by being placed in a burning brazen bull.

These "Paulicians" (also called "Thonraki," "Bogomils," or "Albigenses") believed that "One unleavened loaf and wine are to be offered in the eucharistic sacrifice.... (They) maintained a steady war against images, Mariolatry, and much else that the degenerate Greek world had adopted from Paganism ... We also know ... that the Pauliani, who were the same people who at an earlier date, were Quartodecumans, and kept Easter (sic) in the primitive manner at the JEWISH date. Ananias (early seventh century) (of Shirak says) ... 'But the Pauliani also keep the feast of the Pascha on the same day (as the JEWS), and whatever be the day of the full moon, they call it Kuriake, as the JEWS call it SABBATH, even though it be not a (weekly) SABBATH.'... They are accused by their Armenian opponents of setting at naught all the feasts and fasts of the Church, especially Sunday. They kept the Festival of a Birth of Christ ... 'The same St. Gregory (of Narek),' continues Sahak, 'appointed SABBATHS, and fasts, and abstinences in fulfillment of vows.' ... the Paulicians observed the SABBATH and not the Sunday ... for they were probably the remnant of an old JUDAEO-CHRISTIAN Church, which had spread up through Edessa into Siuniq and Albania.... The early Armenian Christians ... spoke of REST-HOUSES, SYNAGOGUES, of proseuchae, and of shrines ... but hardly at all of churches; and individuals, especially if they were elders, were prone ... to celebrate the Agape and Eucharist in their own houses ... as well as collect in them the firstfruits of the offerings. Sahak insists that these rites must be performed in church ... and the firstfruits are to be taken to the house of the head-priest ... We know that the Pauliani continued to keep the PASSOVER on the fourteenth of Nisan with the JEWS." (The Key of Truth trans. by Fred C. Conybeare pp.38,49,104,152,162). Polycarp followed John in keeping PASSOVER on the 14th (Eusebius E.H. 5:24). Polycrates followed Polycarp (Ante-Nicene Fathers 8:773-774) and now the Paulicians followed Polycrates.

"But I have a few things against thee, because thou hast there them that hold the doctrine of Balaam, who taught Balak to cast a stumblingblock before the children of Israel, to eat things sacrificed unto idols, and to commit fornication" (Rev. 2:14).

What was the "DOCTRINE of Balaam"? Balaam was the son of Beor (Num. 22:5). Beor was Edomite (Gen. 36:31-32; 1 Chr. 1:43). Balaam was willing to curse Israel (Num. 22:15-17; Deut. 23:4) "for REWARD" (Jude 11). Balaam was a soothsayer (Joshua 13:22) who had "an heart exercised with COVETOUS practices, which have forsaken the right way ... who loved the WAGES of UNRIGHTEOUSNESS" (2 Pet. 2:15). In other words, these Christians were willing to compromise to earn more money. Religious mixture with idols and racial mixture with the daughters of Moab (mingling the "holy seed" -- Ezra 9:1-2) -- "religious equality and racial integration." In ancient Pergamos (where Satan's seat was) there were Christians called Ophites who made an alliance with the serpent worshippers there. But more importantly, Christians have participated in false Papal Roman ("where Satan's seat is") religious customs such as Easter and X-mass (fornication -- Ps.106:28). "They joined themselves also unto Baal-peor, and ate the sacrifices of the dead" (Ps. 106:28) which is where the custom of eating ginger-bread men at X-mass time originated.

"So hast thou also them that hold the doctrine of the Nicolaitans, which thing I hate" (Rev. 2:15).

The Paulicians were "spread over Asia Minor and Armenia from the 5th century onwards.... (They were founded by Constantine of Mananali who) "based his teaching on the Gospels and the Epistles of Paul, repudiating other scriptures (Actually "it is more probable that they did not possess" other portions of the Bible -- Miller's Church History) ... (Paulicians) rejected the Eucharistic rites and doctrine of the Greeks.... we reckon the cross and the church and the priestly robes and the sacrifice of mass for nothing ... They assailed the cross, saying that ... we ought not to worship the tree, because it is a cursed instrument.... they smashed up crosses when they could.... (The Key of Truth) warns us that all the apostles constitute the Church universal and not Peter alone; and in the rite of election, i.e. of laying on of hands and reception of the Spirit ... The monkish garb was revealed by Satan ... The same hatred of monkery characterized the Thonraki and inspires the Key of Truth.... They called their meetings the Catholic Church, and the places they met in places of prayer ... The Thonraki equally denied the name church to buildings of wood or stone, and called themselves the Catholic Church (Universal Church).... baptismal water of the Church was mere 'bath-water,' i.e. they denied it the character of a reserved sacrament. But there is no evidence that they eschewed water baptism. The modern Thonraki baptize in rivers ... They PERMIT-TED EXTERNAL CONFORMITY with the dominant church, and held that Christ would forgive it ("doctrine of the Nicolaitans" -- comment mine). The same trait is reported of the Thonraki ... They rejected the orders of the Church, and had only two grades of clergy, namely associate itinerants ... (Acts xix. 29) and copyists ... (who) dressed like other people; the Thonraki also scorned priestly vestments" (Encyc. Brit. 20:959-961).

"Repent; or else I will come unto thee quickly, and will fight against them with the sword of my mouth" (Rev. 2:16).

Yes, martyrs "were counted by hundreds of thousands ... whose slayers invariably took their orders from the persecuting clergy of old and new Rome.... its members were deported by hundreds of thousands to Thrace. There they throve for centuries, and the spread of their tenets into Bohemia (Czechoslovakia), Poland, Germany, Italy, France" (p.104, Key of Truth).

In 679 A.D. Pope Agathon persecuted the Paulicians. Under Pope Sergius II (844-847), the Empress Theodora (wife of the Eastern Emperor Theophilus, 829-842), tried to exterminate the Paulicians. She restored image-worship which had been abolished many years, thereby "casting a stumbling-block" before the church and causing it to "commit fornication."

"He that hath an ear, let him hear what the Spirit saith unto the churches; To him that overcometh will I give to eat of the hidden manna, and will give him a white stone, and in the stone a new name written, which no man knoweth saving he that receiveth it" (Rev. 2:17).

The pot of "hidden MANNA" which Aaron put in the Ark of the Testimony (Ex. 16:33-34) in the Holy of Holies which nobody could enter but the High Priest symbolizes Jesus -- "the BREAD of LIFE" that came down from heaven (John 6:35) and is hidden in heaven. Also in ancient courts of Justice a prisoner's fate was determined by WHITE and black STONES. When there was a majority of WHITE STONES thrown into an urn, the prisoner was ACQUITTED. In 29 A.D. the Roman Senate decided to show its appreciation of one of the founders of the new Empire that the Emperor Augustus should have a new name, so he was given the name Augustus (meaning sacred or divine). All emperors after him were called Augusti. Jesus gave his leading apostles NEW NAMES (Peter -- Cephas; James and John -- Boanerges; Saul -- Paul) and will make them divine.

The Thyatira Era Was Called Waldensian
(1170-1517 A.D.)

"And unto the angel of the church in Thyatira write; These things saith the Son of God, who hath his eyes like unto a flame of fire, and his feet are like fine brass; I know thy works, and charity, and service, and faith, and thy patience, and thy works; and the last to be more than the first" (Rev. 2:18-19).

"Thyatira" literally means "to be ruled by a woman." The city of Thyatira was noted for its BRONZE smiths who crafted BRONZE helmets. Therefore Christ refers to his feet like BRONZE. Thyatira began with the Waldenses. At first the Waldensians were basically Roman Catholics who believed laymen had a right to preach without a license (Enchiridion Fontium Valdensium G. Gonnet (ed.), 1958, p.168).

Waldensians were not Sabbath-keepers in the beginning. But their "LAST works (were) better than the first" (Rev.2:19) -- possibly a pun on the first day and LAST DAY of the week. Also whole-hearted MARTYRDOM, the last act of a Christian, being better than half-hearted obedience, the first act of a Christian. The mistaken concept that they kept the Sabbath arose partly because sources in the original Latin described the Waldenses as keeping the "dies dominicalis" or Lord's day (Sunday) but the word for "Sunday" was translated "Sabbath" as early as the time of the Reformation. Also, Waldenses were called "Sabatati, Insabbatatos, Insabatati, Xabatenses and other variants. Writers have supposed this referred to the Sabbath. But instead, "They are called ... Xabatenses from Xabata (sandal)" (ibid., G. Gonnet, 1958, p.144) because Waldensian ministers wore a special kind of open sandal. The word for "shoe" in modern Romance languages is a cognate of this word: French "sabot," Spanish "zapato," Portugese "sapata," Italian "ciabatta," and Provincal "sabata."

"The name Waldenses was given to the members of an heretical Christian sect which arose in the south of France about 1170.... insisting on a high moral standard, and upholding the words of Scripture against the traditions of an overgrown and worldly church.... In France, at Embrum, Peter de Bruys founded a sect known as Petrobrusians, who denied infant baptism, the need of consecrated churches, transubstantiation, and masses for the dead. A follower of his, a monk, Henry, gave the name to another body known as Henricians, who centered in Tours (Encyc. Brit. 28:255-257). Another preacher at this time was called Arnold. They were charged by the Catholic Church with remaining faithful to the WHOLE LAW of God and of observing the SABBATH (Ecclesiastical History by Peter Allix pp. 168-169).

"It was at this time (1170) that a rich merchant of Lyons, Peter Waldo, sold his goods and gave them to the poor ...The Lombard sect (taught) ... that the Roman Church was the scarlet woman of the Apocalypse, whose precepts ought not to be obeyed, especially those appointing fast days.... Attacked in Dauphine and Piedmont at the same time, the Vaudois were hard pressed; but luckily their enemies were ENCIRCLED by a FOG when marching upon their chief refuge in the valley of the Angrogne, and were REPULSED with GREAT LOSS.... Their ministers ... were admitted to office, after receiving the communion, by the imposition of hands of all ministers present. They went out to preach two by two, and the junior was bound absolutely to obey the senior ... they prayed to the Virgin and saints, and admitted auricular confession, but they denied purgatory and the sacrifice of the mass, and did not observe fasts or festivals.... Oecolampadius gave them further instruction, especially emphasizing the wrongfulness of their OUTWARD SUBMISSION to the ordinances of the church: "God," he said, "is a jealous God, and does not permit his elect to put themselves under the yoke of Antichrist." (Encyc. Brit. 28:255-257)

According to The Ancient Churches of Peidmont by Peter Allix, page 154, we read that "He lays it down also as one of their (Waldensian) opinions; that the LAW OF MOSES is to be kept according to the letter, and that the keeping of the SABBATH, circumcision, and other legal observances, ought to take place." A report of an inquisition before whom were brought some Waldenses of Moravia in the middle of the fifteenth century declares that among the Waldenses "not a few indeed celebrate the SABBATH with the Jews" (Johann von Dollinger's Reports on the History of the Sects of the Middle Ages, Munich, 1890, 2nd part, p.661).

"Notwithstanding I have a few things against thee, because thou sufferest that woman Jezebel, which calleth herself a prophetess, to teach and to seduce my servants to commit fornication, and to eat things sacrificed unto idols" (Rev. 2:20).

But who is JEZEBEL? She is mentioned in 1 Kings 16-18. She taught Israel to worship IDOLS and to burn incense to Ashtaroth, the "Queen of Heaven" (1 Ki. 16:31; Jer. 44:18) in the same way that Papal Rome, the "whore" and "mother of harlots" (Rev. 17), taught veneration of SAINTS and worship of the "Virgin MARY." Jezebel maintained 850 FALSE PROPHETS of Ashtoreth and Baal (1 Ki. 18:19) just as Papal Rome employs a large PRIESTHOOD teaching the worship of "Mother and Child." She used King Ahab over the TEN northern TRIBES as a puppet for her evil plottings (1 Kings 9:7) just as the Papacy used the TEN KINGS of Europe as puppets for evil plottings of the Vatican. Jezebel "SLEW the PROPHETS of the Lord" (1 Ki.18:13) just as Papal Rome SLEW millions of Protestant REFORMERS. Numerous Catholic paintings of Mary in the Art Galleries of the world (such as the London Tate Gallery) have a label underneath which reads, "The Queen of Heaven." Many Catholics pray to Mary but Jesus declared, "I am the way, the truth and the life: no man comes to the Father, but by me" (John 14:6). "For there is ... one mediator between God and men, the man Christ Jesus" (1 Tim. 2:5). Jezebel was violently killed by SEXLESS eunuchs (2 Ki. 9:30-37) just as the Papacy will be destroyed by ATHEISTIC Communists (Rev. 17:15-18) -- both immune from the evil charms.

"And I gave her space to repent of her fornication; and she repented not. Behold, I will cast her into a bed, and them that commit adultery with her into great tribulation, except they repent of their deeds. And I will kill her children with death; and all the churches shall know that I am he which searcheth the reins and hearts: and I will give unto every one of you according to your works" (Rev. 2:21-23).

By comparing Revelation 2:21-23 with Revelation 16:9-11 ("they repented not to give him glory ... and repented not of their deeds") we see that the "space to repent" was 1260 years and Jezebel's "CHILDREN" are defined as (Protestant) "CHURCHES" imitating the Roman Catholic Church. Thyatira therefore extends at least to the Protestant Reformation. Rome didn't reform in the Reformation even though both Wycliffe and Luther sought to reform from within, but found it impossible. "We would have healed Babylon, but she is not healed" (Jer. 51:9).

"But unto you I say, and unto the rest in Thyatira, as many as have not this doctrine, and which have not known the depths of Satan, as they speak; I will put upon you none other burden. But that which ye have already, hold fast till I come. And he that overcometh, and keepeth my works unto the end, to him will I give power over the nations: And he shall rule them with a rod of iron; as the vessels of a potter shall they be broken to shivers: even as I received of my Father. And I will give him the morning star. He that hath an ear, let him hear what the Spirit saith unto the churches" (Rev. 2:24-29).

The "depths of Satan" refer to deeper understanding by initiation into certain mysteries of "Gnostic" type sects. The "ROD of IRON" may refer to the "REED like a ROD" (Rev. 11:1) used to measure the temple. The word "REED" in Hebrew is "kaneh" from which we get the "CANON" of scripture. Scripture that can't be bent, twisted or distorted is "IRON" Scripture. To be given the "MORNING STAR" or "day star" (2 Pet. 1:19), which symbolizes Jesus Christ (Rev. 22:16), is to be given the same ETERNAL LIFE that our Savior has. John Wycliffe is known as "the morning star of the Reformation" because he heralded the rising of the Sun of Righteousness by being the first to translate the whole Bible.

"Not a few, but many know what are the errors of those who are called Pasagini ... First, they teach that we should obey the SABBATH. Furthermore, to increase their error, they condemn and reject all the church Fathers, and the whole Roman Church." (D'Achery, Spicilegium I, f.211-214; Muratory Antiq. med. aevi. 5,f. 152, Hahn, 3, 209) Gilly writes in Waldensian Researches, page 61, note 2 that "Passagii and Passagini, or the inhabitants of the passes, from the Latin word passagium, is one of the names given by ancient authors to the Waldenses."

The Lutheran historian Mosheim describes the twelfth century by saying: "In Lombardy, which is the principal residence of the Italian heretics, there sprung up a singular sect, known ... (as) Passaginians.... Like the other sects already mentioned, they had the utmost aversion to the dominion and discipline of the church of Rome; but they were at the same time distinguished by two religious tenets which were peculiar to themselves. The first was a notion that THE OBSERVANCE OF THE LAW OF MOSES, in everything except the offering of sacrifices, WAS OBLIGATORY UPON CHRISTIANS; in consequence of which they ... abstained from those meats, the use of which was prohibited under the Mosaic economy, and celebrated the JEWISH SABBATH. The second tenet that distinguished this sect was advanced in opposition to the doctrine of three persons in the divine nature." (Eccl. Hist. part 2, chap.5, sec.14, p.127)

"The Waldenses took the Bible as their only rule of faith, abhorred the idolatry of the papal church, and rejected their traditions, holidays, and even Sunday, but kept the seventh-day SABBATH, and used the apostolic mode of baptism." (<u>Facts</u> <u>of</u> <u>Faith</u>, Christian Edwardson, p.121)

THE WALDENSIAN CANDLESTICK.

"The Light Shineth in Darkness"

Church Eras (Sardis to Laodicea)
Chapter 3
The Sardis Era Was Called Anabaptist
(1320-1789 A.D.)

John wrote, "And unto the angel of the church in Sardis write; These things saith he that hath the seven Spirits of God, and the seven stars; I know thy works, that thou hast a name that thou livest, and art dead. Be watchful, and strengthen the things which remain, that are ready to die: for I have not found thy works perfect before God" (Rev. 3:1-2).

Sardis (lit. "That which is left" or "remnant") who "hast a name that thou livest, and art dead" (Rev.3:1), was Christianity during the dark ages. In the days of King John, even the throne of David was subject to the Pope. One of the true churches during this time was the "Anabaptists." But "ready to die" would refer to Huguenots, Hussites, Lollards and Anabaptists. They were all ready for martyrdom.

"Remember therefore how thou hast received and heard, and hold fast, and repent. If therefore thou shalt not watch, I will come on thee as a thief, and thou shalt not know what hour I will come upon thee" (Rev. 3:3).

On Saint Bartholemew's Day in 1572 A.D. the Huguenots were massacred because they were not watching.

"Thou hast a few names even in Sardis which have not defiled their garments; and they shall walk with me in white: for they are worthy. He that overcometh, the same shall be clothed in white raiment; and I will not blot out his name out of the book of life, but I will confess his name before my Father, and before his angels. He that hath an ear, let him hear what the Spirit saith unto the churches" (Rev. 3:4-6).

"A few names" may refer to such men as John Wycliffe who began the Reformation in England (1320-1384 A.D.). He translated the Latin Vulgate Bible into English and sent his "Lollard" preachers to preach throughout the land. Another man is Martin Luther who nailed his 95 theses to the Wittenburg Church door in 1517. Also William Tyndale who issued the first English edition of the New Testament (1526 A.D.). When the Roman Emperor gained some great victory, and desired to celebrate it in Rome, he and his chief men walked in WHITE garments called TOGAS. God is clothed "with LIGHT as with a garment" (Ps. 104:2).

"They who maintain the SATURDAY SABBATH to be in force, comply with the Anabaptists" (Francis White's Treatise of the Sabbath Day, p.132). Russen, speaking of heresies, says: "Under this head I would conclude some of them under those of Anabaptists, who have been inclined to this personal reign of Christ, and have embraced the SEVENTH-DAY SABBATH." (On Anabaptists, London, 1703, p.79). "Anabaptists ... denied the validity of infant baptism ... The earliest Anabaptists of Zurich allowed that the ... Waldensians had, in contrast with Rome and the Reformers, truth on their side, yet did not claim to be in their succession ... deferring baptism to the age of 30, and rejecting oaths, prayers for the dead, relics and invocation of saints. The Moravian Anabaptists, says Rost, went barefooted, washed eachother's feet (like the Fraticelli) ... The Lord's Supper, or bread-breaking, was a commemoration of the Passion, held once a year. They sat at long tables, the elders read the words of institution and prayed, and passed a loaf round from which each broke off a bit and ate, the wine being handed round in flagons.... there was no Trinity of Persons ... The Anabaptists were great readers of Revelation and of the Epistle of James, the latter perhaps by way of counteracting Luther's one-sided teaching of justification by faith alone. Luther feebly rejected this scripture as "a right strawy epistle." English Anabaptists often knew it by heart." (Encyc. Brit. 11th ed.1:904-905) The Anabaptists became the SEVENTH-DAY Baptists of America.

The Philadelphia Era Was Called Church Of God
(1517-1986 A.D.)

"And to the angel of the church in Philadelphia write; These things saith he that is holy, he that is true, he that hath the key of David, he that openeth, and no man shutteth; and shutteth, and no man openeth; I know thy works: behold, I have set before thee an open door, and no man can shut it: for thou hast a little strength, and hast kept my word, and hast not denied my name" (Rev. 3:7-8).

What is the "KEY of DAVID"? Isaiah 22:22 says, "The KEY of the house of DAVID will I lay upon his shoulder." What KEY? In 2 Samuel 7:8-17 God promised DAVID an everlasting THRONE over Israel. Jesus is a royal son of David (Luke 1:32) and therefore is heir to the BRITISH THRONE. Papal Rome locked away the Bible with her "KEYS (authority) of St. Peter" when she RULED BRITAIN but DAVID'S royalty on the BRITISH THRONE (2 Sam. 23:5) took the Pope's place as head of the Church of England and with Christ's invisible authority opened the Bible by printing it and translating it into more than 1000 different languages. The Protestant Reformation had begun. By 1558 A.D. God had closed the door to the Pope ruling Britain. Queen Elizabeth was enthroned and the Protestant Church established in England.

What is the "OPEN DOOR" set before the church (Rev.3:8)? A great trade route passed through Philadelphia of commerce and prosperity. The Bible defines this symbol as an "OPPORTUNITY" (Acts 14:27; 1 Cor.16:9; 2 Cor.2:12; Col.4:3). First of all, that would be a PROTESTANT SOVEREIGN in Britain beginning with Henry VIII. Second, the RELIGIOUS FREEDOM granted by the U.S. Constitution ratified in 1789 which no man has been able to shut. (The French Revolution which destroyed Papal Rome's Catholic power also occurred in 1789.) It was the only official document in the world ratified by a national government, granting FREEDOM of WORSHIP, FREEDOM of SPEECH and FREEDOM of the PRESS -- like a prison DOOR OPENED so Peter could escape (Acts 12:10). Other "OPEN DOORS" naturally followed, such as printing, radio, TV, and airplane travel -- "a DOOR of utterance to speak the mystery of Christ" (Col.4:3). Also Jesus said, "I am the door" (John 10:9).

"Behold, I will make them of the synagogue of Satan, which say they are Jews, and are not, but do lie; behold, I will make them to come and worship before thy feet, and to know that I have loved thee. Because thou hast kept the word of my patience, I also will keep thee from the hour of temptation, which shall come upon all the world, to try them that dwell upon the earth" (Rev. 3:9-10).

What is the "SYNAGOGUE of SATAN"? The word "SYNAGOGUE" is found in James 2:2 referring to a true Christian assembly, but here it refers to a false Christian assembly -- CATHOLICS. The ROMAN CATHOLIC clergy and laity must bow down to the Protestant sovereign of the British Empire. CATHOLICS must also respect the laws and Protestant religions of the United States. Isaiah 60:14 says "they that despised thee shall bow themselves down at the soles of thy feet." "Because thou hast kept the word of my PATIENCE" (Rev.3:10) is defined in Revelation 14:12 as "Here is the PATIENCE of the saints; here are they that KEEP THE COMMANDMENTS of God, and the faith of Jesus." Yes, "thou ... hast KEPT MY WORD, and hast not denied my name" (Rev.3:8). How do people deny Christ? "In WORKS they deny him" (Tit.1:16).

What is the "HOUR of TEMPTATION"? The city of Philadelphia in Asia Minor suffered frequent EARTHQUAKES which are referred to as the "HOUR of TEMPTATION." Those who could afford it, lived outside the city. God promised to keep the church safe from this SHAKING -- as safe as stable pillars in his Temple. In the same way, Protestant Great Britain and Protestant United States have been kept from the "political EARTHQUAKES" of the French Revolution and Napoleon Bonaparte's devastation. Protestant Britain and America have been kept free of invaders in both World Wars. "I will appoint a place for my people Israel, whence they shall NEVER be MOVED, and where the son of wickedness shall AFFLICT them NO MORE as beforetime" (Isa. 49:12).

"Behold, I come quickly: hold that fast which thou hast, that no man take thy crown. Him that overcometh will I make a pillar in the temple of my God, and he shall go no more out: and I will write upon him the name of my God, and the name of the city of my God, which is new Jerusalem, which cometh down out of heaven from my God: and I will write upon him my new name. He that hath an ear, let him hear what the Spirit saith unto the churches" (Rev. 3:11-13).

Nationally speaking, "hold that fast which thou hast (Henry VIII and Parliament abrogated Papal supremacy in England in 1534; the 39 Articles ratified by British Parliament in 1571; the Act of Settlement in 1689 requiring the British monarch be a Protestant; along with that came the Coronation oath requiring monarch to defend Protestant

Faith), that no (Jesuit) man take thy (Protestant British) crown" lest it revert to Papal supremacy again (e.g. "Bloody Mary;" Guy Fawkes) and Catholic idolatry.

The Church of the Reformation took a new name. Until the sixteenth century it was never heard before in history. Reformers and martyrs had been known as Wycliffites, Lollards, etcetera. But in 1521, at the Diet of Spires, they called themselves "Protestants" for the first time meaning "Witnesses for the Truth." The Greek word for "witness" is "martus" and also means "martyr."

Philadelphia (lit. "Brotherly love") began in America when "Stephen Mumford, the first SABBATH-KEEPER in America, came from London in 1664." (Hist. of the Seventh-day Baptist Gen. Conf. by James Basiley, pp.237-238). After seven years, a SEVENTH-DAY congregation of seven members was raised up from these people. They identified it as (a part of) the church of God (Seventh-day Baptist Memorial 1:36). It was located in Newport Rhode Island. In 1682 William Penn established and settled the town of "Philadelphia" in America. The first American Congress met there in 1774 A.D. The "Declaration of Independence" was established there in 1776 A.D. Philadelphia became the capital of the United States until 1800 A.D. The British and Foreign Bible Society was founded in 1804 which has printed the Bible in over 1000 languages. The American Bible Society was founded in 1816, the National Bible Society of Scotland in 1861 and the Hibernian Bible Society of Ireland in 1806. Missionary societies were also launched at this time. In 1792 the Baptist Missionary Society started in Britain; the Anglican Church Missionary Society in 1800; the Wesleyan Missionary Society in 1796; and the London Missionary Society in 1795. Later in 1860 when the SEVENTH-DAY Adventists organized into a denomination, many members of the true church fellowshipped with them. Ellen Gould White (whose name in Latin is 666: l=50, l=50, v=5, l=50, d=500, v=5, v=5, i=1) rejected the name "Church of God" on the grounds that it would "excite suspicion, conceal absurd errors, and be a mark of fanaticism" (Loughborough's Rise And Progress Of S.D.A.'s, 1892, pp.227-228). But the true church "hast not denied my name" (Rev.3:8). Her visions also discouraged marriage, meat, milk and eggs (Testimonies 2:68,400; 3:21; 5:366) reminding us of 1 Tim.4:1-3. Others organized into the Church of God (SEVENTH DAY) which believed in the SABBATH, clean and unclean meats, Wednesday crucifixion and Saturday resurrection, that the Holy Spirit is not a person, that there is no everburning hell, death is like sleep until the resurrection, baptism by immersion, the "Lord's Supper" on the 14th of Nisan, footwashing, the biblical name "Church of God," and that Sunday, Christmas, Easter, Lent and Halloween are of pagan origin (Doctrinal Beliefs of the C.O.G.S.D.)

Herbert W. Armstrong came into contact with this church in 1927 and was ordained in 1931. In 1934 he began a radio broadcast called "the Radio Church of God" and published the Plain Truth magazine. His ministerial credentials were revoked in 1937 when he insisted on preaching the observance of annual Hebrew festivals and British Israelism. However, he retained almost all of the doctrines of the Church of God (Seventh Day) as well as these two new doctrines. He later changed the name to the Worldwide Church of God. This church also believed in avoiding make-up, drugs and vaccines but followed a form of "blind obedience" to the hierarchy. When Herbert Armstrong died in 1986, Joseph W. Tkach took over and began to move toward mainstream Protestantism. He died in 1995. His son, Joseph Tkach Jr., has continued this trend and now presides over a church that believes in the trinity, Christmas and Easter and has abandoned "British Israelism ... the seventh-day SABBATH ... annual festivals ... triple tithe, and that Christians must not eat foods that were 'unclean.'" ("The Plain Truth," Feb. 1996, p.1) About half of the membership left.

The Laodicean Era is Sunday-keeping Protestants

"And unto the angel of the church of the Laodiceans write; These things saith the Amen, the faithful and true witness, the beginning of the creation of God; I know thy works, that thou art neither cold nor hot: I would thou wert cold or hot. So then because thou art lukewarm, and neither cold nor hot, I will spue thee out of my mouth" (Rev. 3:14-16).

At the Council of Laodicea in 364 A.D., the Roman Catholic Church decreed that "Christians must not Judaize by resting on the Sabbath, but must work on that day, resting rather on Sunday. But, if any be found to be Judaizing, let them be declared anathema from Christ." The "little horn" Papacy "will think to change the times and the laws" (Dan. 7:25), the time for the Sabbath law. Most Protestant churches have continued in this error and therefore agree with this Laodicean decision. The name "Laodicea" means "rule by the people." In other words, it is the era of democracy in the British Empire and the United States. This is a good thing in the sense of tolerating Bible Christians but a bad thing in the sense of tolerating infidels, atheists, Catholics and higher critics.

Laodicea obtained her water from hot springs piped some distance to the city. By the time it reached the city, it was lukewarm, too cool for health baths, not cool enough to drink. To be "hot" is to be enthusiastic and wholly committed. In districts neighboring Laodicea, Christian inscriptions have been discovered which show a remarkable spirit of compromise with, and toleration of, heathenism. Laodicea is "politically correct." The other church eras have something good and something bad said about them. But Philadelphia has only good and Laodicea only bad. Why? Maybe because Philadelphia and Laodicea exist together at the end.

"Because thou sayest, I am rich, and increased with goods, and have need of nothing; and knowest not that thou art wretched, and miserable, and poor, and blind, and naked:" (Rev. 3:17).

Many Americans have chosen to become "rich, and increased with goods" at the expense of obeying God. These Christians have become spiritually "wretched, and miserable, and poor, and blind, and naked" (Rev.3:17). As Christ said, "No man can serve two masters; for either he will hate the one, and love the other; or else he will hold to the one, and despise the other. Ye cannot serve God and mammon (money)." (Matt.6:24). The American lukewarm lifestyle includes watching corrupting TELEVISION just as among Laodicea's ruins there have been discovered THEATERS, especially a very large AMPHITHEATER, capable of seating from thirty to forty thousand people. How many Laodicean Christians spent their time watching THEATER and AMUSING themselves? The city of Laodicea was a strong fortress but its water source was several miles from the city. An enemy could besiege the city easily and cut off the water supply. It was outwardly prosperous, but in reality weak and vulnerable. The same is true of the United States and Great Britain. We are vulnerable to terrorist attack.

"I counsel thee to buy of me gold tried in the fire, that thou mayest be rich; and white raiment, that thou mayest be clothed, and that the shame of thy nakedness do not appear; and anoint thine eyes with eyesalve, that thou mayest see" (Rev. 3:18).

What is "GOLD tried in the FIRE"? It is suffering for a belief, and still believing and obeying it after suffering for it. Resting on the Sabbath often interferes with earning a living. Rest anyway. This is buying real GOLD character (1 Cor.3:9-16; Job 23:10; 1 Pet.1:7). "FIRE" is "TRIAL" and suffering (Ez.38:19; 1 Pet.1:7). WHITE raiment is PURITY (Dan.12:10) and "RIGHTEOUSNESS" (Rev.19:8) which is contrasted to Laodicea which produced a BLACK wool cloth from the black sheep in the neighborhood. Laodicea had a school of medicine and the physicians had OINTMENT to cure physical EYE PROBLEMS but that is again contrasted with "an UNCTION from the Holy One" (1 John 2:20) to cure spiritual BLINDNESS -- "the Holy Spirit which God hath given to them that OBEY him" (Acts 5:32). Most Americans are blind to "British-Israel" truth. Most Americans are blind to the requirement to OBEY "Jewish Law." They mistakenly believe it was "done away with." Laodicea also had a tremendous amount of GOLD and so needed nothing. Christ asks Laodiceans (Americans and British) to buy GOLD character.

"As many as I love, I rebuke and chasten: be zealous therefore, and repent.
Behold, I stand at the door, and knock: if any man hear my voice, and open the door, I will come in to him, and will sup with him, and he with me" (Rev. 3:19-20).

Even Christ has been excluded from Laodicea since he stands at the door and knocks (Rev.3:20) like a diplomat who is "persona non grata" to a foreign government. Americans are too busy on the Sabbath to go to church.

"To him that overcometh will I grant to sit with me in my throne, even as I also overcame, and am set down with my Father in his throne. He that hath an ear, let him hear what the Spirit saith unto the churches" (Rev. 3:21-22).

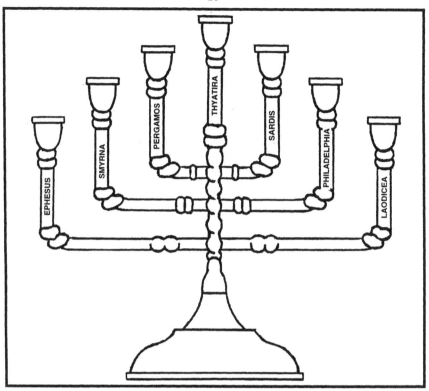

The Seven Seals

Rev.	Church Era	Seal	A.D.	Historical Events
1:4			96	John writes the Revelation
6:1-2	Ephesus	First	96-180	Emperor Nerva to death of Marcus Aurelius -- PROSPERITY
6:3-4		Second	180-284	Commodus to Accession of Diocletian -- CIVIL WAR
6:5-6		Third	211-244	Caracalla to death of Gordian III -- Oppressive Taxation -- SCARCITY
6:7-8		Fourth	244-284	Philip the Arabian to death of Numerianus -- FAMINE
6:9-10	Smyrna	Fifth	284-313	Era of Diocletian to Conversion of Constantine and Licinius' Edict of Toleration (Jan. 13, 313) -- MARTYRS
6:12-17	Pergamos	Sixth	313 to 395	Conversion of Constantine to death of Theodosius -- FALL OF PAGANISM (includes the "halt" or interval of calm from 322 to 395
7:1-4				
8:1-6		Seventh	395	Death of Theodosius (Jan. 17) to revolt of Goths the same year ("space of half an hour"), on division of the Empire

John Saw Constellations in Heaven
Chapter 4

Then "After this I looked, and, behold, a door was opened in heaven: and the first voice which I heard was as it were of a trumpet talking with me; which said, Come up hither, and I will shew thee things which must be hereafter. And immediately I was in the spirit: and, behold, a throne was set in heaven, and one sat on the throne. And he that sat was to look upon like a jasper and a sardine stone: and there was a rainbow round about the throne, in sight like unto an emerald. And round about the throne were four and twenty seats: and upon the seats I saw four and twenty elders sitting, clothed in white raiment; and they had on their heads crowns of gold. And out of the throne proceeded lightnings and thunderings and voices: and there were seven lamps of fire burning before the throne, which are the seven Spirits of God" (Rev. 4:1-5).

Astronomically the Milky Way "rainbow" sits over Cepheus' throne. Ursa Minor consists of seven main stars (lamps). Astronomically, there are 24 stars in Ursa Minor (the Little Flock).

What does the DOOR mean? Jesus said, "I am the DOOR" (John 10:9). An "open DOOR" also means "OPPORTUNITY" (Acts 14:27; 1 Cor.16:9; 2 Cor.2:12; Col.4:3). The Father sits on the throne "whom no man hath seen, nor can see" (1 Tim. 6:16; Ex. 24:10-11; Isa. 6:1-5). He is hidden in a blaze of glory. "JASPER" is various colors but "SARDINE" is fiery red for justice.

What does "a RAINBOW ... like ... an EMERALD" mean? Birth order is "Reuben ... Simeon ... Levi ... Judah ... Dan ... Naphtali ... Gad ... Asher ... Issachar ... Zebulun ... Joseph ... Benjamin" (Gen. 29:31; 30:6-24; 35:16-18). Stone order "according to their birth" (Ex. 28:9-10) on the breastplate is "sardius (flesh color) ... topaz (yellow) ... carbuncle (green) ... emerald (green) ... sapphire (celestial blue) ... diamond (clear) ...jacinth (orange) ... agate (variegated black/white) ... amethyst (violet) ... beryl (sea green) ... onyx (variegated red/white) ... jasper (dark-green)" (Ex. 28:17-20) "every one with his name shall they be according to the twelve tribes" (Ex. 28:21). Therefore, combining both lists we get: Sardius -- Reuben, Topaz -- Simeon, Carbuncle -- Levi, Emerald -- Judah, Sapphire -- Dan, Diamond -- Naphtali, Ligure -- Gad, Agate -- Asher, Amethyst -- Issachar, Beryl -- Zebulun, Onyx -- Joseph (The High Priest's Ephod contained two onyx stones, one on each shoulder -- for Ephraim and Manasseh [Gen.49:24]), and Jasper -- Benjamin. A multicolored RAINBOW is God's promise to not destroy every living creature with a flood (Gen. 9:8-17). An EMERALD RAINBOW is just that part of the spectrum that deals with God's promise to JUDAH -- a perpetual throne culminating in the "Lion of the tribe of Judah" (Gen. 49:10; 2 Sam. 7:12-16; Ps. 89:1-4; Jer. 33:17; Rev. 5:5).

Who are the "24 ELDERS"? There were 24 priestly shifts who served in "the house of the Eternal" from the descendants of Aaron (1 Chr. 24:1-19). There were also 24 Levitical shifts who "should prophesy with harps, with psalteries, and with cymbals" and "with song" (25:1-31). These were "the example and shadow of heavenly things" (Heb. 8:5; 1 Chr. 28:12-19). The twelve PATRIARCHS of Israel in the Old Testament and the twelve APOSTLES of our Lord in the New Testament "shall sit upon twelve thrones judging the twelve tribes of Israel" (Matt. 19:27-28). They are a fitting parallel for the spiritual temple of the church. Our 24-hour day may be based on this.

"And before the throne there was a sea of glass like unto crystal: and in the midst of the throne, and round about the throne, were four beasts full of eyes before and behind. And the first beast was like a lion, and the second beast like a calf, and the third beast had a face as a man, and the fourth beast was like a flying eagle. And the four beasts had each of them six wings about him; and they were full of eyes within: and they rest not day and night, saying, Holy, holy, holy, Lord God Almighty, which was, and is, and is to come" (Rev. 4:6-8).

What is the "SEA of GLASS"? Astronomically it is the starry heaven. "And they saw the God of Israel, and there was under His feet as it were a paved work of a sapphire stone (celestial blue); and as it were the body of HEAVEN in His clearness" (Ex. 24:10). Historically in Revelation 17:15 "many waters" are interpreted as "peoples, and multitudes and nations and tongues." In Luke 21:25 the "sea and the waves roaring" is a figure for "distress of nations with perplexity." The converse of these metaphors, a sea so calm that it looks like a sheet of glass, and so still that all sediment has settled to the bottom making it clear as crystal, would be people at peace, united and harmonious.

The "CROWNS" are astronomically "Corona Borealis" pictured alternately as a laurel wreathe of seven stars. Historically floral wreathes were awarded to the victors at Greek games after a successful struggle. They were not the crowns we normally think of today as gold metal.

Lightning, thunder and voices recall God's presence on Mount Sinai (Ex. 19:16). "Seven LAMPS" are the Menorah Seven-branched Candlestick representing the seven CHURCHES.

Who are these "FOUR BEASTS"? The original Greek here translated "beasts" should be translated "living creatures." Two gold cherubim formed part of the mercy seat on top of the Ark of the Covenant over which their wings were stretched. God dwelt between the cherubim (Ex.25:17-22; Isa. 37:16). Each cherub had four faces -- an ox, man, lion, and eagle (Ez.10:14,21). The curtains and veils of the Tabernacle were woven with figures of cherubim. In Solomon's Temple the walls and doors were carved with cherubim (Ex. 26:1,31; 1 Ki. 6:23,29,31). What do these CHERUBIM symbolize? The twelve tribes of ISRAEL encamped in four groups under the four leading tribe's standards -- Judah (lion), Ephraim (ox), Reuben (man) and Dan (eagle) -- east, west, south and north of the Tabernacle (Num. 2:3-31). Also the four main CONSTELLA-TIONS are Leo (a lion), Taurus (a bull), Aquarius (a man pouring water) and Scorpio (Anciently known as the flying eagle. Also Aquila [the eagle] is nearby. In Java and Brazil Scorpio is a serpent.) all rotating around God who dwells "in the sides of the north" (Isa. 14:13). "For promotion cometh neither from the east, nor from the west, nor from the south" (Ps. 75:6; Isa. 40:22). The CHERUBIM symbolize the ISRAELITE encampment and the ISRAELITE encampment symbolizes these CHERUBIM. Both are SERVANTS of God. The glass-like crystal SEA corresponds to the vast expanse of SPACE. The many EYES anciently symbolized the many STARS. Each cherub had SIX WINGS just as the four main constellations have subordinate CONSTEL-LATIONS: TWO decans above and TWO decans below and ONE to the left and ONE to the right.

"And when those beasts give glory and honour and thanks to him that sat on the throne, who liveth for ever and ever, The four and twenty elders fall down before him that sat on the throne, and worship him that liveth for ever and ever, and cast their crowns before the throne, saying, Thou art worthy, O Lord, to receive glory and honour and power: for thou hast created all things, and for thy pleasure they are and were created" (Rev. 4:9-11).

Just as Moses was learned in the wisdom of the Egyptians and defeated Egypt, so also John is learned in the wisdom of the Chaldean astrologers and defeats Babylon.

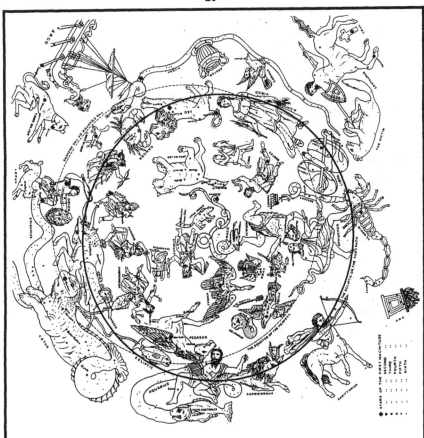

Reuben -- Aquarius (Gen. 49:4).

Simeon -- Gemini (Gen. 49:5).

Levi -- Ara (Deut. 33:10).

Judah -- Leo (Gen. 49:9).

Zebulun -- Argo (Gen. 49:13; Deut. 33:18).

Issachar -- Libra (Gen. 49:14).

Dan -- Scorpio (& Aquila) (Gen. 49:17).

Gad -- Orion (Gen. 49:19: Deut. 33:20).

Asher -- Capricorn (Cornucopia) (Gen. 49:20).

Naphtali -- Cassiopeia (Gen. 49:21).

Joseph or Ephraim -- Taurus (Deut. 33:17).

Manasseh -- Sagittarius (Gen 49:23-24).

Benjamin -- Lupus (Gen. 49:27).

The Sealed Scroll is Title Deed to Earth
Chapter 5

We read, "And I saw in the right hand of him that sat on the throne a book written within and on the backside, sealed with seven seals" (Rev. 5:1).

Astronomically, Cepheus (enthroned king) takes Lyra (alternately the scroll) sealed with seven stars (seals). Historically, this scroll has chapters 6 through 11 on one side giving progressive historic events to the end of this age, and 12 through 22 on the other giving additional details and taking us to the Millenium and beyond (cp.Ez. 2:9-10). This "Revelation of Jesus Christ, which God gave unto him" (Rev. 1:1) is our Redeemer's title deed to legal possession of the earth and its inhabitants. In Daniel 12:9 we read, "Go thy way, Daniel: for the words are closed up and sealed till the time of the end." Here the seals are being opened for John.

If a poor man sold his estate, two documents were drawn up. One containing all the particulars of the mortgage, the other containing the names of the witnesses of the mortgage. The first was carefully sealed, the second was not sealed. So this roll is said to be written within (where it contained the details of the mortgage) and written without (where it contained the names of the witnesses). The next of kin to the poor man, if he wished, could redeem his land by buying it back. Thus he became the "redeemer" or "goel." John wept not only because he didn't understand, but also because nobody could give mankind back what mankind lost. Only the Lamb -- our Redeemer -- could buy the earth and its inhabitants back from Satan.

"And I saw a strong angel proclaiming with a loud voice, Who is worthy to open the book, and to loose the seals thereof? And no man in heaven, nor in earth, neither under the earth, was able to open the book, neither to look thereon. And I wept much, because no man was found worthy to open and to read the book, neither to look thereon. And one of the elders saith unto me, Weep not: behold, the Lion of the tribe of Juda, the Root of David, hath prevailed to open the book, and to loose the seven seals thereof. And I beheld, and, lo, in the midst of the throne and of the four beasts, and in the midst of the elders, stood a Lamb as it had been slain, having seven horns and seven eyes, which are the seven Spirits of God sent forth into all the earth. And he came and took the book out of the right hand of him that sat upon the throne" (Rev. 5:2-7).

Astronomically, Hercules is the "strong angel" next to the book. Leo is Judah's constellation. Aries is wounded in the forehead by El Natik ("wounded") and takes Lyra out of Cepheus's hand. Hydra is the Root of David. Aries has seven prominent stars. Historically who is the "LAMB"? John 1:29 says, "The next day John seeth Jesus coming unto him, and saith, Behold the LAMB of God who taketh away the sin of the world." He buys back the earth and its inhabitants with his blood. What do the seven HORNS and seven EYES mean? Isaiah 11:2-3 names the seven attributes of the Holy Spirit: "wisdom ... understanding ... counsel ... might ... knowledge ... fear of the Eternal ... quick understanding." Luke 4:18-19 tells us five of the seven purposes of the Messiah's ministry: "to PREACH the GOSPEL to the poor ... to HEAL the brokenhearted, to PREACH DELIVERANCE to the captives (on the Jubilee year), and RECOVERING of SIGHT to the blind, to SET at LIBERTY them that are bruised (on the Jubilee year), To PREACH the acceptable YEAR of the Lord (the Jubilee year)." Isaiah 61:1-2 gives the other two: "To PROCLAIM ... the day of VENGEANCE of our God (the Day of Atonement of the Jubilee year); to COMFORT all who mourn." Since the Lamb is seated "at the right hand of God" (Heb. 12:2), he takes the scroll from the "right hand" of God.

"And when he had taken the book, the four beasts and four and twenty elders fell down before the Lamb, having every one of them harps, and golden vials full of odours, which are the prayers of saints. And they sung a new song, saying, Thou art worthy to take the book, and to open the seals thereof: for thou wast slain, and hast redeemed us ("them" in orig. Greek. -- The four beasts are speaking) to God by thy blood out of every kindred, and tongue, and people, and nation; And hast made us (Greek "them") unto our God kings and priests: and we (Greek "they" -- the Redeemed) shall reign on the earth" (Rev. 5:8-10).

Astronomically, Leo and Aquarius have the two golden vials -- Crater and the Bucket -- while Taurus and Scorpio have Gemini's Harp and Lyra. Historically, what is the KINGDOM of GOD? This kingdom has not yet been established with our Lord ruling the earth from Jerusalem and the saints ruling under him as immortal kings and priests and the twelve disciples sitting on thrones "judging the twelve tribes of ISRAEL" (Matt. 19:28; Luke 12:32; 22:30). But it has nonetheless been established since the day Moses organized ISRAEL into a human kingdom (Ps. 114:1-2; Ex. 19:6). The Kingdom of God is the Kingdom of ISRAEL (Acts 1:5; 2 Chr. 13:8; 9:8). The positions of human king and priest were given to ISRAELITES (Ex. 19:5-6; 1 Pet. 2:9-10). The kingdom of God is the kingdom of Christ (Eph. 5:5) and the Kingdom of Christ is the Kingdom of DAVID (Luke 1:32; Isa. 9:6; Jer. 23:5). When Jesus said, "The kingdom of God shall be taken from you (Edomite, Shammaite Jews), and given to a nation bringing forth the fruits thereof" (Matt. 21:43), he was still speaking about a nation composed of ISRAELITES. Many ISRAELITES had migrated to the British Isles where Protestant Christianity took root. This British Empire, along with the United States, is the human Kingdom of God today. Queen Elizabeth sits on the throne of David today.

"And I beheld, and I heard the voice of many angels round about the throne and the beasts and the elders: and the number of them was ten thousand times ten thousand, and thousands of thousands; Saying with a loud voice, Worthy is the Lamb that was slain to receive power, and riches, and wisdom, and strength, and honour, and glory, and blessing. And every creature which is in heaven, and on the earth, and under the earth, and such as are in the sea, and all that are in them, heard I saying,

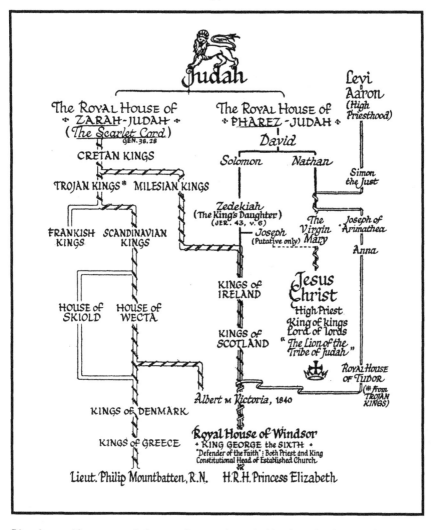

Blessing and honour, and glory, and power, be unto him that sitteth upon the throne, and unto the Lamb for ever and ever. And the four beasts said, Amen. And the four and twenty elders fell down and worshipped him that liveth for ever and ever" (Rev. 5:11-14).

God gave Adam dominion over the earth (Gen. 1:26). But Adam obeyed Satan (Gen. 3:6) thereby making Satan the "god of this world" (2 Cor. 4:4). Jesus our Messiah is our Kinsman-Redeemer -- a close relative (Lev. 25:23-28; Ruth 4:1-12; Jer. 32:6-12). "The right of redemption is thine to buy it" (Jer. 32:7). Christ "hast redeemed us to God by thy blood" (Rev. 5:9). The near kinsman redeemed (bought back) persons and lands (Lev. 25:25,48; Gal. 4:5; Eph. 1:7-14) by saying, "I will do the part of a kinsman to thee" (Ruth 3:13). He bought the land and slaves back from their captors (Jer. 50:33-34). He bought it "before the elders of my people" (Ruth 4:4) who are witnesses. Our Lord was crucified before the elders. "Ye were not redeemed with corruptible things, like silver and gold, from your vain conversation (conduct) ... But with the precious blood of Christ" (1 Pet. 1:18-19). Christ is here seen in the Holy of Holies on the Day of Atonement accepting the title deed. Satan just rented the land and people. Christ's blood bought back the earth and its inhabitants. Just as the title deed was put in a clay jar and buried, so our Lord's human body was put in a sepulcre (Jer. 32:15). Just as the title deed was sealed with seven seals of seven families of Israel as proof of the transaction, so also the body of Christ (the true Church of seven eras) was given the Holy Spirit verifying Christ's death and resurrection. We are sealed with the Holy Spirit (2 Cor. 1:22) which is the "earnest (downpayment) of our inheritance until the redemption (buy back) of the purchased possession" (Eph. 1:13-14). We are "sealed unto the day of redemption" (Eph. 4:30) or Day of Atonement on the Jubilee year when land reverts back and debt slaves are freed. Christ quoted from the first part of Isaiah 61:2 in Luke 4:17-19 when he came the first time just before a Jubilee to call it the "acceptable year of the Lord." He may quote from the second part when he comes again on the Day of Atonement of a Jubilee to call it the "day of vengeance" (Tribulation period). Our "Redeemer ... shall ... plead their cause" (Jer. 50:34). How? He pleaded Israel out of Egyptian bondage with 10 plagues of the Exodus, and he pleads Israelites out of "Babylon" with 7 trumpet plagues of Revelation (Rev. 12:1-9). At the end of the plagues,"the kingdoms of this world (both land and people) are become the kingdoms of our Lord and Savior" (Rev. 11:15). He opens the seals under which are found successive historical steps that recover the purchased possession of earth and its inhabitants. Seven seals are broken from the title deed on the Day of Atonement during the Jubilee year, the seventh containing seven Trumpets. Seven Trumpets are blown around "Jericho" during the Feast of Unleavened Bread, the seventh containing seven Cups. Seven drops from the Passover "Cup of Freedom" (a.k.a. "cup of wrath" -- Rev. 14:10; 16:19; 17:4; 18:6; Ps. 75:8) are poured out, the seventh ushering in the Messiah's return. From Seals to Trumpets is Pagan emperors to "Christian" emperors. From Trumpets to Cups is "Christian" emperors to Roman Popes. Gibbon's Decline and Fall of the Roman Empire is a secular record that unintentionally confirms the accuracy of the Apocalypse since Gibbon was an unbeliever who sneered at John's Revelation, yet his work confirms this inspired history of Europe.

The Rise and Decline of
the Roman Empire
(96 to 395 A.D.)
(Chapter 6)

We have the pre-written history of Europe from chapter 6 to 11 of Revelation. Supplementary visions are found in chapters 12 to 14, and then the history resumes from chapters 15 to 22. Revelation 6 begins John's record of the visions he saw as Christ broke, one after the other, the seals binding the scroll. The prophecies then revealed were "shortly to come to pass" (Rev. 1:1), or soon after 96 A.D. As each seal was broken, more of the scroll was unrolled, and Christ translated the written contents into dramatic action before John's gaze. The stage is the "earth" meaning the territory of the Roman Empire.

"And I saw when the Lamb opened one of the seals, and I heard, as it were the noise of thunder, one of the four beasts saying, Come and see. And I saw, and behold a white horse: and he that sat on him had a bow; and a crown was given unto him: and he went forth conquering, and to conquer" (Rev. 6:1-2).

Astronomically, the sun moving through Aries is the seal, and the crescent moon moving through Aries is the seal broken by him. Sagittarius is given Corona Borealis. Historically, the correct translation is "Come" (RV) not "Come and see" (KJV) since the beast is talking to the horseman, not to John. The HORSE symbolizes Sagittarius with his bow. Historically a HORSE symbolizes the ROMAN EMPIRE as ancient Roman coins and standards demonstrate. In Revelation 19:11-16 the "King of kings" rides on a white HORSE also. God led his "house of ISRAEL ... like a HORSE" (Isa. 63:7,13). The "house of JUDAH ... his goodly HORSE in the battle" (Zech 10:3). Therefore, the Roman Empire is largely composed of ISRAELITES at this time. Virgil's Aeneid written in 19 B.C., tells about Trojans under Aeneas who founded Rome. Who were the Trojans? The "TROJANS were called DARDANI" (Lemp. Clas. Dict., p.193). "DARDA" (KJV margin of 1 Chr.2:6) called "DARDANUS" by Josephus, was the Egyptian founder of TROY (and the Kingdom of Priam) on the southern shore of the strait called "DARDANELLES." He was from Judah. Upon Christ's head are many crowns (Greek "diadema"). Both riders are kings who demand to be worshipped and both are victorious. But we shouldn't confuse them. One is the Jewish Messiah; the other a pagan Roman Jewish "messiah." "For many shall come in my name (claiming to be "God" or "Augustus"), saying I am Anointed; and shall deceive many" (Matt.24:4-5). The white horse here symbolizes Imperial Rome because Roman emperors invariably rode white horses in their victory celebrations. The national badge of CRETE was a BOW and arrow. The CRETANS manufactured the BOW. The CRETAN Apollo first invented the BOW. Thus Cherethites were David's bodyguard and were called "BOW-

34

bearing Cretans" (Pindar Ode 5). Thucydides relates how ARCHERS were fetched from CRETE during the Pelopponesian War by the belligerent parties. All Roman Emperors had been of Italian extraction prior to Nerva. Nerva, the first Emperor of the period, was a CRETAN. The other four emperors who reigned during the age of prosperity were not his descendants, but according to Roman law of adoption were reckoned as such. They were known as the CRETAN dynasty. The rider's "crown" is "stephanos" in Greek meaning a circle of laurel leaves (Greek crown for VICTORS in Pythian games) -- not a jewelled diadem. From 81 A.D. its use was confined to the reigning emperors till 292 A.D. when Diocletian wore a diadem in imitation of barbarian kings. This is the peaceful, prosperous, united empire from 96 to 180 A.D. of Nerva, Trajan, Hadrian and the Antonines ending in Marcus Aurelius. But it was PAGAN. It did go forth "conquering and to conquer" because Trajan conquered Dacia (Romania) and annexed the kingdom of the Nabateans as the province of Arabia. He temporarily took control of Armenia and Mesopotamia from the Parthians. Marcus Aurelius triumphed over Germans and Sarmatians.

The Cretan Emperor M. Aurelius, with a Laurel Crown, on a White Horse (top). A Cretan Coin showing Apollo with his Bow (right).

"And when he had opened the second seal, I heard the second beast say, Come and see. And there went out another horse that was red: and power was given to him that sat thereon to take peace from the earth, and that they should kill one another: and there was given unto him a great sword" (Rev. 6:3-4).

Astronomically when the crescent passed through Centaur the next seal was stripped away and John saw this constellation in a red sunrise. Historically, the next stage of Roman history was CIVIL WAR from 185 A.D. (accession of Commodus) to 284 A.D. (Diocletian's accession). During this period there were no less than 32 Emperors opposed by 27 Pretenders (according to Sismondi), who took the "great sword" -- the Roman short sword (Gr. "machaira"). Emperor Commodus was ASSASSINATED in 192 A.D. The many armies throughout the empire REVOLTED from allegiance to one emperor, and created numerous rival emperors many of whom were in turn MURDERED. The rival armies under their respective generals in the provinces brought wide-spread

CIVIL WAR and REVOLUTION; whole armies MASSACRED one another and red blood drenched the empire. These are the "WARS and rumors of WARS" (Matt. 24:6).

Gibbon says of this era, "The power of the sword had begun its reign, and military rule was supreme. The tyranny of Commodus, the civil wars occasioned by his death, and the new policy introduced by Severus, had all contributed to increase the dangerous power of the army, and to obliterate the faint image of laws and liberty that was still impressed upon the minds of the Romans. This internal change undermined the foundations of the empire" (ch. 6).

The "giving of the sword" was fulfilled when Commodus exalted Perennis (who aspired to the Empire) to practically despotic authority as Captain of the Praetorian Guards (ch.4, Gibbon). In theory the Praetorian commander represented the Emperor; the action of Commodus transferred in practice supremacy to the army which it wasn't slow to use. Septimus Severus (193-211) aggravated this military despotism, thereby leading to further revolutions and bloodshed.

"And when he had opened the third seal, I heard the third beast say, Come and see. And I beheld, and lo a black horse; and he that sat on him had a pair of balances in his hand. And I heard a voice in the midst of the four beasts say, A measure of wheat for a penny, and three measures of barley for a penny; and see thou hurt not the oil and the wine" (Rev. 6:5-6).

Astronomically, this is Centaur holding Libra as seen in the black of night after the sun-seal has been stripped away and in its place a crescent moon. A "MEASURE" equalled approximately ONE QUART. A PENNY was equal to the DAILY WAGE of a laborer during Roman times (Matt. 20:1-16 -- "He agreed with the laborers for a PENNY a DAY"). When bread is eaten by weight, it is a sign of SCARCITY. As Jesus said, "there shall be FAMINES" (Matt. 24:7). The balances were used as a common symbol in Rome for justice and commerce and hence were often a badge of the emperor or provincial governors as seen on Roman coins. The rider is a tax-gatherer. What caused this economic depression and famine? Gibbon says of this period, "The industry of the people was discouraged by a long series of oppressions." and the financial oppression was "a noxious weed of luxurious growth, DARKENING the Roman world with its deadly SHADE." The HEAVY TAXATION was the result of reckless extravagance in the reigns of Caracalla and Elagabalus -- dissolute emperors -- who for ten years exhausted the resources of the Empire in supporting the army. TAXES to support the armies, the court and the capital city, could be paid either in money or the equivalent value of produce such as wheat, wine and oil. Roman TAXATION by this official tax gatherer caused black DEPRESSION. One of the chief causes of decay was EXCESSIVE TAXATION from 200 to 250 A.D. Not just local, provincial taxes. In 212 A.D., the Emperor Caracalla issued his famous decree extending the privilege of Roman citizenship to all free men within the Empire. Such a "favor" was actually a curse since it carried with it MORE TAXES. This TAXATION to maintain the armies, coupled with the EXTRAVAGANT administration of the Empire, proved to be so burdensome that AGRICULTURE was RUINED, and fertile provinces were LEFT UNCULTIVATED in desolation, ECONOMIC DEPRESSION and gloom. TAXATION was brought to such a pitch that vast tracts of country went OUT of CULTIVATION -- the tiller of the soil feeling NO ENCOURAGEMENT to RAISE CROPS merely to hand over to the revenue officer. An idea of the extent of the taxation, which crushed alike every part of the empire, may be gathered from the fact that when a new government took over, taxes were instantly reduced to one thirtieth part of what they were during the reigns of Caracalla and Elagabalus. Alexander Severus came to the throne after the assassination of Elagabalus, and he wasn't unjust with regard to the wine and oil. In other words, although wheat should be at FAMINE prices owing to the FISCAL EXTORTIONS of the first part of the seal, prices were lowered instead. The prices given for wheat and barley enable us to date the prophecy since they are the exact market prices during the reign of Alexander Severus.

The Greek verb "adikeo," translated "hurt" in verse 6, means "to be unjust." The command should be translated "and see thou BE NOT UNJUST with regard to the oil and the wine,"-- that is, when collecting taxes, take only the FAIR EQUIVALENT in PRODUCE. It was wine and oil that had been HEAVILY TAXED. Severus lowered the taxes, reduced the price of provisions, and the interest on money. But all his efforts to change the color of the horse were inadequate. The previous evils were too deeply planted to be removed in a short time, and the army became discontented with the economy of Severus.

Left: Emblem of Roman Propraetors. A pair of balances was the tax collector's badge of office. Right: The balance on an Imperial Coin of Alexander Severus. Taxes were paid in wine, oil, barley and grain.

"And when he had opened the fourth seal, I heard the voice of the fourth beast say, Come and see. And I looked, and behold a pale horse: and his name that sat on him was Death, and Hell followed with him. And power was given unto them over the fourth part of the earth, to kill with sword, and with hunger, and with death, and with the beasts of the earth" (Rev. 6:7-8).

Astronomically this is the crescent moon (Grim Reaper's Scythe of Death) sitting on Centaur followed by Crater (the pit of Hades). Historically, the "FOURTH part" is a play on words. First, it is the FOURTH empire in succession from Babylon -- namely the whole Roman Empire. Second, ONE QUARTER of the citizens from all parts of the Roman Empire fell victim to war, famine, disease and wild beasts. Third, Diocletian divided the empire into FOUR PARTS, called prefectures, over each of which a prince, or prefect, exercised authority in subjection to the emperors. The four parts at this time were: 1. the East (including Egypt, Syria, Asia Minor etc.); 2. Illyricum; 3. Gaul (France, Spain, Britain, etcetera) and 4. Italy The principal or leading fourth was the prefecture of Italy -- headquarters of the Roman Empire. The events of the fourth seal especially affected this FOURTH section of the empire. From 250 to 300 A.D., disastrous WARS raged both within the Empire and against enemies on the borders. DISEASE followed the bloodshed. Also the ruin of agriculture through excessive taxation brought inevitable FAMINES; and, as civilization waned, the wild BEASTS which multiplied ravaged the inhabitants. During this time there were 39 emperors and not one died a natural death. Virtually all were assassinated. Maximin had Severus assassinated. Once he became emperor, he had 4000 nobles put to death. Commanders, governors and nobles were executed at the slightest accusation. He confiscated taxes for his own use and the use of his army. He stripped temples of gold and silver. This all led to public revolt and civil WAR. Finally Maximin was killed by his troops. The early church historian Eusebius, writing of this period, says, "Death waged a desolating war with two weapons, FAMINE and PESTILENCE ... Men, wasted away to mere skeletons, stumbled hither and thither like mere shadows, trembling and tottering. They fell down in the midst of the streets ... then, drawing their last gasp cried out, HUNGER! ... Some indeed were already the food of the dogs." Gibbon says, "From A.D. 248 to the death of Gallienus there elapsed twenty years of shame and misfortune ... FAMINE was followed by epidemical DISEASES, the effect of scanty and unwholesome food. Other causes must, however, have contributed to the furious PLAGUE which, from the year A.D. 250 to the year 265, raged without interruption in every Province, every city, and almost every family in the Roman Empire. During some times, five thousand persons died daily in Rome ... So great was the mortality that we might expect that war, PESTILENCE and FAMINE had consumed in a few years the half of the human species." Arnobius described the state of the Roman Empire in 296 A.D. by saying,"Men complain: There are now sent us from the gods PESTILENCE, DROUGHTS, WARS, SCARCITIES, LOCUSTS, wars with wild BEASTS, battles with LIONS, and destruction from venomous CREATURES." These are the "PESTILENCES" (Matt. 24:7).

Before going further, it is worth noting that national decline in the United States has proceded along these same lines: From 1776 to 1867 the U.S. expanded and conquered territory successfully as a WHITE horse. From 1861 to 1865 came the RED horse of civil war with lingering after-effects. From 1929 to 1939 came the BLACK horse of Great Depression. Then from 1941 to 1945 (W.W. 2) and from 1950 to 1953 (Korea) and from 1964 to 1973 (Viet Nam), etcetera, the PALE horse of death and hell have been the fruit of war. What is next for the United States? It has already begun. In 1962 the U.S. Supreme Court banned voluntary, public prayer (Engel v. Vitale) and in 1963 voluntary, public Bible-reading in public school (Abington v. Schempp).

Since 1963, SAT scores and productivity plummetted while fornication, crime, suicide and divorce sky-rocketed. Then came "Waco Texas" adding up to 666 if A=6, B=12, C=18, etc. After 9-11-2001 the Patriot Act was passed and Americans lost their Bill of Rights.

"And when he had opened the fifth seal, I saw under the altar the souls of them that were slain for the word of God, and for the testimony which they held: And they cried with a loud voice, saying, How long, O Lord, holy and true, dost thou not judge and avenge our blood on them that dwell on the earth? And white robes were given unto every one of them; and it was said unto them, that they should rest yet for a little season, until their fellowservants also and their brethren, that should be killed as they were, should be fulfilled" (Rev. 6:9-11).

All the constellations (representing souls) are under Ara (the Altar). The horse with a single rider has disappeared because "military emperors" (27 B.C. to 284 A.D.) have now passed away and Israel is moving west. Hitherto the empire had been governed as one unit. But in 292 A.D. Diocletian divided the empire into four parts, each under its own ruler. Maximian, Galerius and Constantine therefore helped him govern.

These "souls" are Christians martyred by pagan Rome. "They shall deliver you up to be afflicted, and shall KILL you; and ye shall be hated of all nations for my name's sake" (Matt. 24:9). The Brazen Altar in the Court of the Temple was the place where priests burnt the carcasses of the sacrificial animals and around which the blood of the animals was sprinkled. These SACRIFICIAL ANIMALS typified CHRIST'S SACRIFICE and therefore the martyrs in this vision must also be CHRISTIANS who SUFFERED at the hands of the same Roman Empire. Leviticus 4:7 says, "Thou shalt pour all the blood ... at the BOTTOM of the altar." The blood of the victims was poured out UNDER the altar. They were "UNDER" the Altar indicating they were UNDER the New Covenant and would have Eternal Life. Their sacrifices were well pleasing to God (2 Tim. 4:6). Under the Mosque of Omar, where the Temple once stood, is an underground cave. In the roof of this cave there was a hole which connected with the floor above where the brazen altar stood. Through that hole the blood of victims poured down into the cave.

The Romans looked upon Christians as enemies since Christians refused to worship the emperor or offer sacrifice to the pagan gods. Also the Bible that Christians followed condemned their heathen sacrifices. Hence when the Romans offered Christians the alternative of engaging in such heathen ceremonies or of being put to death, multitudes chose public martyrdom and so died literally "for the Word of God, and for the testimony which they held" that Jesus was the Christ. "Present your bodies a LIVING SACRIFICE" (Rom. 12:1). Persecution of Christians took place under Emperor Diocletian from 303 to 313 A.D. and this was the longest, fiercest and most universal. It was Smyrna's "tribulation for ten days" (years) (Rev. 2:8-10). DIOCLETIAN published his edict at Nicomedia on February 24, 303 and it lasted until his death and Licinius's "Edict of Toleration" on January 13, 313. Churches were demolished, the Scriptures burnt, Christians put outside the protection of the law, prevented from holding any office, and imprisoned, tortured, and cruelly slain. The era of Diocletian was the "Age of the Martyrs."

When Cain slew righteous Abel, Abel's blood cried out to God for justice (Gen. 4:10). When PAGAN Rome slew Christians, the Christians' blood also cried out (Rev. 6:10). "WHITE ROBES" symbolize "RIGHTEOUSNESS" (Rev. 19:8). The first group of martyrs were told to "rest yet for a little season" meaning sleep in death "until their brethren should be killed as they were." Their brethren were the second group of martyrs to be killed at the hands of PAPAL Rome. The "day of vengeance" (Jer. 46:10) is coming and God says, "Vengeance is mine; I will repay, saith the Lord" (Rom. 12:19).

"And I beheld when he had opened the sixth seal, and, lo, there was a great earthquake; and the sun became black as sackcloth of hair, and the moon became as blood; And the stars of heaven fell unto the earth, even as a fig tree casteth her untimely figs, when she is shaken of a mighty wind. And the heaven departed as a scroll when it is rolled together; and every mountain and island were moved out of their places. And the kings of the earth, and the great men, and the rich men, and the chief captains, and the mighty men, and every bondman, and every free man, hid themselves in the dens and in the rocks of the mountains; And said to the mountains and rocks, Fall on us, and hide us from the face of him that sitteth on the throne, and from the wrath of the Lamb: For the great day of his wrath is come; and who shall be able to stand?" (Rev. 6:12-17).

John doesn't see the second coming here. Instead he sees terror-stricken people who think it is the "day of his wrath." But that event doesn't come till the eleventh chapter. Other similar descriptions of the Day of the Lord occurred at the downfall of Babylon in 539 B.C. (Isa. 13:9-10), destruction of Judah in 604 B.C. (Zeph. 1:14-16; Jer. 4:23-25), the fall of Israel in 721 B.C. (Hos. 10:8) and of Egypt (Ez. 32:7-8). The EARTHQUAKE is political upheaval. It signifies "the REMOVING of those THINGS that are SHAKEN ... that those THINGS which cannot be shaken may REMAIN.... a KINGDOM which cannot be moved" (Heb. 12:27-28). The "Lord shall punish ... the HIGH ONES ...the KINGS ... Then the MOON shall be confounded, and the SUN ashamed" (Isa. 24:21-23). The Lord's "fury" is "upon all their ARMIES ... all the HOST of HEAVEN shall be dissolved ... fall down" (Isa. 34:2-4). DIOCLETIAN the "SUN" was eclipsed. The "MOON" was the pagan CLERGY who obtained their glory from Diocletian's favor. "STARS" were GENERALS. As Jesus said, "Immediately after the tribulation of those days shall the SUN be darkened, and the MOON shall not give its light, and the STARS shall fall from heaven" (Matt. 24:29). Eusebius describes the ruling Roman GOVERNMENT as "celestial powers, the SUN, the MOON and the STARS" (Eccl. Hist. 10:4). A mighty WIND is an ARMY (Jer. 4:11-13; 49:36; 51:1-2; Dan.7:2-3). A MOUNTAIN is a KINGDOM (Isa. 2:2; Jer. 51:25; Dan. 2:35; Micah 4:1). Since the SUN, MOON and STARS were worshipped alongside other heathen gods in the pantheon of Rome, this verse has a double meaning: "Upon their gods also, the Lord executed judgments" (Nu. 33:4) in Pharaoh's Egypt.

Diocletian sent Constantius to govern Britain. He married a British lady named Lady Helena, a native of York. Their son was called Constantine, and his mother, Helena, appears to have early taught him the Christian faith. Constantius died at York in 306 A.D. Constantine his son traveled to Rome to deliver Christianity from Diocletian. Eusebius records that on the eve of battle, he saw at mid-day the two initial letters of Christ in Greek, X (Chi) and P (Rho) in the sky and above them was written in Latin: "In Hoc Signo Vinces" or "By This Sign Conquer." A dream followed in which he was directed to put the cross on his banners if he wished for victory. He did so. This was a small fulfillment of "Then shall appear the SIGN of the Son of Man in HEAVEN" (Matt. 24:29). He put this symbol on his banner or Labarum. In the Battle of "Milvian Bridge" he defeated the army of Maxentius (successor of Maximian) in October 27, 312 A.D. about nine miles from Rome. Maxentius was drowned in the River Tiber while fleeing. Constantine defeated the rival pagan emperors in 313 A.D. and became Emperor himself (324-337 A.D.). Constantine abandoned the dragon standards of the Roman armies and adopted instead "the Sign of the Cross" which seemed to assure him of victory after victory over fear-stricken pagan armies (cp. Isa. 44:28). Constantine issued the Milan Edict in 313 A.D. giving complete tolerance to all religions, including Christians. Later in his rule, he suppressed heathen sacrifices, destroyed pagan temples, and tolerated no other public form of worship than Christianity. This is why heathenism came to be called "pagan" because it could only be practices in the "pagi" or villages (Pagus meaning rural) from where we get the word "peasant." He also elevated Christians to high offices in the State, and displaced pagans. Heathen priests lost their great power over the people. The Roman population thought the Day of Wrath had come but it was just a type and forerunner. "A stone (Constantine's British & Gallic -- Israelite -- troops) ... smote the image upon its feet" (Dan. 2:34). It was more superficial than substantial. Neverthless, Diocletian was so panic-stricken that he died insane in 313 A.D. Maximinian committed suicide. Galerius was smitten in 310 A.D. with an incurable disease. In 311 A.D., softened by suffering, he allowed Christians to rebuild their places of worship. Then he died. After this Maximin was struck with a sudden plague all over his body. He died in 313 A.D. Licinius lost his life in battle against Constantine. Newton quoting Eusebius says, "Galerius, Maximin and Licinius made even a public confession of their guilt, recalled their decrees and edicts against the Christians and acknowledged the just judgments of God and of Christ in their destruction" (p.461, Newton's Dissertations on the Prophecies). These "kings of the earth" experienced "the wrath of the Lamb." Later, Julian the Apostate in 363 A.D. gave orders for the rebuilding of Jerusalem's Temple to disprove the origins of Christianity by strengthening their enemies the Jews. But "horrible balls of fire breaking out near the foundations, with repeated attacks, rendered the place inaccessible to the scorched workmen" (Amm. Marc.). He reigned one year and eight months. While dying from a Persian lance on the battlefield, he cried, "O Galilean, Thou hast conquered." Pagans hid their idols and heathen rites in the dens and caves. As Gibbon says, "The ruin of the pagan religion is described by the Sophists as a dreadful and amazing prodigy, which covered the earth with DARKNESS, and restored the ancient dominion of chaos and of NIGHT" (ch. 28,).

Angles, Saxons, Jutes & Danes
Arrive Safely in the British Isles
(Chapter 7)
(from 449 A.D. onward)

We read "And after these things I saw four angels standing on the four corners of the earth, holding the four winds of the earth, that the wind should not blow on the earth, nor on the sea, nor on any tree. And I saw another angel ascending from the east, having the seal of the living God: and he cried with a loud voice to the four angels, to whom it was given to hurt the earth and the sea, Saying, Hurt not the earth, neither the sea, nor the trees, till we have sealed the servants of our God in their foreheads" (Rev. 7:1-3).

Astronomically, the four are Leo, Taurus, Aquarius and Scorpio. The eastern ascending angel is Perseus stepping up with Medusa's Head. The SEAL of the Holy Spirit turns hearts from stone to flesh while MEDUSA'S HEAD turns hearts from flesh to stone. Historically, chapter 7 is a continuation of the sixth seal. An interval of PEACE and CALM settled upon the Roman Empire after Constantine's triumph over paganism. Testimonies of contemporary writers bear this out. "Some medals of Constantine are still preserved with the head of this emperor on one side and the inscription: CON-STANTINUS AUG.; and on the reverse: BEATA TRANQUILLITAS, Blessed Tranquility" (Dissertations on the Prophecies by Dr. Thomas Newton, p. 463). During this time of TRANQUILITY, the servants of God were being sealed in their foreheads. Constantine defeated the Goths in 322 A.D. He not only repulsed their invasion of Roman territory, but carried the war into their own country, extracting from them humiliating terms of PEACE, with the result, as Gibbon tells us, that "the threatening tempests of barbarians, which so soon subverted the foundations of Roman greatness, hung SUSPENDED on the frontiers." This tranquility lasted till about 402 A.D.

The SEA TOSSED up by the WIND means NATIONS (Rev. 17:15) in TURMOIL or AN-ARCHY (Isa. 57:20; Dan. 7:2-3). All human RULERS are TREES (Dan. 4:20-22;. Ez. 31:3; Judges 9:8-15; Ps. 52:8). The Goths (west), Vandals (south), Huns (east) and Heruli (north) did come against Rome from all four sides just like the four winds. The westward march of Israel from "Pontus, Galatia, Cappadocia, Asia (Minor), and Bithynia" (1 Pet. 1:1-2; 2:9-10) across the Roman "earth" was possible by holding back the four "WINDS" of WAR (Jer.4:11-13; 49:36; 51:1-2; Dan.7:2-3) so Anglo-Saxons, Jutes and Danes could enter the "Isles afar off" (Jer. 31:1,4, 9-11) -- the British Isles. These islands once formed part of the continent. The shallow English Channel is only 20 to 30 fathoms with submerged forests still standing there. Then they were "CUT OUT ... without hands" (Dan. 2:45) during Noah's Flood. The winds started to blow when Alaric the Goth invaded Italy in 402 A.D. and sacked Rome itself on August 24, 410. Meanwhile, in 409 A.D. an imperial missive from Honorius resigned defense of

Britain to the natives. In order to protect Italy, the Roman army evacuated the British Isles completely by 410 A.D. Native kings quickly reasserted their independence. Jutes began to arrive in the British Isles in 449 A.D. Saxons in 477 A.D. Angles 507A. D., Scandinavians 802 A.D., Danes 866 A.D. and Normans in 1066 A.D.

"Ye shall go forth as calves (Eglah) of the stall" (Mal. 4:2). Ephraim is an EGLAH (Jer. 31:18; Hos. 4:16; 5:5-6; 10:11) -- a bullock, heifer or calf. The AEGLI (Herod. 3:92) were sometimes known as AGGAI where the first "G" in Greek has the sound of "N," hence ENGLISH. The Angel of the Lord led the way as they travelled toward the "appointed place" (2 Sam. 7:10) in the British Isles (Isa. 41:1; 49:1). "BRIT-ISH" means "Covenant Man" in Hebrew. The Anglo-Saxon Chronicle (891 A.D.) says the British came from Armenia -- where Israel was taken captive (2 Ki. 17:6). There is a pass even today known as the "Israel Pass" through the Caucasus Mountains from whence CAUCASIANS get their name. "They have broken up, and have passed through the gate, and are gone out by it" (Micah 2:13). Herodotus says the SCYTHIANS (Scotch) came from "across the Araxes" into CIMMERIA (Her. 4:11) or the Crimea. Hence the Welsh call themselves CYMRY. "I will sift the house of Israel among all nations, like corn is sifted in a sieve: yet shall not the least grain fall upon the earth" (Amos 9:9). "They shall be wanderers among the nations" (Hos. 9:17). But "they shall remember me in far countries" (Zech. 10:9). "O Israel ... I am with thee to save thee: though I make a full end of all the nations whither I have scattered thee (the Roman Empire in this case) yet will I not make a full end of thee" (Jer. 30:10-11). "They went from one nation to another ... He suffered no man to do them wrong: yea, he reproved kings for their sakes" (Ps. 105:13-14). Second Esdras 13:39-43 describes the ten tribes as escaping to Arsareth. The city of Sereth is in Thrace. Here we find the names BRITO-Lagae, SAXON ("In Isaac shall thy seed be called" -- Gen. 21:12), PICT (Viking), CYMRY, Scythia (SCOT) and Wallachia (WELSH).

The sealing is protection from the punishment directed against the Roman Empire for idolatry. We are "SEALED with the HOLY SPIRIT of promise ... and grieve not the HOLY SPIRIT whereby ye are SEALED unto the day of redemption" (Eph. 1:13; 4:30). God has "SEALED us, and given the earnest (downpayment) of the SPIRIT in our hearts" (2 Cor. 1:21-22). Just as in ancient times servants were marked on their foreheads with the NAME of their MASTERS to distinguish who owned them, the Roman Catholic Church was beginning to teach that salvation could be obtained through "the sign of the cross" made at infant baptism and that there was no salvation outside of her membership, that she was the "Israel of God" -- the inheritor of all the covenants and promises of God to racial Israel. "Arise ye, and depart, for this is not your rest, because it is polluted; it shall destroy you, even with a sore destruction" (Micah 2:10). This vision was intended to correct that false doctrine and to contrast it with the truth. Revelation 22:4 says, "And they shall see his face; and his NAME shall be in their FOREHEADS." Ezekiel 9:1-6 says, "Set a MARK upon the FOREHEADS of the men that sigh and that cry for all the abominations that be done." "And these words, which I command thee ... shall be as frontlets between thine eyes" (Deut. 6:4-9). In other words, GOD'S LAW in their MINDS is the SEAL (Gr. "sphragis" -- genuine stamp or signet) in their FOREHEADS.

"And I heard the number of them which were sealed: and there were sealed an hundred and forty and four thousand of all the tribes of the children of Israel. Of the tribe of Juda were sealed twelve thousand. Of the tribe of Reuben were sealed twelve thousand. Of the tribe of Gad were sealed twelve thousand. Of the tribe of Aser were sealed twelve thousand. Of the tribe of Nepthalim were sealed twelve thousand. Of the tribe of Manasses were sealed twelve thousand. Of the tribe of Simeon were sealed twelve thousand. Of the tribe of Levi were sealed twelve thousand. Of the tribe of Issachar were sealed twelve thousand. Of the tribe of Zabulon were sealed twelve thousand. Of the tribe of Joseph were sealed twelve thousand. Of the tribe of Benjamin were sealed twelve thousand" (Rev. 7:4-8).

Joseph represents Ephraim (Gen. 48:15-20). But Joseph had a double portion granted to him (Ez. 47:13), so Manasseh is one of the twelve. Why is Dan not present in this numbering? Deborah asked the question, "Why did Dan remain in ships?" (Judges 5:17). Dan was able to escape to the British Isles centuries before the main body of Israelites arrived (2 Sam. 7:10; Isa. 24:15). "Dan shall leap from shame" (Heb. "Bashan") (Deut. 33:22) of captivity. He was absent in the geneology (1 Chr. 5:17). Danites didn't need protection. The tribe of Dan is certainly not excluded from a portion of land nor from a city gate (Ezek.48:1-32). Homer, Aeschylus, Pindar, Euripides, and Strabo mention the "Danai" of Greece who were originally "slaves in Egypt," "the Divine Seed," who had escaped from their brother Egyptus, and were the children of Bela (Bilhah). First Maccabees 12:5-23 and Josephus' Antiquities 12:4:10 mention that the Lacedemonians were "of the stock of Abraham" just like the Jews. Ancient historians trace the Lacedemonians to the Heraclidae or descendants of Hercules who was Samson of the tribe of Dan (Judges 13:2, 24-25). In the Gulf of Corinth in Greece, near the modern Lepanto, was a town called Calydon (Heb. "All of Dan"). In Scotland is Caledonia. The Danube (Dan's Swelling), Daneister (Dan's Hiding Place), Danapris (Dan's Villages) and Don all show his migrations. "The Dannans were a people of great learning, they had overmuch gold and silver ... they left Greece after a battle with the Assyrians, and for fear of falling into the hands of the Assyrians came to Norway and Denmark (Dannemark) and thence passed over to Ireland" (Keating's History of Ireland, p.40). "The colony called Tuatha-de-Dannan conquered the Firbolgs and became Masters of Ireland ... were highly skilled in architecture and other arts from their long residence in Greece and intercourse with the Phoenicians" (Annals of Ireland by the Four Masters, p.121). In the Lough of Belfast we find Donaghadee ("Dan My Witness"). Dannans arrived in Ireland in 1200 B.C. Milesians conquered them in 1000 B.C. Milesians were also called Gadelians from a leader called Gadhol (Heb. "Great") (Keating's History, p.30) (The tribes of Dan and Gad).

"After this I beheld, and, lo, a great multitude, which no man could number, of all nations, and kindreds, and people, and tongues, stood before the throne, and be-fore the Lamb, clothed with white robes, and palms in their hands; And cried with a loud voice, saying, Salvation to our God which sitteth upon the throne, and unto the Lamb. And all the angels stood round about the throne, and about the elders and the four beasts, and fell before the throne on their faces, and worshipped God, Saying, Amen: Blessing, and glory, and wisdom, and thanksgiving, and honour, and power, and might, be unto our God for ever and ever. Amen. And one of the elders answered, saying unto me, What are these which are arrayed in white robes? and whence came they? And I said unto him, Sir, thou knowest. And he said to me, These are they which came out of great tribulation, and have washed their robes, and made them white in the blood of the Lamb. Therefore are they before the throne of God, and serve him day and night in his temple: and he that sitteth on the throne shall dwell among them. They shall hunger no more, neither thirst any more; neither shall the sun light on them, nor any heat. For the Lamb which is in the midst of the throne shall feed them, and shall lead them unto living fountains of waters: and God shall wipe away all tears from their eyes" (Rev. 7:9-17)

Astronomically, Ursa Major is the innumerable multitude while Ursa Minor is the 144,000 "little flock." Both Cassiopeia and Virgo hold palm branches. Historically, Matthew 24 runs parallel to the first six seals in Revelation 6:1-17. Both accounts answer the question, "What shall be the sign of thy coming, and of the end of the world?" (Matt. 24:3). Both have a double application, first to the era from 96 - 395 A.D. ending in the coming of Constantine to rule and his era of tolerance. Second to the era from 1776 A.D. to the end-time and the coming of Jesus the Messiah to rule and his Millenium. Now Revelation 7:14 mentions the "Great Tribulation" which occurred just prior to Constantine -- under Diocletian -- from 303 to 313 A.D. It is the fifth seal. This "Great Tribulation" will occur again in end-time America. Pagans blamed Christianity for the evils that had befallen the Roman Empire and will blame Christians for the evils that will befall the United States. The "great sound of a trumpet" (Matt. 24:31) is the seventh trumpet of Revelation (under the seventh seal). They "gather together his elect" (24:31) first in the British Isles in 460 A.D. and second in British Columbia and Australia in the end-time. Isaiah 49:6 says Israel would be "a light to the gentiles, that thou mayest be my salvation unto the end of the earth." "In thee and in thy seed shall all the families of the earth be blessed" (Gen. 22:18). God wanted complacent Israel to flee west because this "Great Tribulation" lasted TEN years in the East but lasted only EIGHT years further West, and only TWO years in the extreme West of Europe (France & Britain) because these latter provinces were ruled over by Constantius, who hated the decree. Perhaps the Governor of Washington State and the Premier of Vancouver Island will provide the safest havens in the future. Many persecuted Gentiles, such as Huguenots, fled to the British Isles in obedience to the command "Come out of her (papal Europe), my people" (Rev. 18:4). But "builders" have rejected these three stones. In the case of BRITAIN, the Roman legions left in 410 A.D. In the case of VANCOUVER ISLAND, the Russians only claimed north of 54 degrees 40 minutes. Spanish ceded to America all claims north of 42 degrees and Americans never claimed the island. In the case of AUSTRALIA, Spain, France, Portugal and Holland all saw that Australia and Tasmania were desolate and concluded they were useless. Furthermore, commercial builders have rejected all three stones (Britain, Vancouver Island & Australia) because they are less accessible due to being islands rather than mainland.

John 12:13 says Jesus rode into Jerusalem and they took palms and waved them saying "Hosanna" meaning "Save now." Israel's deliverance from Egypt was celebrated with palms in hand during the Feast of Boothes. This fruit harvest festival typified the spiritual harvest of the whole human race here portrayed. These are non-Israelites by birth who accept Christ as their savior and obey the Bible. Strangers could become Israelites by obeying Bible law (Eph. 2:12; Rom. 11:17). True Christianity spread first to the BRITISH Isles because Jesus said to his disciples, "Go not in the way of the Gentiles, and into any city of the Samaritans enter ye not: but go rather to the lost sheep of the house of ISRAEL" (Matt. 10:5-6).

Tertullian (155-222 A.D.) wrote: "The extremities of Spain, the various parts of Gaul, the regions of BRITAIN which have never been penetrated by Roman arms have received the religion of Christ." (Tertullian Def. Fidei, p.179). Eusebius (260-340 A.D.) wrote: "The Apostles passed beyond the ocean to the Isles called the BRITANNIC Isles." (De Demonstratione Evangelii) Dorotheus Bishop of Tyre wrote in 303 A.D.: "Aristobulus whom Paul saluted, writing to the Romans (Rom. 10:16) was Bishop of BRITAIN." and "Simon Zelotes preached Christ through all Mauretania, and Africa the Less. At length he was crucified at BRITANNIA, slain and buried." (Synopsis De Apostal) Chrysostom (Patriarch of Constantinople) (347-407 A.D.) wrote: "Though thou shouldest go to the ocean to the BRITISH Isles, there thou shouldest hear all men everywhere discoursing matters out of the Scriptures with another voice but not another faith." (Chrysostom Orat O Theos Xristos) Gildas (425-512 A.D.) wrote: "Christ the True Sun, afforded His light, the knowledge of His precepts to our island in the last year as we know of Tiberias Caesar." (37 A.D.) (De Excidio Britanniae, Sect. 8, page 25) William of Malmesbury (1080-1143 A.D.) wrote in his De Antiquitate Glastonie, that Joseph of Arimathea brought the pure Apostolic Gospel to Glastonbury not long after the resurrection of our Lord. Polydore Virgil (1470-1555 A.D.) wrote: "BRITAIN partly through Joseph of Arimathea ... was of all kingdoms the first that received the Gospel." Archbishop Ussher (1581-1656 A.D.) wrote: "the mother church of the BRITISH Isles is the Church in Insula Avalonia called by the Saxons Glaston."

Even the Roman Church Councils of Pisa 1409 A.D., Constance 1417 A.D., Sienna 1424 A.D., and Basle 1434 A.D. all admitted that: "The churches of France and Spain must yield in points of antiquity and precedence to that of BRITAIN, as the latter Church was founded by Joseph of Arimathea immediately after the passion of Christ."

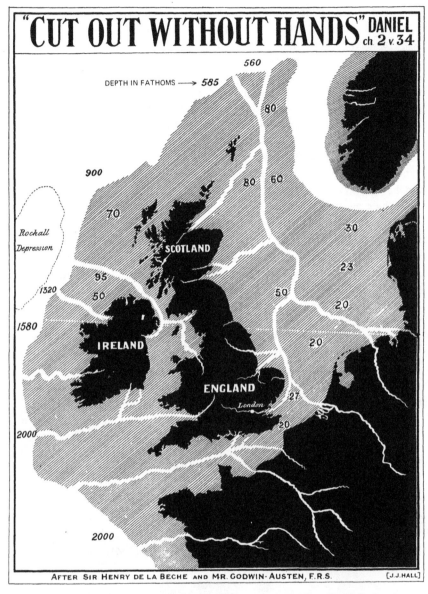

Showing how the British Isles were "cut out without hands"
from the mountain of Europe.

Goths and Huns Overthrow
Western Roman Empire

(395 A.D. to 476 A.D.)
(Chapter 8)

John wrote "And when he had opened the seventh seal, there was silence in heaven about the space of half an hour. And I saw the seven angels which stood before God; and to them were given seven trumpets" (Rev. 8:1-2).

Astronomically, Ursa Minor contains seven prominent stars (angels) that stand before Cepheus (enthroned king) forming an alternate bugle constellation and an alternate shofar (ram's horn) constellation. As the sun enters Scorpio, Scorpio blows the west wind into his shofar. As the sun enters Aquarius, Aquarius blows the south wind into his shofar. As the sun enters Taurus, Taurus blows the east wind into his shofar and as the sun enters Leo, Leo blows the north wind into his shofar. Then the three woes keep rotating till all seven shofars are blown. Historically, what does "ABOUT ... HALF an HOUR" mean? If one day is a year of 360 days (Num. 14:34; Ez. 4:6), and if there are "twelve hours in a day" (John 11:9), then 360 divided by 24 gives a "half hour" as 15 days which is 15 years. This describes the comparative peace under Emperor Theodosius the Great in the Roman Empire from October 3, 382 , when the final treaties with the remaining Gothic forces were signed, to January 17, 395 A.D. when he died which is "ABOUT" 15 years (12 years 3.5 months).

Why switch from SEALS to TRUMPETS? Because we have switched from PAGAN emperors to "CHRISTIAN" emperors. What do the TRUMPETS mean? "If the TRUMPET give an uncertain sound, who shall prepare himself for the BATTLE?" (1 Cor. 14:8). TRUMPETS symbolize WAR (Jer. 4:5; Hosea 8:1; Joel 2:1). The FOUR TRUMPETS probably let loose "the FOUR WINDS" (Rev. 7:1).

The ancient city of Jericho prevented Israel from entering into Canaan to establish the Kingdom of God until after "seven trumpets of Ram"s horns" were blown (Joshua 6:16) on the Feast of Unleavened Bread. In the same way, the Roman Empire now becomes "Jericho" preventing Anglo-Saxon Israel from arriving in the British Isles. True Christians are being persecuted by Roman Catholics. Therefore, seven trumpet blasts of punishment are needed (Nu. 10:1-10; Amos 3:6; Zeph. 1:14-16; Joel 2:1). The first six days they marched once around (Joshua 6:11-14) corresponding to the first six seals. The seventh day they marched seven times around (Joshua 6:15-16) corresponding to the seventh seal which contains seven trumpets.

"And another angel came and stood at the altar, having a golden censer; and there was given unto him much incense, that he should offer it with the prayers of all saints upon the golden altar which was before the throne. And the smoke of the incense, which came with the prayers of the saints, ascended up before God out of the angel's hand" (Rev. 8:3-4).

Astronomically, Aquarius offers incense from his "censer" Bucket on Ara, and the smoke of the Milky Way incense floats before the throne of Cepheus. Historically, the incense-offering ritual is described in Leviticus 16:12. This "Angel" must be Jesus the Messiah because in the original Tabernacle in the wilderness, the "golden censer" was found only inside the Ark of the Covenant (a type of Christ) in the Holy of Holies (Heb. 9:4); and none but the High Priest could enter that holiest place. He is the one and only "Mediator between God and men, the Man Christ Jesus" (1 Tim. 2:5) "who ever liveth to make intercession" (Heb. 7:25). This "Angel" gathers the prayers of all the saints or Christian martyrs who were persecuted by the Roman Empire, among which was this prayer recorded in Rev. 6:10: "How long, O Lord, holy and true, dost thou not judge and avenge our blood on them that dwell on the (Roman) earth?" Like incense, these prayers "Ascend up before God."

"And the angel took the censer, and filled it with fire of the altar, and cast it into the earth: and there were voices, and thunderings, and lightnings, and an earthquake. And the seven angels which had the seven trumpets prepared themselves to sound. The first angel sounded, and there followed hail and fire mingled with blood, and they were cast upon the earth: and the third part of trees was burnt up, and all green grass was burnt up" (Rev. 8:5-7).

The exclusive right of the High Priest of Israel was to have a golden censer in his hand -- so this is Jesus the Messiah (Heb. 4:14). Just as "there went out a decree from Caesar Augustus that all the WORLD (Greek "oikoumene") should be regis-tered" (Luke 2:1) meaning the ROMAN world, so also the "fire" is cast "upon the EARTH" (Greek "ge") (Rev. 8:5) meaning the ROMAN earth -- not the globe. Hail, fire and blood were three of the plagues of Egypt God sent to liberate ancient Israel so they could escape to the Promised Land. Just as hail-storms originate from the cold NORTHEAST and sweep across Europe, Alaric the Goth came from the NORTHEAST. "HAIL" means "BATTLE and WAR" (Job 38:22-23). In Ezekiel 10:2, when "coals of FIRE" were scattered "over the city" of Jerusalem, it meant "I will bring a SWORD upon you saith the Lord God" (Ez. 11:8). "FIRE" cast on the evil Roman Empire is God's "FURY" "because of the evil of your doings" (Jer.21:12).

What were those evils? Worshipping saints, martyrs, angels and relics rather than Christ our Lord. Making priests the "mediators" who "forgive sins." Using images and idols in worship. The pagan Eunapius in 396 A.D. exclaimed, "The monks kneel before dead men's bones, pickled, salted, covered with filth and dust. These are their intercessors with the gods now-a-days." And the Manichaean Faustus in 400 A.D. wrote, "You have but exchanged the old idols for martyrs, and offered to the latter the same prayers as to the former." To whom much is given, much is required (Luke 12:48; Amos 3:2) whereas God overlooks mistakes done in ignorance (Acts 17:30).

49

The level of responsibility increased as Rome went from pagan to "Christian."

Gibbon says that between 375-476 A.D., "The greater part of the Roman world was shaken by a violent and destructive EARTHQUAKE ... and they considered these alarming strokes as the prelude only of still more dreadful calamities. Alaric's and Rhadagaisus's Gothic revolt, breaking their alliance with Rome in 395 A.D., may also be the "thunders ... lightnings ... EARTHQUAKE" (Rev. 8:5). Emperor Theodosius died in 395 A.D. Alaric's Visigoths then swept down upon the Western Roman Empire and devastated it with fire and sword. Rhadagasius's 250,000-man army of Vandals, Suevi and Burgundians is described by Gibbon: "The consuming flames of war spread from the banks of the Rhine over the greatest part of the seventeen provinces of Gaul; the scene of plenty was suddenly changed into a desert." The first four trumpets are Gothic trumpets because they foreshadow four different invasions of Gothic peoples upon the Western section of the Roman Empire to destroy it. Who were the GOTHS? "The old geographer Ortelius, in his description of Tartary, notes the kingdom of Arsareth, where 'the TEN TRIBES retiring took the name of GAUTHEI, because they were very jealous for the glory of God.'" (Lights and Shadows by Elizabeth Wilson, pp.154-155). Tacitus informs us they spoke "the Gallic tongue" which probably got its name from "Galilee" (Isa. 9:1). Perhaps this is why Alaric showed mercy to the Christian churches, while sacking villas and palaces. Through the ministry of Ulphilas, a section of the Goths had accepted Christianity.

This Western section was one "third part" of the entire Roman Empire. At that time the Roman Empire was divided into three parts -- the Western Roman (Latin), the Eastern Constantinople (Greek), and the middle Illyrian Praefecture (Oriental). During the fourth century, the Empire was on three occasions divided into three parts under the rule of three emperors -- at Constantine's conversion 312 A.D.; at his death in 337 A.D. and from the years 383 to 387 A.D. History wonderfully confirms the accuracy of the first six trumpets. Three different races, Goths, Arabs and Turks each invaded a different third of the Roman Empire which John predicted long before in Revelation 8 and 9.

In another sense, the western "third" of the empire was part of the "third" empire in succession -- the Eastern Greek empire. Diocletian partitioned the empire in 292 A.D. Constantine named the capital Constantinople in 328 A.D. thereby fulfilling 2 Thess.2:7. The emperor who ruled from Rome was an emperor in name only. He was subject to the ruler of a revived Greek Empire set up at Constantinople. The first four trumpets brought enemies upon an empire which had become Eastern or Greek in character as well as capital, and which is therefore described as "third" rather than "fourth" in the book of Revelation.

In the ten years from 400 to 410 A.D., Alaric's Gothic hordes attacked Gaul, Spain and Italy. The Goths laid Italy waste three times by destroying the green vegetation and fruit trees as they went. Alaric beseiged Rome three times -- 408 A.D., 409 A.D. and 410 A.D. -- the third time destroying the city, sacking it for three days and selling

50

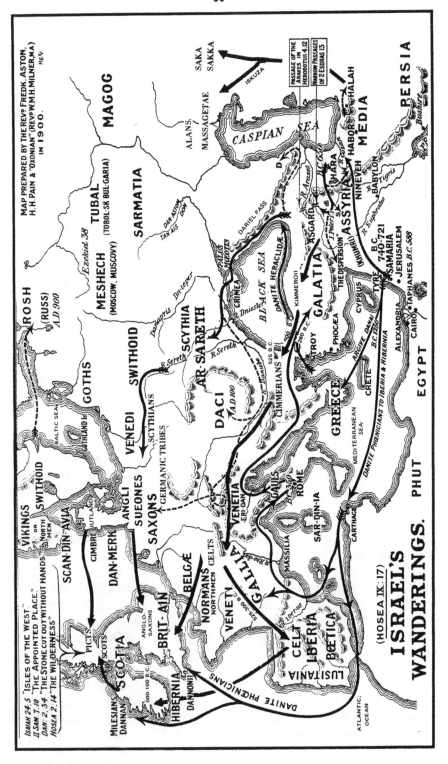

ISAIAH 24.5 "ISLES OF THE WEST"
II SAM. 7:10 "THE APPOINTED PLACE"
DAN: 2.34 "THE STONE cut out without HANDS."
HOSEA 2:14 "THE WILDERNESS"

MAP PREPARED BY THE REV? FREDK. ASTON,
H.H. PAIN & "OXONIAN" (REV?W.M.H. MILNER, M.A.)
IN 1900. REV

ROSH
(RUSS.) A.D. 900

MAGOG

SAKA
SAKKA

ISKUZA

PASSAGE OF THE
ARATES IN
HERODOTUS 4.12

NARROW PASSAGES
OF 2 ESDRAS 13

PERSIA

MEDIA

HABOR HALAH

NINEVEH ASSYRIA
(KHUMRI)
BABYLON

B.C.
740-721

SAMARIA
• JERUSALEM
TYRE B.C.1300

CAIRO TAPHANES B.C.588
ALEXANDRIA

EGYPT

PHUT

GOTHS

MESHECH
(MOSCOW, MUSCOVY)

TUBAL
(TOBOL-SK BUL-GARIA)

SARMATIA

MAGOG

Ezekiel 38

CASPIAN SEA

ALANS,
MASSAGETAE

DAN ASTER
TANAIS DON

SWITHOID

VENEDI

SCYTHIANS

GERMANIC TRIBES

AR-SARETH

SCYTHIA

DACI
A.D.100

R. Sereth

Dnieper

Dniester

CRIMEA

PALUS
MÆOTIS

BLACK SEA

DANITE HERACLIDE

KIMMEROII

CIMMERIANS

ASGARD

GALATIA

THE DISPERSION

CYPRUS

CRETE

GREECE

MEDITERRANEAN
SEA:

DANITE PHŒNICIANS TO IBERIA & HIBERNIA

CARTHAGE

VIKINGS

SWITHOID

SCAN-DIN-AVIA

DAN-MERK

CIMBRI

NORTH
MEN

ANGLI

SUEONES

SAXONS

BELGÆ

NORMANS
NORTHMEN CELTS

VENETI

GALLIA

SAR-DIN-IA

ROME

MASSILIA

GAULS

VENETIA
ERI-DAN

PICTS

SCOTS

SCOTIA

HIBERNIA
DANNONI

BRIT-AIN

ANGLO-
SAXONS

CELT

IBERIA

BÆTICA

LUSITANIA

ATLANTIC
OCEAN

DANITE PHŒNICIANS

MILESIANS
DANNAN

500-100 B.C.

(HOSEA IX:17)

ISRAEL'S
WANDERINGS.

thousands of its inhabitants into slavery. Gibbon describes their siege of Rome in apocalyptic terms: "The inhabitants were awakened by the tremendous sound of the Gothic TRUMPET." Alaric died in 410 A.D. Roman soldiers evacuated from Britain to help save and defend their own empire, leaving Britain built and prepared, but empty, for Anglo-Saxon Israel. Alaric's Goths destroyed not only the VINEYARDS and FARMS but also these Roman soldiers. Figuratively speaking, "All flesh is GRASS" (Isa. 40:6; 51:12) and "the glory of man like the FLOWER" (1 Pet. 1:24; James 1:10). All human rulers are TREES. "The TREE ... it is thou" (Nebuchadnezzar) (Dan. 4:20-22). "The Assyrian was a CEDAR" (Ez. 31:3; Judges 9:8-15). King David sang, "I am like a green OLIVE TREE " (Ps. 52:8). Green trees signify the righteous and dry trees the wicked (Ez. 20:46-47; 21:3-4; Luke 23:31). "Hail, fire and blood" remind us of the plagues upon Egypt to free God's people Israel from heathen tyranny. The Gothic invasions -- the hail of arrows, the fire of torches and arson and the blood of the slain -- caused Roman legions to withdraw from England and Wales, thus freeing British Israel from the yoke of Imperial Rome.

"And the second angel sounded, and as it were a great mountain burning with fire (volcano) was cast into the (Roman) sea: and the third part of the (Roman) sea became blood; And the third part of the creatures which were in the (Roman) sea, and had life, died; and the third part of the ships were destroyed" (Rev. 8:8-9).

What does the burning mountain mean? "O destroying mountain, saith the Lord ... I will ... make thee a burnt (-out) mountain" (an extinct volcano) (Jer. 51:25) describing the aggressive kingdom of Babylon. From 429 to 477 A.D., Genseric threw a large army "into the sea" and his aggressive Vandals waged war on the coasts of the Mediterranean Sea from Gaul and Spain. They crossed the Mediterranean from Gibraltar to Africa and burned Hippo in 430 A.D. and conquered Carthage in 439 A.D. Priscus the poet referred to the Vandals as "Burning Byrsa." (Byrsa was the hill on which Carthage was built.) There they built ships and committed piracy against Rome's navy and ships. They captured Sicily, Sardinia, Corsica, Majorca and Minorca. Rome was sacked (June 15-29, 455 A.D.) and thousands of its inhabitants enslaved. Jerusalem's temple furnishings which Titus had deposited in the Temple of Peace in Rome nearly 400 years ago, were carried off by Genseric to Carthage. The Western Roman navy was defeated in 457 A.D. In 468 A.D. fireships were driven amongst 1,113 ships that had sailed to attack Cathage from Constantinople. In the obscurity of the night, the fire of the Vandal volcano defeated this Eastern Roman navy in 468 A.D. Genseric the Great was known as the "tyrant of the seas." He is reputed to have said, "Let us make for the dwellings of men with whom God is angry." Genseric died in 477 A.D.

"And the third angel sounded, and there fell a great star (meteor) from heaven, burning as it were a lamp (torch), and it fell upon the third part of the rivers, and upon the fountains of waters; And the name of the star is called Wormwood: and the third part of the waters became wormwood; and many men died of the waters, because they were made bitter" (Rev. 8:10-11).

A falling "STAR" is a short-lived "RULER" (Dan. 8:10; 12:3). A chronicler in 444 A.D. likened Attila (433-453 A.D.) to a baneful meteor that blazed in the heavens that year foreboding a brief period of ruin and WAR. This imagery indicates Attila was Satanic (Luke 10:18; Rev. 12:8-9; Rev. 9:1). Attila ruled over a territory bordered by the Danube, the Volga and the Baltic. He had a large head, square shoulders, swarthy complexion, deep eyes and flat nose. In 450 A.D. he ravaged the upper Danube, and followed the Rhine from Basle to Belgium and made its valley desolate. Attila became known as "the scourge of God." Defeated in the battle of Chalons in 451 A.D., Attila and his Huns made the Alpine lake and river country and the valleys of the Po all desolate (Lombardy). He sacked the cities of Padua, Verona, Milan and Turin. Upon reaching Rome, he was persuaded to turn back by Pope Leo. Refugees were driven to marshy islands where they founded Venice. In 453 A.D. Attila retired to Buda where he died the same year. The absinthe plant -- Wormwood -- grows freely in the Alps and is bitter and is associated with gall in Scripture (cp. Deut. 29:18). Wormwood (Apsinthos) is the name of a river in the Illyrian region ruled by Attila. Therefore, the same name gives us both the local origin of the "great star" and the effect of his war on the Roman third. Attila burnt cities, massacred and enslaved inhabitants and generally caused despair, famine and bitterness. The Huns devastated the inhabitants of the Italian Alps -- the source of the rivers, causing pollution and disease for those who drank. He died in 453 A.D. having had a brief, meteoric career.

"And the fourth angel sounded, and the third part of the sun was smitten, and the third part of the moon, and the third part of the stars; so as the third part of them was darkened, and the day shone not for a third part of it, and the night likewise" (Rev. 8:12).

Odoacer was chieftain of the Heruli. His father Edecon had been ambassador and secretary to Attila the Hun. Odoacer was of the Arian Christian sect which denied the Deity of the Lord Jesus. He received a prophecy from a hermit who said, "Go to Italy and you shall rise to honour and cast away your coarse garment of skin for nobler vestures and your wealth will be equal to the liberality of your mind." Odoacer brought his mercenaries and quickly rose to be a general in the Western Roman Empire. Odoacer's Heruli finally conquered Rome itself terminating Imperial rule by banishing Emperor Romulus Augustulus in 476 A.D. By a strange coincidence the names of the two great founders of the city and the monarchy were united in their last emperor. Jerome said, "The world's glorious sun has been extinguished." Odoacer governed Italy from 476 to 490 A.D. Theodoric the Ostrogoth destroyed the Heruli and their kingdom at Rome and Ravenna and ruled Italy as an independent sovereign from 493 to 526 A.D. The Kingdom of Lombardy was set up in 570 A.D. If the sun is the supreme ruler, the moon and stars are subordinate rulers (Gen. 37:9-10). There is a parallel here between the punishment on Pagan Rome (Rev. 8:7,8,10,12) and the punishment on Papal Rome (Rev. 16.). In both the same four symbols are used: "Earth," "Sea," "Rivers" and "Sun" (ruler). See Isaiah 13:10, Amos 8:9 and Acts 2:20. After 476 A.D. the Roman Empire divided into ten independent nations, the feet of ROMAN IRON and GOTHIC CLAY (Dan. 2:42). "We (ISRAEL) are the CLAY" (Isa.

64:8; cp. Jer. 18-19 & Rom. 9:21). Today their names are Germany, Austria, France, Belgium, Luxemburg, Holland, Switzerland, Italy, Spain and Portugal. Israelite clay is mixed in these nations.

In 2 Thessalonians 2:3-4 we read "That man of sin (shall) be revealed, the son of perdition; who opposeth and EXALTETH HIMSELF ABOVE all that is CALLED GOD, or that is WORSHIPPED; so that he AS GOD sitteth in the TEMPLE of GOD (Naos), showing himself that HE IS GOD."

First of all, the "temple of God" in the original Greek is not the Jewish Temple. It is "Ho Naos touTheou" while the word used for the Jewish Temple is "Hieron." The word "Naos" means "a dwelling" and is defined in Ephesians 2:20-22, 2 Thessalonians 2:4, 1 Corinthians 3:16-17 and 2 Corinthians 6:16 as the "Church." "Know ye not that YE ARE the TEMPLE (Naos) of GOD, and that the spirit of God dwelleth in you? If any man defile the temple (Naos) of God, him shall God destroy: for the temple of God is holy, which TEMPLE (Naos) YE ARE" (1 Cor. 3:16-17). Second, what is "CALLED GOD" or "WORSHIPPED" in the Catholic Church? Any Catholic would immediately say "the HOST." There are many idols in that church, but only one thing called "GOD" -- the WAFER used in Mass, which is truly WORSHIPPED by all faithful Catholics. Catholics even PRAY to it. Third, at the time of the coronation of a new Pope, the host is consecrated and placed on the high altar in St. Peter's at Rome. It is now CALLED GOD. ABOVE the high altar there is a THRONE built into the architecture. When the mass is over, "The Pope rises and wearing his mitre, is LIFTED by the cardinals, and is placed by them UPON the altar to sit there. One of the bishops kneels and begins the Te Deum (we praise thee Oh God). In the meantime the cardinals kiss the feet of the Pope" (Ceremoniale Romanum by Marcelles, 16th cent. Archbishop). This ceremony is called by Roman Catholic writers "the Adoration" and has been observed for many centuries. For Pius IX a medal was struck to celebrate the occasion, and on it is the inscription "Quem creant adorant" or "whom they create (viz. the Pope) they adore." Such language is blasphemous in the extreme. During the coronation of a new Pope there are no less than five distinct adorations, at each of which the canons and clergy of St. Peter's, with their cardinal high priest leading them, come and kneel before the Pope and kiss his feet. At this time also the Pope is CARRIED UP to the THRONE ABOVE the high altar where he sits literally "ABOVE that which is CALLED GOD." Fourth, does the Pope actually exalt himself verbally above God? Pope Pius XI said, "You know that I am the Holy Father, the representative of God on the earth, the vicar of Christ, which means that I am God on earth" ("The Bulwark" October 1922, p. 104). "A holy priest is a savior and another christ" (The Priest, His Dignity and Obligations, St. John Eudes, p.12). "There is more certainty in doing the will of God by obedience to superiors than by obedience to Jesus Christ, should He appear in person to give His commands" (Liguori's True Spouse of Christ, pp. 93 & 162). Pope Nicholas said, "I am all in all and above all, so that God Himself, and I, the Vicar of God, have both one consistory, and I am able to do almost all that God can do ... Wherefore, if those things that I do be said not to be done of man, but of God, what can you make me but God? Again, if prelates of the church be called and counted of Constantine for gods, I then, being above all prelates, seem by this reason to be above all gods. Wherefore, no marvel if it be in my power to dispense with all things, yea, with the precepts of Christ." (End of Age, p.191) Pope Pius X in 1895 said, "The Pope is not only the representative of Jesus Christ, but he is Jesus Christ Himself hidden under the veil of the flesh. Does the Pope speak? It is Jesus Christ who speaks. Does the Pope accord a favour or pronounce an anathema? It is Jesus Christ who pronounces the anathema or accords the favour. So that when the Pope speaks we have no business to examine. We have only to obey. We have no right to criticize his decisions or discuss his commands. Therefore, everyone who would wear the crown ought to submit himself to Divine Right." Fifth, is the antichrist an individual or a dynasty? Daniel 7:17 speaks of four world-ruling empires and says, "These great beasts which are four are FOUR KINGS which shall arise out of the earth." Does this mean four individual kings? No. Instead it refers to the Babylonian, Medo-Persian, Greek and Roman Empires all ruled by a DYNASTY over each. Again the ten horns of Daniel 7:20,24 are proven by fulfillment to be ten kingdoms into which the western Roman Empire was divided at its fall. These ten kingdoms are called "KINGS" (Dan. 7:24), yet they have each existed 14 centuries as a SUCCESSION of KINGS. Side by side with these a little horn "which had eyes (the See of Rome), and a mouth that spake very great things" ran its course. Therefore, this antichrist is a SUCCESSION of POPES.

In 2 Thessalonians 2:7 we read that "he who now hindereth will continue to hinder until he be taken out of the way. And then shall that wicked one be revealed, whom the Lord shall consume." Pagan Roman Caesars hindered until they were taken out of the way in 476 A.D. Then Papal Rome was able to take their place and be revealed. In the same way, American presidents stand for freedom of religion and separation of church and state. Until they are taken out of the way, they will hinder the rise of an intolerant Catholic America.

"And I beheld, and heard an angel flying through the midst of heaven, saying with a loud voice, Woe, woe, woe, to the inhabiters of the (Roman) earth by reason of the other voices of the trumpet of the three angels, which are yet to sound!" (Rev. 8:13).

Astronomically Pegasus the flying horse may say "Woe, woe, woe" as he gallops endlessly. Historically the first four Trumpets (stages in decline of "Christian" Roman Emperors), like the first four Seals (stages in decline of the pagan Roman Emperors), stand apart from the last three, and resemble one another. The three woes are:
1. Fifth Trumpet: Arabs conquer the Southern third of the Roman Empire.
2. Sixth Trumpet: Turks conquer the Eastern third of the Roman Empire.
3. Seventh Trumpet: The French Revolution.

Notice that the first six trumpets of Revelation 8 and 9 predicted the division of the Roman Empire into thirds. The Goths conquered the Western third of the Roman Empire which we've just covered. Arabs conquered the southern third and Turks the eastern third as we shall see.

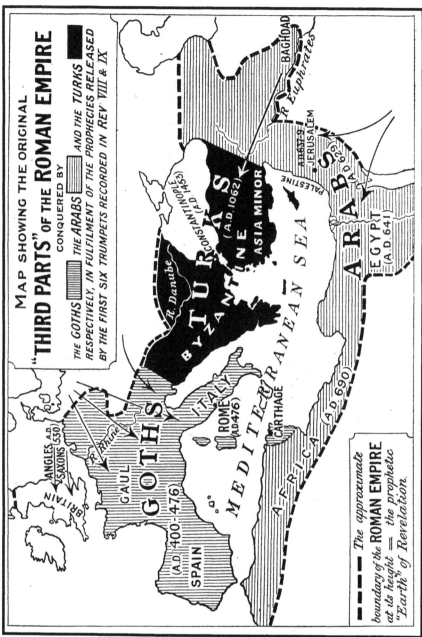

MAP SHOWING THE ORIGINAL "THIRD PARTS" of the ROMAN EMPIRE

CONQUERED BY

THE GOTHS THE ARABS AND THE TURKS RESPECTIVELY, IN FULFILMENT OF THE PROPHECIES RELEASED BY THE FIRST SIX TRUMPETS RECORDED IN REV. VIII & IX

The approximate boundary of the ROMAN EMPIRE at its height = the prophetic "Earth" of Revelation.

"The third part of trees were burned up ... and the third part of the sea became blood; And the third part of the creatures which were in the sea ... died; and the third part of the ships were destroyed ... and the third part of the waters became wormwood ... the third part of the sun was smitten, and the third part of the moon, and the third part of the stars ... the third part of men killed" (Rev. 8:7 to 9:18).

The Seven Trumpets

Rev.	Church Era	Trumpet	A.D.	Historical Events
8:7	Pergamos	First	395-410	Ravages of Alaric the Goth in Greece, 395; in Italy 402.
8:8		Second	429-477	Ravages of Genseric the Vandal; plunders Rome (June 15-29, 455)
8:10		Third	433-453	Ravages of Attila the Hun (Commenced after sounding of 2nd Trumpet began in 429)
8:12		Fourth	476	Odoacer, Heruli king, deposed last Emperor, Romulus Augustulus.
8:13	Thyatira	Interval	476-612	From Fall of Western Roman Empire to Rise of Islam
9:1-11		Fifth	612-762	Saracenic "Woe Trumpet," 150 years (9:5) -- First "Woe"
9:12	Sardis (1558-1850)	Interval	762-1062	
9:13-21		Sixth	1062-1917	Turkish Second "Woe." Fall of Constantinople and Eastern Roman Empire, May 29, 1453. "Dried up" (Rev. 16:12) historically ("times fulfilled") on release of Jerusalem, Dec. 9, 1917 (Luke 21:24); officially by expulsion of House of Othman from Turkey, and abolition of Caliphate, March 6, 1924.
16:13-14	Philadelphia & Laodicea (1870-present)	Interval	1917-present	Bolshevism -- Third "Woe" "cometh quickly" after 2nd Woe (11:14)
11:15-19		Seventh	present	Era of "the Day of the Lord" (climax of Armageddon), Judgment of the Babylonian counterfeit system preparatory to the Millenium.

57

Moslem Arabs Attack Idolatrous
South Roman-Byzantine Empire
(612-762 A.D.)
Chapter 9:1-12

John wrote "And the fifth angel sounded, and I saw a star fall from heaven unto the earth: and to him was given the key of the bottomless pit. And he opened the bottomless pit" (Rev. 9:1-2)

Astronomically, the constellation Cassiopeia (Enthroned Woman) is alternately symbolized by a "Laconian Key" which opens Crater (the Bottomless Pit). Historically, who is the STAR? The "STAR" that fell from heaven is SATAN because Christ said, "I beheld SATAN as lightning FALL from HEAVEN" (Luke 10:18). "How art thou FALLEN from HEAVEN, O LUCIFER ... thou shalt be brought down ... to the sides of the PIT" (Isa. 14:12-15). Furthermore, verse 11 confirms this by calling him "DESTROYER." When paganism was overthrown, Satan fell (Rev. 12:9). But Satan then opened the prison of evil spirits and inspired an Arab of Mecca in 605 A.D. named Mohammed. "For there shall arise false Christs and false Prophets ... behold I have told you before ... if they say unto you behold he (Mohammed) is in the desert (of Arabia), go not forth: behold he (the Pope) is in the secret chamber (Cardinals sealed inside Sistine Chapel whenever they vote for a new Pope), believe it not" (Matt. 24:24).

What is the KEY? Papal KEYS of St. Peter (cp. Matt. 16:19; Rev. 1:18; 3:7) came from the KEY of Janus and KEY of Cybele just as India's Brahmatma has two crossed KEYS on his tiara and just as Mithraism's KEYS symbolized the Sun-god's authority. All these religions inherited their KEYS from the Pontiff of ancient Babylon. The KEY has been the emblem of the family of Mohammed because of its role as guardian of the sacred, black Kaaba stone of Mecca. The Moorish followers of Islam displayed the KEY on their banner as they advanced across north Africa into Spain. The KEY was also engraved upon the arch of Alhambra, the Moorish palace in Granada. Furthermore, the Koran says, "Did not God give to his Legate (Mohammed) the power of heaven which is above, and the fire which is beneath? With the KEY did he not give him the title and power of a porter that he may open to those whom he shall have chosen?"

What is the SMOKE of the PIT? One day at age 40, he entered the mouth of the CAVE of Hera at the foot of Mount Hera, three miles from Mecca. He was shaken by an unseen power. A light flashed and the Angel Gabriel (Satan impersonating Gabriel) stood before him. Mohammed said "the Angel Gabriel" dictated to him the Koran in this CAVE which was the "bottomless PIT." His experiences were similar to the witch of Endor hearing the prophet Samuel, or the "voices" heard by Joan of Arc or the "visions" of Lourdes and Fatima. He ran home and told his wife (a wealthy widow named Kadijah who was 15 years older than him) he was possessed of a devil and had gone mad. She told him he was a prophet. He went into trances in which he had visions of the supposed sensual delights of Paradise, of the material torments of hell, and so on, all of which showed that he was a medium for Satan. Those who witnessed Mohammed fall into his strange trances, described him as one indwelt or possessed by genii or spirits. He wrote the Koran to imitate scripture while denying Jesus was anything but a good man. The Koran says that Noah's flood occurred in Moses' time (Sura 7:136 cf. 7:59); that Abraham attempted to sacrifice Ishmael, not Isaac, and that Mohammed is the Comforter rather than the Holy Spirit. "Take not the Jews and the Christians for your friends ... Allah's curse be on them: how they are deluded away from the truth" (Sura 5:51; 9:30). He publicly declared himself a prophet in 610 A.D. Notice that both "little horns" of Daniel began in 606-610 A.D.

"And there arose a smoke out of the pit, as the smoke of a great furnace; and the sun and the air were darkened by reason of the smoke of the pit. And there came out of the smoke locusts upon the earth: and unto them was given power, as the scorpions of the earth have power" (Rev. 9:2-3).

Astronomically, John saw Scorpio ascending from the burning altar Ara. According to the Aztecs, Corvus is another scorpion. The Milky Way billowing up from Ara is the smoke. Who are the LOCUSTS? In Hebrew the word for LOCUST is "ARBEH" and for Arab is "ARBI." Exodus 10:13 says, "the EAST wind brought the LOCUSTS" (on Egypt). What country was EAST of Egypt? ARABIA. Midianites (Arabs) come as LOCUSTS for multitude (Judges 6:5). "In the Bedoween romance of Antar the LOCUST is introduced as the national emblem of the ISHMAELITES.... Mohammedan tradition speaks of LOCUSTS having dropped into the hands of Mohammed, bearing on their wings this inscription, 'We are the army of the Great God.'" (Forster's Mohammedan-ism Unveiled 1:217). The teaching of the Koran is described as smoke that darkens the sun or obscures the Byzantine Emperor's influence as well as the idolatrous Eastern Orthodox Church. Out of the pit come LOCUSTS like SCORPIONS which both come from ARABIA. The swarms of Saracen or ARABIAN LOCUSTS overspread the east and partially the west part of the Roman Empire. The Koran promises endless sensual pleasures as the reward of death in battle.

Why SCORPIONS? Rehoboam's reply to the deputation who wanted him to lighten the tax burden was, "I will chastise you with SCORPIONS" or impose OPPRESSIVE TAXES. In 612 A.D. Mohammed publicly proclaimed his mission to convert all so-called Christians and infidels to the Koran. These were Greek and Latin "CHRISTIANS" who were image-worshippers and idol-worshippers in practice -- who weren't "SEALED with the Holy Spirit" (Eph. 1:13) because they didn't depart "from iniquity" (2 Tim. 2:19). Moslems called them "dogs and infidels" and treated them accordingly. Arabs offered conquered peoples the choice of accepting the Koran, or of PAYING TRIBUTE MONEY, or of death by the sword. Christians could buy their liberty to continue in their own religion, but only at the cost of HEAVY TRIBUTE. This is the meaning of "as the torment of a scorpion."

Also the Arabs pulled along in their REAR, "SCORPION" ARTILLARY which looked like "tails of scorpions." They employed in their military operations formidable MISSILES which they styled 'SCORPIONS." These missiles were of a chemical mixture which was the forerunner of gunpowder. An Arab writer in 1249 speaks of them: "The SCORPIONS surrounded and ignited by nitrated powder, glide along like serpents with a humming noise, and when exploded, they blaze brightly and burn. Now, to behold the matter expelled was as a cloud extended through the air, which gave forth a dreadful crash like thunder, vomiting fire on every side and breaking down, burning, and reducing all things to ashes." This was known as Saracen fire -- later as Greek fire.

"And it was commanded them that they should not hurt the grass of the earth, neither any green thing, neither any tree; but only those men which have not the seal of God in their foreheads" (Rev. 9:4).

Mohammed wrote, "The sword is the key of heaven and hell; a drop of blood spent in the cause of God ... is of more avail than two months fasting and prayer." Unlike ordinary locusts, the Arabs did not lay waste the countryside. The Koran says, "Destroy no FRUIT TREES, nor any FIELDS of CORN, cut down no FRUIT TREES." Caliph Abu Beker ordered his Arabian officers and soldiers: "When you fight the battles of the Lord, acquit yourselves like men, without turning your backs. But let not your victory be stained with the blood of women or children. Destroy no PALM-TREES, nor burn any FIELDS of CORN; cut down no FRUIT-TREES, nor do any mischief to cattle, only such as you kill to eat ... You will find another sort of people that belong to the Synagogue of Satan, who have shaven crowns: be sure you cleave their skulls and give them no quarter till they either turn Mahomedans or pay tribute" (Gibbon's Decline and Fall, ch. 51:10 or vol. 5:189). Compare this with the wilful destruction of the Gothic invasion in Revelation 8:7 where we saw "all GREEN GRASS burned up." Symbolically green trees signify the righteous and dry trees the wicked (Ez. 20:46-47; 21:3-4; Luke 23:31).

"And to them it was given that they should not kill them, but that they should be tormented five months: and their torment was as the torment of a scorpion, when he striketh a man. And in those days shall men seek death, and shall not find it; and shall desire to die, and death shall flee from them" (Rev. 9:5-6).

Biologically a literal locust plague lasts from April to September and scorpions are only active in five hot months. Historically this locust plague would last "FIVE MONTHS" which is 5 x 30 = 150 days which means 150 years in prophecy. In 612 A.D., Mohammed proclaimed his mission. In 622, the first year of the Mohammedan calendar, the prophet fled from enemies to Medina (the Hegira) where he organized his converts into an army. In 632 A.D. Mohammed died. In 632 A.D. the war against Christendom began when Arab armies moved out of Arabia. Just as natural locusts are bred in holes in the earth, the Arabs swarmed out of the DEAD SEA area -- the water of the Dead Sea is 1,300 feet below the Mediterranean and typified the "BOT-

TOMLESS PIT." Under succeeding Caliphs the Arabs conquered Palestine and Syria in 637-639 A.D. Egypt by 641 A.,D. All northern Africa by 690 A.D. and Spain by 713 A.D. -- all countries where locusts are known to exist naturally. Their SWIFT conquest is represented by their "WINGS." Also their cavalry had an east and west wing. Thus history gives us the years 612 to 632 for the beginning of the "locust woe" and 150 years later is 762 to 782 A.D., when the Mohammedan woe ceased its aggressive torment, having conquered another "THIRD PART" (Southern and Southeastern) of the former Roman Empire by the sword.

After their severe defeat at Tours in 732 A.D., by Charles Martel, the Caliph Almansor built Baghdad (called the City of Peace) in the year 762 A.D. as the new capital of his empire and moved from Damascus 500 miles east, and then the Saracens ceased their aggression like locusts. This was exactly 150 years after 612 A.D. when Mohammed proclaimed his mission. Cardinal Baronius says that in 761 A.D. the Christian remnant in the mountains of Spain began to roll the tide of war back upon their Saracen oppressors. It is interesting that they were defeated in Savoy, Piedmont and southern France -- the home of Waldenses and Albigenses -- since they were to hurt only corrupt Christians. In 755 A.D. the General Council of Constantinople passed a public condemnation on all images. Also in 755 A.D. a second Caliph was recognized in the West and Africa revolted. Both events occurred exactly 150 years after Mohammed received the "key" (9:1 -- 605 A.D.). Islam was no longer united. The Moslems never seriously harmed the Jews either. Jews profited by Moslem conquests and the Jewish golden age, since their dispersion, was their life under the Moors in Spain. In 771 A.D. -- the last year of the 150-year period from 622 -- Charlemagne began his long reign as sole ruler of France. Under him, Christian Europe became a single Empire and no longer feared an Arab menace. In 782 A.D., by the Treaty of Constantinople, the eastern Byzantine Roman Empire agreed to pay regular tribute to the Caliph of Baghdad exactly 150 years after Mohammed died and the war against idolatrous Christianity began in 632 A.D.

Since, "FIVE MONTHS" are mentioned twice (9:5,10) in the Fifth Trumpet, some expositors believe 300 years (150 x 2) is the full limit from 632 to 932 A.D. History bears this out. Through luxury and licentiousness the Arabs began to decline. The last Caliph of eminence was slain outside the walls of Baghdad near the Euphrates in 932 A.D. The Caliphate at Baghdad was stripped of its temporal power in 934 A.D. From the taking of Damascus or Jerusalem in 637 A.D. we add 300 years to get 937 A.D. In 936 A.D. Persia advanced on Bagdad and stripped the Caliph of his secular office of supremacy. Why not just say "ten months" instead then? Because natural locusts only appear FIVE MONTHS in the year.

On the Christian side, some desired to martyr themselves for Christ, rather than convert, but were AFRAID ("desire to die, and death shall flee"). On the Moslem side, death in battle with an infidel would ensure Paradise, so naturally Moslems sought this glorious death. But they rarely found it because their RECKLESS COURAGE combined with their prophetic destiny destroyed all opposition.

"And the shapes of the locusts were like unto horses prepared unto battle; and on their heads were as it were crowns like gold, and their faces were as the faces of men. And they had hair as the hair of women, and their teeth were as the teeth of lions. And they had breastplates, as it were breastplates of iron; and the sound of their wings was as the sound of chariots of many horses running to battle" (Rev. 9:7-9).

Astronomically this is Centaur with his breastplate of iron, Sagittarius [whom Caesius claimed was "Ishmael"], Pegasus and Leo pulling the chariot of Auriga with the star Capella -- the Charioteer with his Chariot superimposed (Isa. 66:15). Anciently, Leo, Ursa Major and Ursa Minor were all given the chariot symbol as well. Historically, Arabs were skilled HORSEMEN who wore YELLOW TURBANS -- the Sabean "turbans" (Ez. 23:42 Fenton) ("crowns of gold"). Unlike the Goths or Romans who were clean-shaven, they wore BEARDS ("faces ... as men") and had LONG HAIR flowing to their shoulders in the days of Mohammed ("as women"). They invented the use of CHAIN ARMOUR and Mohammed declared in the Koran: "God has given coats of mail to defend you in your wars" ("breastplates as it were of iron") from whom the Crusaders learned its use. Their horses were protected by SHEET METAL, making a clattering sound in battle. Gibbon wrote, "The charge of the Arabs was not like that of compact infantry; their military force was chiefly formed of cavalry." The Arab poem "Antar" composed about the 6th century describes a typical Arab, "He adjusted himself properly, twirled his whiskers, and folded up his hair under his turban, drawing it from off his shoulders. ... Horsemen clad in iron."

"And they had tails like unto scorpions, and there were stings in their tails: and their power was to hurt men five months. And they had a king over them, which is the angel of the bottomless pit, whose name in the Hebrew tongue is Abaddon, but in the Greek tongue hath his name Apollyon. One woe is past; and, behold, there come two woes more hereafter" (Rev. 9:10-12)

Both names mean 'Destroyer." One of the titles of the Turkish Sultan was 'Hunkiar' meaning "Slayer of Men." One woe is past, and, behold, there come two woes more hereafter" (Rev. 9:12). This verse occupies about 130 years.

The "king of fierce countenance" (Dan. 8:23) is the entire dynasty of Caliphs whose Islamic creed is essentially warlike. They "understand dark sentences" in the Koran. They are not "by his own power" -- not Mohammed's own flesh and blood descendants (cp. Dan. 8:22,24). "By peace ("Salama" or Islam) he shall destroy many" (Dan. 8:25). Moslems believe it is not necessary to keep treaties with infidels and so use "crafty deceit." "But he shall be broken without (human) hand" (Dan. 8:25). Both the Arab and Turkish Empires collapsed as a result of internal corruption. Quarrels over the Caliphate resulting in the rival Umayyaid and Abassid Dynasties as well as Islam splitting into Sunni and Shia sections caused the collapse of the Arab Empire. "Many shall be purified and made white and tried" (Dan. 11:33) because of martyrdoms under pagan Rome and Papal Rome. Daniel 11:40-45 mentions the "King of the South" (Arab Moslem Empire) conquering "south" (Arabian Peninsula), "east" (Mesopotamia and Persia) and into the "pleasant land" (Syria and Palestine). Professing Eastern Christians were cast to the ground and stamped upon by Moslems. Between 634 and 644 A.D., the Caliph Omar was responsible for the destruction of some 4000 places of Christian worship. Christians under Moslem rule were restricted in their worship, trade, commerce, dress and travel. The Turks entered the "glorious land" but Ammon, Edom and Moab escaped the Ottoman Empire because they were wandering Arab tribesmen who already accepted Islam. Egypt "shall not escape" when in 1516-1517 the Ottoman Emperor Selim I marched into Egypt and stripped it of its wealth and moved 500 Egyptian families from Cairo to Constantinople. In 1550 the Turks made Libya pay tribute. "All the princes who were before tributary or confederate to the late Sultan of Egypt even to the most mighty king of Ethiopia without delay entered into like subjection with the Turks" (Rycaut's Turkish History1:375). Both the "King of the South" and the "King of the North" (Turkish Ottoman Empire) push at "him" -- apostate Christianity -- who doesn't regard the "desire of women" (celibate), speaks "against the God of gods" (blasphemes), honors the gods of forces or the god that protects (guardian or patron saints) as well as honouring a god hitherto unknown, with gold, silver and precious stones whenever they worship the Host or wafer-god set up in a gold or silver monstrance adorned with precious stones (Dan. 11:36-39). The Pope "shall exalt himself ... above every god" (11:36). The "King of the North" causes the banks of the Euphrates to "overflow" (Dan. 11:40). Verse 41 should read, "He shall enter also into the glorious land, and many shall be overthrown." (Crusades) Gibbon says, "Jerusalem ... soon became the theatre of nations" (Decline 10:375). The "tidings out of the east and north" that "trouble him" are Russia's victories against the Ottoman Empire. From the mid-1700s onward, Russian attacks upon the northeast border of Turkey became increasingly frequent. Turkish armies and navies attacked Russia "with great fury" but unsuccessfully. In 1768, Turkish armies were badly defeated and in 1770 the Turkish navy was obliterated. In 1774 and 1777 more defeats occurred. In 1806 the Russians seized Moldavia and Wallachia, and destroyed another Turkish fleet. In 1826, Turkey surrendered all fortresses in Asia to the Russians. Russia again defeated the Turks in the Crimean War of 1853. During the First World War, the Turks established their military headquarters in Jerusalem at Mount Zion. He planted the "tents of his army" "between the seas and the glorious holy mountain" (Dan. 11:45). General Allenby drove them out in December 1917. Turks subsequently lost Baghdad, Damascus and Aleppo in 1918 -- three capitals of the pre-Roman King of the North. Deserted by their German allies, the Turks surrendered. He came "to his end and none" helped him (Dan. 11:45). Within six years the Ottoman Emperor had been deposed, the Caliphate abolished and Turkey declared a Republic under Mustapha Kemal. From the Hegira in 622 A.D. to the surrender in 1917 A.D. was 1335 years (Dan. 12:12). From the Hegira in 622 A.D. to 1844 A.D. when the Sultan of Turkey issued a Decree of Religious Toleration for Moslems who convert to Christianity was 1260 days (Dan. 12:7). From 622 A.D. till 1912 A.D. when the Balkan War occurred that greatly weakened Turkey is 1290 years. From 634 A.D. when the Caliph Omar, who conquered Jerusalem and established the Arab empire, began to rule, to 1924 when the Islamic Caliphate was abolished was 1290 years (Dan. 12:11). From 632 A.D. when the Caliphate was established to 1922 when the Turkish Ottoman Empire came to an end with the abdication of the Sultan was also 1290 years.

Mohammed

Also spelled Muhamed, Mahomet or Maometis. In Greek, Maometis adds up to 666. Notice: μ (40) + α (1)+ o (70) + μ (40) + ε (5) + τ (300) + ι (10) + ς 200 = 666. **The Quran has 6,666** ayats or verses in it. Furthermore, the Greek 666 in Revelation 13:18 (Chi, Xi & Stigma) can also read "bismillah" in Arabic meaning "in the name of Allah." The Greek stigma is the same as Arabic BSM sound. Allah is spelled like the letter E on it's back with an extra small leg. If you tilt the letter 90 degrees to the left laying the E on it's back, it spells Allah in Arabic. Xi & Stigma read right to left with the period first because it's at the end of the verse. See Codex Vaticanus which has both a period and Alif. Last are the crossed swords of Allah (Chi), commonly seen with this phrase "bismillah." John saw χξϛ´ on the foreheads (green martyr's headbands) and right arms (green arm bands) and on Muslim coins.

χξϛ´.

64

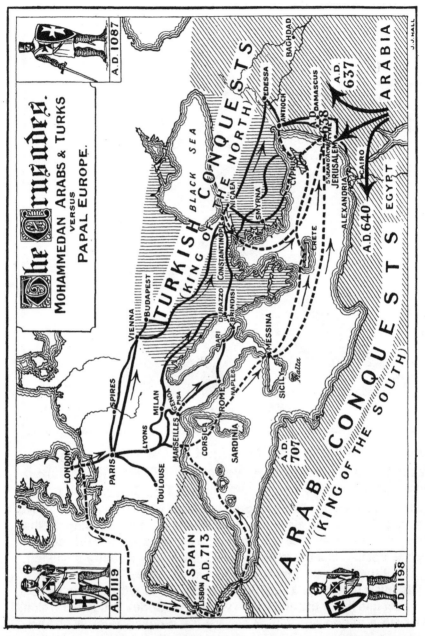

"And at the time of the end shall the King of the South (Arabs who conquered Egypt) push at him (Papacy), and the King of the North (Turks who conquered Syria) shall come against him (Papacy) like a whirlwind ... and he shall enter into the countries (of Asia Minor) and shall overflow and pass over" (the Mediterranean Sea into Europe) (Dan. 11:40).

Moslem Turks Attack Idolatrous Eastern Greek Byzantine Empire
(1062-1453 A.D.)
Chapter 9:13-21

John wrote "And the sixth angel sounded, and I heard a voice from the four horns of the golden altar which is before God, Saying to the sixth angel who had the trumpet, Loose the four angels who are bound in the great river, Euphrates" (Rev. 9:13-14).

Astronomically there are four bright stars in the Eridanus (Euphrates) River. Historically, the next scourge of Christendom, the TURKS or second woe, arose in the east 130 years after the first woe of the Arabs. Revelation 9:12 occupies this interval. Both were MOSLEM. The TURKS were to "slay" what the Arabs only "torment." The TURKS were the "little horn" of Daniel 8. The home of the original TURKISH people was in the delta of the River EUPHRATES -- hence the use of the EUPHRATES symbolism. The river symbolically "OVERFLOWED its banks" as the Seljuk (1062 to 1299 A.D.) then Othman dynasties (Ottomans became independent in 1299 A.D.) expanded. (Later, in Rev. 16:12, as the Turkish Empire decays, we read that "The River Euphrates DRIED UP."). There were FOUR SULTANATES of Turks bordering on the EUPHRATES corresponding to the "FOUR ANGELS" and "FOUR HORNS" of the altar. They were Baghdad, Damascus, Aleppo and Iconium. There were also FOUR great WAVES of Turkish hordes poured into the provinces of the eastern GREEK third of the Roman Empire, spread over a period of nearly FOUR HUNDRED years. (Esau had "FOUR hundred men" -- Gen.33:1. Turks controlled Jerusalem for 400 years: 1517-1917 -- cp. Gen. 15:13). According to the Historian's History of the World, "The mystic number FOUR is taken as the base of the governmental hierarchy in honour of the FOUR angels which carry the Koran, and the FOUR Caliphs, disciples of Mohammed." They are associated with names famous in history -- Togrul Beg, Alp Arslan, Tamerlane, Bajazet, and so on, the leaders of the Ottomans or Turcomans. They are sent to punish the "FOUR heads," "FOUR wings" (Dan. 7:6) and "FOUR notable HORNS" (Daniel 8:8,22) of Alexander's GREEK Empire now in Roman form.

"And the four angels were loosed, who were prepared for an hour, and a day, and a month, and a year, to slay the third part of men" (Rev. 9:15).

Togrul Beg was invited by the Caliph of Baghdad to quell a rebellion by his subjects. When he completed this task, Togrul was declared Lieutenant of the Caliph and invested with the title of Protector and Governor of the Moslem Empire. He went to war against the Eastern Byzantine Empire, defeating their army and slaying an estimated 100,000 Greeks. He and his successors conquered Armenia, Asia Minor, Arabia Felix,

Jerusalem and the neighborhood of Constantinople. The Crusaders then intervened to recover the Holy Land; and their attempts lasted from 1097 A.D. to 1291 A.D. when they were driven from Palestine. Then the Turks crossed into Europe conquering more and more of the remaining "third" -- Bulgaria (1389), Salonica (1430), Serbia (1438) and Greece (1446). By 1453 practically the whole Eastern Roman Empire had fallen to the Turks except its capital, Constantinople, which fell 29th of May.

The beginning of the Turkish power was when Togrul Beg, their first military leader, married the daughter of the Caliph of Baghdad (the head of the Arab-Moslem religion), and became the head of the Mohammedan faith in 1062 A.D. He died the same year and was succeeded by Alp Arslan, the "valiant lion" who, setting out from Baghdad, "passed the Euphrates at the head of the Turkish cavalry" (Decline and Fall, Gibbon ch. 57, p.12) in 1062 A.D. and waged a holy war against Greek Christendom which by this time had once again become idolatrous because the Empress Irene convened the Second Council of Nicea which declared idols lawful and by the Ninth Century idolatry reigned supreme in both east and west. Finally the Turkish mission of destruction was completed in the capture of Constantinople in 1453 A.D. and the Greek or Byzantine "THIRD" of the Roman Empire passed to the Turks under the Sixth Trumpet. This third was killed politically and religiously if not physically. The city named for the first Christian emperor was now in the hands of Islam and its Cathedral of St. Sophia, the center of Eastern Orthodoxy, was turned into a Moslem mosque. The Goths already had the western THIRD under the first Four Trumpets and the Arabs the southern THIRD under the Fifth Trumpet. From 1062 A.D. to 1453 A.D. is 391 years, which agrees with the prophetic period mentioned in verse 15: An hour, day, month and year using the day-for-a-year principle represents one month, one year, thirty years and 360 years. Total is 391 years and one month.

A second method of figuring the time interval is even more precise than the previous method. There are two Greek words for "year." The first is "kairos" meaning 360 days and the second is "eniatos" meaning 365 days 5 hours 49 minutes. John used the second. Nowhere else in scripture is "eniatos" used. Therefore an "hour" calculates out to 30 days since there are "twelve hours in a day" (365/12 = 30.4). The "day" is one year. The "month" is 30 years. The "year" is 365 years 91 days. The total is 396 years, 121 days. From 18th of January 1057 A.D. when Togrul Beg left Baghdad at the head of a Moslem Turkish force on a career of conquest to the 29th of May, 1453 A.D. (Gibbon's Decline and Fall 7:199; Langer's Encyc. of World History p.327) when Constantinople fell is 396 years, 130 days. This is 9 days over. If the prophecy had said "two hours," May 29th would be 21 days under.

A third way to figure the 391-year interval is from 1453 A.D. to 1844 A.D., which is the 1260th lunar year of the Hegira or flight of Mohammed (Dan. 12:7; 622 + 1260 = 1844), when Britain and other Christian European nations forced the Sultan to sign the Decree of Toleration which abolished the death penalty for conversion from Islam to Christianity or any other religion. Also 1290 lunar years from 622 A.D. is 1873. From that date on she began to decline until by 1917 (622 + 1335 = 1917) on the 1335th lunar year, Turkey was driven from Jerusalem and Palestine by Great Britain's General Allenby. "And I will lay my vengeance upon Edom by the hand of my people Israel" (Ez. 25:14). Then in 1948, Zionist Jews challenged Britain's right to Palestine. "The house of Israel ... are they unto whom the inhabitants of Jerusalem have said, Get you far from the Eternal; unto us is this land given in possession" (Ez. 11:15).

To digress, in 1299, the Turkoman power was revived under Ortogrul, father of Othman (whence the term Ottoman), who united together the four sultanates of Turks bordering on the Euphrates -- at Baghdad founded in 1058; at Damascus and Aleppo in 1079; and at Iconium in 1080 -- aptly prefigured in the four angels bound in the Euphrates. "On the 27th of July, 1299, Othman first invaded the territory of Nicomedia" (Gibbon ch. 64). Ortogrul had previously obtained the FIRST Ottoman Turk VICTORY over Christians by capturing the city of Kutani in 1281. The Ottoman Turks obtained their LAST VICTORY by taking the Cameniec territory from the Poles in 1672, this conquest marking the limits of their territorial expansion which never extended beyond the original boundaries of the Byzantine Empire The 391 years between 1281 A.D. and 1672 A.D. is yet a fourth way to figure the interval.

Twenty-seven years later the "drying up" of the Ottoman Empire (Rev. 16:12) began in earnest in 1699, by the Treaty of Carlowitz, following the wars with Austria and Russia, and it has never ceased to recede till finally extinguished on March 6th, 1924, 666 years (the number of a man representing a dynasty -- Rev. 14:18) from the birth of its founder, Othman, in 1258. The office of Sultan-Caliph was abolished by Mustafa Kemal (Ataturk) on March 1924. This is confirmed in Daniel 12:11, being 1290 solar years from 634 A.D., when Omar (the "desolator"), who set up the "abomination" here referred to, succeeded to the Caliphate.

"And the number of the army of the horsemen were two hundred thousand thousand: and I heard the number of them. And thus I saw the horses in the vision, and them that sat on them, having breastplates of fire, and of jacinth, and brimstone: and the heads of the horses were as the heads of lions; and out of their mouths issued fire and smoke and brimstone" (Rev. 9:16-17).

Astronomically, the head of a lion is held by Orion. An army of 200 million stars. Historically Togrul's successor was Alp Arslan whose name means the "valiant lion." Other Turkish leaders had similar names. Revelation 9:16 mentions "two hundred thousand thousand" cavalry or "twice ten thousand times ten thousand" (Revised Version). The number of horsemen used by the Turks, not all at once, but over the course of 1062 to 1453 A.D. may have been this high. Two myriads of myriads, a myriad being 10,000. Turks were in the habit of reckoning their forces by "myriads" or groups of 10,000 men which they termed "tomans." "Breastplates of fire (RED), and of jacinth (BLUE) and brimstone (YELLOW)" because these were the MILITARY COLORS of the Turkish Cavalry from their beginning to the Nineteenth century. Daubuz remarks that Ottomans wore SCARLET, BLUE and YELLOW from their first appearance. The lion-head was then, and is now, a notable ensign among the Turks.

"By these three was the third part of men killed, by the fire, and by the smoke, and by the brimstone, which issued out of their mouths. For their power is in their mouth, and in their tails: for their tails were like unto serpents, and had heads, and with them they do hurt" (Rev. 9:18-19).

The Turks defeated the Romans by using "Brimstone" or sulfur which is the basis of GUN POWDER (saltpetre, sulfur and charcoal) at a time when it had been recently invented. The Turks were the first to use cannons. Sultan Mohammed hired a Greek Christian engineer to cast cannons in a foundry to batter down the wall of Constantinople. Men were "killed, by the fire ... smoke and brimstone, which issued out of their mouths. For their power is in their mouth, and in their tails; for their tails were like serpents, and had heads, and with them they do hurt" (Rev. 9:18-19). Cannons of the fifteenth century were called "basilisks" -- a name given to a fabulous serpent, the breath ("fire and brimstone") -- and even the look -- of which the ancients considered fatal. CANNONS pulled by horses are long and thin and round, so look like SERPENTS. When pulled they become TAILS; when swung around and fired the artillery becomes the "HEADS of LIONS" (Rev. 9:17) or ROARING GUNS, because the horse is now behind. For similar scriptural symbolism see Hab. 1:8; Joel 2:4-8; Isa. 5:21-30.

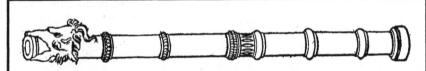

Contemporary engraving of a 15th century Turkish cannon. Note serpent's tail coming out of lion's head (see Elliott's Hor. Apoc. 1:514).

"And the rest of the men which were not killed by these plagues yet repented not of the works of their hands, that they should not worship devils, and idols of gold, and silver, and brass, and stone, and of wood: which neither can see, nor hear, nor walk: Neither repented they of their murders, nor of their sorceries, nor of their fornication, nor of their thefts" (Rev. 9:20-21).

Those who "worship demons and idols" (Rev. 9:20) were Roman Catholics and Greek Orthodox. Pagans worshipped through visible images, thereby compelling the actual spirit to be present. Mary-worship and saint-worship has followed the same principle. Proponents claim they do not actually worship the image. But the second commandment plainly forbids even the bodily act or posture, whatever be the intention behind it. Using Mary and the saints as mediators between God and men contradicts 1 Timothy 2:5 mentioning the "one mediator ... Jesus Christ." "Murders" (Rev. 9:21) refer to Paulicians (679), Albigenses (1208-1218, 1229) of France, Waldenses (1237) in the Alps, Hussites and Moravians in Germany (1413) and the Lollards of England (1413) who were all regarded as "heretics" and killed. Rome has never repented of these murders, and would kill "heretics" today if she had the power. "Sorceries" (Rev. 9:21)

69

refer to pretended miracles and revelations such as Transubstantiation and visions. "Fornication" (Rev. 9:21) was caused by enforced celibacy, auricular confession, monasteries and nunneries. "Thefts" (Rev. 9:21) refer to the sale of indulgences for release from an imaginary purgatory, masses for the dead and otherwise extracting money from the dying, paying for religious offices and fictitious relics instead of trusting in the fully-paid pardon of Christ's sacrifice. Just as the Egyptian plagues didn't cause Egypt to repent but instead Pharaoh's heart was hardened; so also the trumpet plagues didn't cause the Roman Empire to repent but instead the Pope's heart was hardened. There was no repentance till the Reformation.

"Power ... in their (horse's) TAILS" (9:19) may also refer to the official badge of the Sultans and Pashas which was HORSE-TAILS attached to crescents. The Sultan had seven HORSE-TAILS borne before him, the Pashas (governors) had one, two or three HORSE-TAILS according to their rank. They were responsible for all the oppression, injustice, cruelty and harsh taxation in the Ottoman Empire. How did this ensign originate? In their early days, the Turkish tribes carried the ensign representing the horse-like tail of a yak. "A general of theirs, not knowing how to rally his troops, they having lost their ensigns, cut off a horse's tail, and fixed it on the end of a spear: the soldiers rallying at this signal, gained the victory" (Tournefort's Travels). These standards became known as Tughs.

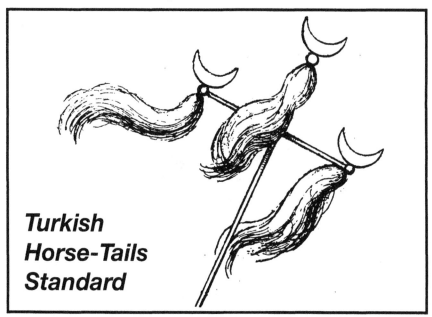

Turkish Horse-Tails Standard

Why did God permit Moslems to defeat Christians? Because these "Christians" taught Transubstantiation and the sacrifice of the Mass, which deny the finished Atonement of Christ. That is why the voice that loosed the evil came from "the four horns of the golden altar" (9:13). The golden altar was the altar of incense in the Jewish Temple. On the Day of Atonement its four horns were anointed with the blood of a lamb without spot or blemish: "He shall put the blood upon the horns of the altar round about" (Ex. 30:10; Lev. 16:18). The blood signified the finished atonement of our Lord Jesus the Messiah. But this was polluted when a monk named Paschasius Radbertus in the middle of the tenth century proclaimed Transubstantiation -- that the bread and wine were changed to the body and blood of Jesus at Communion by the priest's words. The doctrine was accepted by Pope Hildebrand and by 1022 A.D. twelve Protestant martyrs of Orleans were publicly burned at the stake for refusing to believe it. Devotion to saints and the "Virgin Mary" also polluted Christ's atonement. During the tenth century the invention of the Rosary came into use, a chain of beads that count recited prayers (vain repetitions) at a ratio of ten prayers to Mary for every one offered to God.

Who are the Turks? Ezekiel 35 and 36 tell us that those who have trodden down Palestine and Jerusalem are "Edom" or Esau. We know that the Turks are the ones who for centuries have trodden down Jerusalem and Palestine.

The Bible is Translated And Reproduced Using the Printing Press

(1453-1611 A.D.)
Chapter 10

We read, "And I saw another mighty angel come down from heaven, clothed with a cloud: and a rainbow was upon his head, and his face was as it were the sun, and his feet as pillars of fire: And he had in his hand a little book open: and he set his right foot upon the sea, and his left foot on the earth" (Rev. 10:1-2).

Astronomically, the rainbow is the Milky Way upon Orion's head when the sun is in Orion. He holds a SCROLL above his head. Orion's right foot is on the Eridanus ("the sea") and his left on the earth. Historically, in Revelation 10:1-2 we read about an angel -- "the Angel of the Covenant" (Mal. 3:1; Matt. 17:2). His face is like the sun because he is "The Sun of Righteousness" (Mal. 4:2). He is clothed with a cloud because Christ "cometh with clouds" (Rev. 1:7) and "maketh the clouds his chariot" (Ps. 104:3). A rainbow is upon his head because Christ has "a rainbow round about" his throne (Rev. 4:3) and he has feet like "pillars of fire" because Christ's feet are "as if they burned in a furnace" (Rev. 1:15). The Angel's VOICE is like the roar of a lion because He is the "Lion of the tribe of Judah" (Rev. 5:5). The Reformers here discovered the WORD as the "one Mediator between God and men." He had "a little open BOOK." A closed book is one that is not understood (Isa. 29:11-12; Dan. 12:4). Papal Rome had achieved this by keeping the BIBLE in Latin which few could read and hidden away in monasteries. Not content with this, the Papacy forbade the SCRIPTURES: In 1229 the Council of Toulouse stated, "We prohibit also the permitting of the laity to have the books of the OLD and NEW TESTAMENTS ... in the vulgar tongue." Even in England, by the 7th Constitution of Arundel (Oxford, 1408), "no unauthorized person shall translate any part of the Holy SCRIPTURE into English, or any other language." All reading of the WORD of GOD was also forbidden by this Constitution. The Council of Trent in 1559 prohibited reading the BIBLE without written permission because reading it "will cause more evil than good" (to the Papacy). The more the BIBLE is read, the less the Pope is obeyed. In other words, "the Lord shall consume (Him) with the Spirit of His mouth" (2 Th. 2:8) -- the BIBLE. None but Jesus could open this BOOK (Rev. 5:3) so He must be this Angel. He caused it to be printed and translated in English, Dutch, French, German, Spanish and Italian and be in every public library. Perhaps He set his right foot on Britain and His left in the English Channel to symbolize the act of taking possession -- "The earth is the Lord's and the fulness thereof" (1 Cor. 10:26) -- especially Israel. On the Continent, the appeal of the Reformation was to the people ("waters" -- Rev. 17:15) and to the rulers ("mountain" -- Micah 4:1; Jer. 51:25) of Germany for different reasons. The Reformation's success was due to this real, if unacknowledged alliance between the two.

Both the Renaissance and the Reformation began at the start of the sixteenth century. When Constantinople fell to the Turks, the Reformation followed. Why? First because the armies of "Christendom" (Catholics) were fully employed in warding off the Turkish menace, which had now expanded to its greatest limits, giving time for reform (Protestants) to spread and consolidate before persecution could crush the movement. Emperor Charles V, out of fear of the Turk, could not use his full army against Protestants. Also Constantinople had been the center of Greek Christianity, but with the advent of the Turks, scholars fled to the universities of Western Europe, taking with them their knowledge of Greek and also precious Greek manuscripts of the Bible. The result was a revival in the study of the classical languages, Greek being taught in Europe for the first time in 1458 A.D. Such a Renaissance or "New Learning" meant that the Bible which was written in Greek and Latin was studied afresh. In 1516 Erasmus published his famous Greek New Testament, thousands of copies of which were eagerly read by the numerous scholars who had already learned Greek. Translations of the Bible into the languages of the nations automatically followed so that, instead of being closed to the masses, it became an open book for all to read. An English Bible was chained by law to every church.

Also the invention of printing was made at the same time. The invention of movable type and how to make paper from rags and pulp all came when the Bible was rediscovered. Instead of a large book being hand-copied on vellum, a tedious and expensive process, the Bible now became a small book -- one of the first books to be printed. From the sixteenth century onward, millions of Bibles were printed. Notice the list of important dates as follows:

1453 -- Flight of Greek scholars to Western Europe
1454 -- Invention of printing in Germany
1458 -- Greek first taught in European Universities
1476 -- Caxton introduced printing into England.
1516 -- Erasmus printed his Greek New Testament
1518 -- Zwingli printed the first Swiss New Testament
1522 -- Luther's New Testament in German
1526 -- Tynedale's English New Testament. A Swedish Bible.
1535 -- Coverdale's Complete English Bible.
1537 -- A Danish Bible. Matthew's English Bible.
1539 -- The "Great Bible" printed under Coverdale's supervision
and placed by Royal Command in every church for parishoners' use.
1611 -- The King James Authorized Version.

"And cried with a loud voice, as when a lion roareth: and when he had cried, seven thunders uttered their voices. And when the seven thunders had uttered their voices, I was about to write: and I heard a voice from heaven saying unto me, Seal up those things which the seven thunders uttered, and write them not" (Rev. 10:3-4).

Astronomically, Orion's scroll is so powerful it is like a roaring lion which Orion is holding in his other hand. Historically, Revelation 10:3 has the "Angel" crying "with a loud voice, as when a lion roareth" which pictures the Lion of the tribe of Judah shouting through the pages of scripture to the Church of Rome through the writing and preaching of Reformation leaders such as Luther, Zwingli, Calvin and Knox. Historians often refer to Papal Edicts and Bulls as the "thunders" from the seven-hilled city of Rome. Therefore we read that "seven thunders uttered their voices" (Rev. 10:3) in reply. Gibbon even uses the word and says "The spiritual thunders of the Vatican depend on the force of opinion" (ch. 70). Luther said, "Terrible as the lightning and the thunder, fulminatory Bulls and anathemas impended over the heads of those who incurred pontifical displeasure" (Antichrist Revealed, p.47). John was told to "write them not" (10:4) because he was only to "write ... true and faithful" words (Rev. 21:5). Similarly, Luther replied to the Pope's final Bull thundered in June 1520, by gathering an audience outside the walls of Wittenberg where he deliberately burned the Papal Bull and Edicts. In this manner the "seven thunders" were "sealed up" (Rev. 10:4). They were nothing more than the formation of the Society of Jesus by Ignatius Loyola in 1534; the excommunication of Henry VIII and his deposition by Papal Bull in 1536 and the Council of Trent in 1546-1564.

"And the angel which I saw stand upon the sea and upon the earth lifted up his hand to heaven, And sware by him that liveth for ever and ever, who created heaven, and the things that therein are, and the earth, and the things that therein are, and the sea, and the things which are therein, that there should be time no longer: But in the days of the voice of the seventh angel, when he shall begin to sound, the mystery of God should be finished, as he hath declared to his servants the prophets" (Rev. 10:5-7).

Astronomically, Orion's hand is lifted up to heaven as it holds an open scroll. Historically, "There should be TIME no longer" (Rev. 10:6) refers to the fact that a "TIME" is 360 years and that the last one is the "TIME of the End" (Dan.9:35) from 1557 to 1917. The accession of Queen Elizabeth and the permanent establishment of the Protestant Church in England began in 1558. This was the seventh or last TIME of the Gentiles as the Angel said. On December 9th 1917, (during the Festival of Hanukkah) British General Allenby liberated Jerusalem from the Turks. Or alternately, January 15th 1559, Queen Elizabeth was crowned. If we add 365 years to 1559 we arrive at 1924 when the Turkish Caliphate was abolished.

"And the voice which I heard from heaven spake unto me again, and said, Go and take the little book which is open in the hand of the angel which standeth upon the sea and upon the earth. And I went unto the angel, and said unto him, Give me the little book. And he said unto me, Take it, and eat it up; and it shall make thy belly bitter, but it shall be in thy mouth sweet as honey. And I took the little book out of the angel's hand, and ate it up; and it was in my mouth sweet as honey: and as soon as I had eaten it, my belly was bitter" (Rev. 10:8-10).

Then John ate the little book. Historians record that in the Reformation the Bible became the most treasured thing in all the world, diligently read by millions, carried about in the bosom, studied and committed to memory, so SWEET was its heavenly manna to men and women hungry for spiritual guidance. However, along with more knowledge comes more responsibility. After studying and digesting the message of the Bible, Protestants now had to obey it (Jer. 15:16; Ps. 119:103). Roman Catholic doctrine had to be condemned and abandoned. Obedience to the Bible brought "BIT-TER" persecution from Rome.

During the 30 years after Luther's protest, all Europe experienced the Inquisition which condemned multitudes of true Christians to torture and death because they studied the Scriptures. In England, when Tyndale was executed October 6th, 1536, his last words were, "Lord, open the King of England's eyes." Within less than a year, a royal decree ordered a copy of the whole Bible placed in every parish church. By 1540 this order became a reality. Henry VIII and Edward VI both placed Bibles in all churches with the injunction that it be read and taught. Then came Roman Catholic Mary's reign when nearly 300 Protestants, including Latimer, Ridley and Cranmer, were burned alive. During those same years, from 1st October, 1553 to 17th November 1558, on the Continent tens of thousands of Protestants were imprisoned, tortured, buried or burned alive, crucified on trees and badly treated -- merely because they possessed Bibles and had tasted its SWEETNESS.

As Queen Elizabeth passed under a triumphal arch erected in Cheapside a Bible was let down into her hands by a white-robed child called "Truth." The queen received it, kissed it and pressed it to her heart, replying that this present was more acceptable to her than any of the more costly ones the city had given her that day of her accession (Walter's History of England).

"Thou must prophesy again before many peoples, and nations, and tongues, and kings" (Rev. 10:11).

John wrote the Revelation once in his own life while imprisoned on Patmos. The Reformers preached from it "AGAIN" because Revelation was a very popular book.

Protestant Reformation
& Two Witnesses
(1517-1689)
Chapter 11

John says, "And there was given me a REED like unto a ROD: and the angel stood, saying, Rise, and measure the TEMPLE OF GOD, and the altar, and them that worship therein. But the COURT which is without the temple leave out, and measure it not; for it is given unto the GENTILES: and the holy city shall they tread under foot FORTY and TWO MONTHS" (Rev. 11:1-2).

What is the "REED like unto a ROD"? A 12 1/2 foot long measuring device made of iron. In Hebrew the word is "kaneh" and from that we get our English word "CANON" or the books of the Bible recognized as canonical or genuine. The REED is therefore the Bible. Christians are measured by the rule of scripture. God uses it to chasten us because "Shall I come to you with a ROD?" (1 Cor 4:21) and "He that spareth the ROD hateth his son" (Pr. 13:24). "Hear ye the ROD" and "Feed thy people with thy ROD" (Micah 6:9; 7:14), "And I will cause you to pass under the ROD" (Ez. 20:37).

What is the "TEMPLE (naos) of GOD"? The real temple of God always symbolizes the New Covenant CHURCH of Israel because "the HOUSE of GOD ... is the CHURCH of the living God" (1 Tim. 3:15). "Ye are the TEMPLE (naos) of the living God; as God hath said, I will dwell in them" (2 Cor. 6:16). "As living stones, ye are built up a spiritual HOUSE" (1 Peter 2:5). "For the Temple of God is holy, which TEMPLE (naos) are ye" (1 Cor. 3:17).

What is the "COURT of the GENTILES"? When Solomon built the Temple, he added an OUTER COURT to accommodate GENTILES who desired to worship God. The Temple of Israel and the Court of the Gentiles are here contrasted. Protestant churches in Britain, northern Germany, Holland and Scandinavia were measured using Bible standards by the time of the Reformation and suffered affliction. "Show the House of Israel that they may be ashamed of their iniquities and let them measure the pattern" (Ez. 43:10). ROMAN CATHOLIC CHURCHES in southern Germany, France, Spain, Portugal and Italy (and GREEK ORTHODOX CHURCHES) are not measured by Bible standards but follow human traditions and enjoyed wealth and power. Protestant reformers used the Bible to determine what the New Testament congregation should be like, but they didn't try to reform the Roman Catholic or Eastern Orthodox Churches. They left them out or "cast them out."

When are the 42 MONTHS? The four Gentile Empires of Daniel 2 have possessed the Holy Land for a combined total of "42 MONTHS" or 1260 days which symbolize 1,260 years (Num. 14:34; Ez. 4:6): Babylon possessed Palestine for 90 years, from 624 to 534 B.C. Medo-Persia for 200 years, from 534 to 334 B.C. Greece for 304 years from 334 to 30 B.C. and Rome for 666 years from the Battle of Actium in 31 B.C. to the Saracen conquest in 636 A.D. Now 90 + 200 + 304 + 666 = 1,260 years. Just as the Gentiles "tread under foot" the physical Jerusalem for 42 months (1,260 days), (when Omar the Turk took Jerusalem in 637 A.D., add 1,260 more years to get 1897 when the Zionist Movement was founded in Basel, Switzerland by Jews of all nations desiring to settle in the Holy Land. The fig tree represents the Jewish people (Matt. 24:32-33). When they become a nation, Christ's return is "at the doors") so also they "shall" "tread under foot" the "New Jerusalem" or all TRUE CHRISTIANS for 1,260 YEARS because "HEAVENLY JERUSALEM" is the "ASSEMBLY and CHURCH of the FIRSTBORN" wherever they may dwell (Hebrews 12:22-23).

The Roman Catholic Church oppressed true Christians for 1260 YEARS (see Dan. 7:25) until it lost its temporal power. In 606 A.D. Emperor Phocas decreed the Pope "Universal Bishop." Exactly 1260 years later in 1866 A.D. the last two Protestants were burned by Papal decree at Barletta, Italy. In 610 A.D. Emperor Phocas died. Exactly 1260 years later in 1870 A.D. the city of Rome was captured and the Pope lost his temporal power. Constantine ascended the throne in A.D. 312. Claiming to be Christian, but really Catholic, he persecuted "heretics." Exactly 1260 years later, Huguenots were massacred in 1,572. A.D. The "millenium" of Papal Rome was from 533 A.D. when Emperor Justinian decreed the Bishop of Rome "Head of all the Holy Churches" to 1534 when Parliament abrogated Papal supremacy in England.

"And I will give power to my TWO WITNESSES, and they shall prophesy a thousand two hundred and threescore days, clothed in sackcloth. These are the TWO OLIVE TREES, and the TWO CANDLESTICKS, standing before the God of the earth" (Rev. 11:3-4).

Who are the TWO WITNESSES? Astronomically, John saw Castor and Pollux together in Gemini, the constellation that pictures "Simeon and Levi (who) are brethren" (Gen. 49:5). Two Israelites. Deuteronomy 19:15, John 8:17 and 2 Cor. 13:1 require two witnesses to establish any fact. "In the mouth of TWO or THREE WITNESSES shall every word be established" (2 Cor. 13:1).

These TWO WITNESSES are called "TWO CANDLESTICKS" because a candlestick is a CONGREGATION of GOD'S PEOPLE (Rev. 1:20). Zechariah saw in his vision only ONE CANDLESTICK because only the KINGDOM of JUDAH remained in Palestine (Zech. 4:11-14). John saw TWO CANDLESTICKS depicting the KINGDOM of JUDAH as well as the "lost" tribes of the KINGDOM of ISRAEL Christianized by this time. The House of JUDAH and the HOUSE of ISRAEL are the "JEW and the GREEK." Both "shine as lights in the world" (Phil.2:15).

The "TWO OLIVE TREES" symbolize ISRAEL and JUDAH. "ISRAEL ... his beauty shall be like the OLIVE TREE" (Hosea 14:6). "The Eternal called thy name, A green OLIVE TREE... house of ISRAEL and ... house of JUDAH" (Jer.11:16; see also Zechariah 4:3 and Romans 11). King David sang, "I am like a green OLIVE TREE in the house of God" (Ps. 52:8). Isaiah 61:3 also mentions these "TREES of RIGHTEOUSNESS."

Isaiah 43:10 says of Jacob (both houses of JUDAH and ISRAEL), "Ye are my WIT-NESSES saith God." Isaiah 44:8 says, "Ye are even my WITNESSES" (both houses of Israel). Psalm 114:1-2 says, "JUDAH was his sanctuary and ISRAEL his dominion." Yes, "What are these two olive trees? ... the two anointed ones" (Zech. 4:11-14). Joshua was the High PRIEST and Zerubbabel was the KING (Zech. 3:8; 4:9; 4:14). Notice that the KING came from JUDAH and the PRIEST came from LEVI (ISRAELITE). Then in Acts 1:8 Christ says to his disciples, "Ye (the church) shall be WITNESSES unto me ... unto the uttermost parts of the earth." In the Reformation the TWO WITNESSES were English STATE (throne of David of Judah) and the English CHURCH (Protestant Israel) or the British "Jutes" (Judah -- Jer. 3:18) and "Angles" (Ephraim -- Jer. 31:18).

Furthermore, Christ said, "Search the SCRIPTURES for they are they which TESTIFY (or witness) of me" (John 5:39). Many Bibles were also burned just like the Protestant and Jewish martyrs. Yes, "Thy WORD is a LAMP unto my feet, and a LIGHT unto my path" (Ps. 119:105), so the SCRIPTURES are a CANDLESTICK or a LAMP with OIL from an OLIVE TREE.

Therefore, any combination of PROTESTANTS, observant JEWS, throne of DAVID and/or the BIBLE constitutes the TWO and/or THREE WITNESSES needed to establish a fact. These witnesses stand before "the god of the earth" meaning "his holiness the pope" who blasphemously claims to be god.

"And if any man will hurt them, FIRE proceedeth out of their mouth, and devoureth their enemies: and if any man will hurt them, he must in this manner be killed. These have power to shut heaven, that it RAIN NOT in the days of their prophecy: and have power over waters to turn them to BLOOD, and to smite the earth with all PLAGUES, as often as they will" (Rev. 11:5-6).

What is the FIRE? This refers to the power given to Moses (state) and Elijah (church) (Nu.16; 1Ki.17:1; Luke 4:25). Literal FIRE has come from the mouths of Protestant British muskets and cannons and FIRE ships (Isa. 54:17). But symbolically, Jeremiah 5:14 defines the FIRE by saying, "I will make MY WORDS in thy mouth FIRE, and this people wood, and it shall devour them." Furthermore, "must in this manner ber killed" refers to the final judgment of HELL FIRE. "He that hath my word, let him speak my word faithfully. What is the chaff to the wheat? saith the Eternal. Is not MY WORD like a FIRE? saith the Eternal; and like a hammer that breaketh the rock in pieces" (Jer. 23:28-29). No rain implies a SPIRITUAL DROUGHT during the sway of the Papacy just as Elijah foretold a physical drought (1 Ki. 17:1; James 5:17) during the sway of Jezebel "and it rained not on the earth for the space of three years and six months" (1,260 days). "That is why it is called the "Dark Ages" (1260 years) -- "a FAMINE of the

HEARING of the WORDS of the LORD" (Amos 8:2). "Turn waters to blood" denotes the bloodshed of WARS inflicted by God on the enemies of his witnesses (see Rev. 8:8-9). Metaphorically, "WATERS" are "PEOPLES" and they turn to BLOOD and guts when killed. Goths, Vandals, Huns, Saracens and Turks were permitted by the Lord to scourge the "Christian" offenders. Europe's RIVERS, the natural defensive positions, have RUN with BLOOD in warfare. France and Spain in particular, who persecuted Christians, Israelites, Jews and their scriptures, have experienced many wars and revolutions while Anglo-Saxon and Scandinavian countries who persecuted the witnesses far less, have suffered far less.

"And when they shall have finished their testimony, the BEAST that ascendeth out of the bottomless pit shall make war against them, and shall overcome them, and kill them. And their dead bodies shall lie in the street of the GREAT CITY which spiritually is called Sodom and Egypt, where also our Lord was crucified. And they of the peoples and kindreds and tongues and nations shall see their dead bodies THREE DAYS and a HALF, and shall NOT SUFFER their dead bodies to be put in GRAVES. And they that dwell upon the earth shall REJOICE over them, and make MERRY, and shall SEND GIFTS one to another, because these two prophets tormented them that dwelt on the earth. And after THREE DAYS and a HALF the spirit of life from God entered into them, and they stood upon their feet, and great FEAR fell upon them who saw them. And they heard a great voice from heaven saying unto them, COME UP HERE And they ascended up to HEAVEN in a cloud, and their enemies beheld them. And the same hour was there a great EARTHQUAKE, and the TENTH PART of the city fell, and in the earthquake were slain of men SEVEN THOUSAND; and the remnant were AFFRIGHTED, and gave glory to the God of heaven" (Rev. 11:7-13).

Who is the BEAST? The fourth BEAST of Daniel 7:3-8, the red DRAGON or the Pagan Roman Empire now changed to the "Holy Roman Empire." From the twelfth century onward, the Waldenses and Albigenses (in France), the Wycliffites (in England 1350 onward) and the Hussites (followers of Huss and Jerome in Bohemia, 1480 onwards) all finished their testimony by declaring the Papacy was Antichrist and the doctrines of transubstantiation, purgatory, prayers to saints and angels, and infallibility of Papal councils were unbiblical. They asserted that the scriptures were the sole and absolute authority in matters of faith and practice. Therefore, the "Holy Roman Empire" -- the fourth BEAST or red DRAGON -- made war against these "heretics" and used the Inquisition against them.

The "GREAT CITY" of ROME was called by the Reformers "Sodom" because of its pride and sexual impurities; and "Egypt" because of idolatry and oppression of God's people. The Pope thus becomes Pharaoh. Jesus the Messiah was crucified in Judea, a Roman province, by a Roman governor. By the edict of Caracalla, the city of Rome was decreed to be co-extensive with the Roman empire.

Hosea predicted, "after two days he will revive us" (Hos. 6:2). Since "one day is ... a thousand years" (2 Pet. 3:8), two days are 2000 years from when Israel was "torn" and "smitten" (6:1) by captivity in 721-676 B.C. arriving at 1278-1323 A.D. In 1280, in the reign of Edward I, one of England's greatest rulers, rightly called "the English Justinian," England's code of laws received their confirmation. In 1322 the authority of Kings, Lords, and Commons was established under Edward II. In 1324 A.D. John Wycliffe was born -- the Morning Star of the Reformation.

Who were the English witnesses? John WYCLIFFE (1320-1386) translated the Latin Bible into the first English Bible in 1382 to "revive" England. Fifty years after WYCLIFFE'S death, in 1438, priests dug up his bones from the grave and burned them in his village of Lutterworth, and then threw the ashes into the river Swift where they were carried to the Sea. His ashes like his writings spread far and wide. WYCLIFFE'S writings influenced John HUSS of Bohemia and JEROME of Prague. HUSS'S writings then stirred Martin LUTHER of Germany. The Reformation of the "third day" raised England up (Hos. 6:1-2). TYNEDALE'S English Translation in 1526 took the place of Wycliffe's. Copies of it were smuggled into England hidden in bales of cloth.

Queen Mary, daughter of Henry VIII, began to reign in 1553. She reigned only five years till she died childless when smitten by a tumor. But about 288 men, women and children were burnt to death in her short reign. When the Pope of Rome heard of Protestants being burnt, he was glad and there were special celebrations. The first martyr was John ROGERS. He had done much in translating the Bible into English. The date of his martyrdom was February 4th, 1555. On November 10th, 1558 the last martyrs were burnt at Canterbury for a total of THREE YEARS and NINE MONTHS-- "after three days and a half." Then Protestant Queen Elizabeth took the throne.

Another English fulfillment: The Revocation of the Edict of Nantes took place on the 17th of October, 1685. The English Revolution followed in 1688 and the coronation of WILLIAM of ORANGE and Queen Mary took place on the 9th of April 1689. The interval is THREE-AND-A-HALF YEARS. In the reign of William III the Bill of Rights was passed (1699). That bill made it impossible for any but a Protestant to sit on the throne of England. That Bill said to Protestants, "COME UP HERE."

Another English fulfillment: The English Church was established under Theodore A.D. 668. This church has always protested against the arrogancy and supremacy of the Roman Papacy. Adding 1241.88 (1260 x 360/365.25) years brings us to 1910. At the Coronation of King George V in 1910 the Declaration against the errors of Rome was omitted for the first time since William and Mary, 1688. This church witness was thereby silenced.

Another English fulfillment: "The JEWS were expelled from England in 1290 by a Catholic and feudal England and readmitted in 1655 (by Oliver Cromwell) to a Protestant and mercantile England" (p.229, Dimont's Jews, God and History). That is 365 years or "after THREE DAYS and a HALF the spirit of life from God entered into them, and they stood upon their feet, and great FEAR fell upon them who saw them. And they heard a great voice from heaven saying unto them, COME UP HERE. And they ascended up to HEAVEN in a cloud, and their enemies beheld them" (after three-and-a-half centuries). "The JEWS in England quickly rose to high posts" (p.293, ibid.).

The rise of Dutch supremacy coincides with the arrival of JEWS to the Netherlands in 1593 (p.291, ibid.).

Who were the French witnesses? The revocation of the Edict of Nantes and the final massacre of Calvin's HUGUENOTS occurred in 1685 but 105 years later, in 1790, a summons from Louis XVI, invited the common people to come together for the exercise of legislative power in the affairs of the realm. This was the "great voice from heaven" saying "COME UP HERE." They responded in a great CLOUD which inspired FEAR in the mind of king, nobles and clergy. They took possession of supreme power, disestablished the church, confiscated the estates of the clergy and nobles, imprisoned and decapitated the king, abolished all titles, proclaimed faith in God a superstition, and proclaimed France a Republic not a kingdom. Thousands were guillotined who were suspected of sympathizing with the former regime. This was called the "Reign of TERROR." This "EARTHQUAKE" caused a "TENTH of the city to fall." In other words, France was overthrown as a loyal part of the Holy Roman Empire. And "the remnant were AFFRIGHTED, and gave glory to the God of heaven" (Rev. 11:13). When people were tired of the terror, a public decree was made recognizing the existence of God and a future life, and convoking a national assembly in the Deity's honour. The assembly in honour of "the GOD of HEAVEN" was held in the presence of thousands -- Robespierre officiating as priest. The French Revolution bestowed French citizenship on JEWS. Napoleon incorporated them into French life, in effect saying "COME UP HERE." This is the age of Zunz and Vilna Gaon.

From the death of these French witnesses to their resurrection was 105 years. Now THREE-AND-A-HALF LUNAR DAYS, days of the moon instead of the earth, turn out to be 105 earth-days or 105 years exactly. The moon turns upon its axis just once in thirty days. Consequently, one day of the moon is just 30 times longer than one day upon earth. From 1685 to 1790 is 105 years.

Another French fulfillment: The Duke of Savoy, the sovereign of the VAUDOIS, by an edict dated January 31, 1686, forbade the exercise of their religion on pain of death and ordered their churches demolished and their ministers banished. Savoy and French troops attacked them on the 22nd of April 1686. Many Vaudois were killed or imprisoned and permitted to depart about the beginning of December 1686. Papists REJOICED. The VAUDOIS were kindly received by Holland, Brandenburg, Geneva and Switzerland. Towards the end of the year 1689, about THREE-AND-A-HALF YEARS after the attack on the 22nd of April, they passed the Lake of Geneva secretly, and entering Savoy with their swords in their hands they recovered their ancient possessions, and by the middle of April 1690, established themselves in it, notwithstanding the opposition of the troops of France and Savoy; of whom they, who were comparatively few, slew great numbers with inconsiderable loss; causing FEAR and TERROR in their enemies, till the Duke himself, who had now, left the French interest, by his League, and an Edict signed June 4th, 1690, just THREE-AND-A-HALF YEARS after their total dissipation, recalled the rest of them and re-established them with liberty to the French refugees also. This fulfillment includes the resurrection of both the WALDENSES and ALBIGENSES -- two witnesses -- which t refugees also. This fulfillment includes have been a united people, and dwelt together in these valleys of Piedmont ever since the conclusion of the Crusades against the ALBIGENSES in the 13th century.

Another French fulfillment: Huguenots were lured to Paris for the wedding of Henry of Navarre, leader of the Huguenots, to Margaret, sister of the French king. This royal marriage alliance was supposed to end wars of religion. But on August 24th at 3 A.M. in the morning, Papists wearing white arm bands and white crosses in their hats for identity, slaughtered defenseless Huguenots for three days. By the fourth day the slaughter had stopped. Protestants were massacred at Paris beginning on the eve of St. Bartholemew's Day, 1572. Thirty or forty thousand HUGUENOTS were slain in a few days. "Their dead bodies lay in the streets of the great city" because they WEREN'T allowed to be BURIED due to being "heretics." The usual death for "heresy" was burning, the ashes being afterwards thrown to the winds or cast into rivers. The practice of exhuming bodies of heretics already buried was derived from paganism; but Papal practice went even a step further, in holding a formal process against a dead body, if after death suspected of heresy. Then massacres began in other major towns: Lyons, Rouen, Dieppe, etcetera. It is estimated that 70,000 HUGUENOTS perished (Elijah's 7000?). Queen Catherine de Medici, mother of reigning King Charles IX, became known as "Queen JEZEBEL." When news reached Rome September 8th, 1572, the people REJOICED and SANG Te Deums and Pope Gregory XIII issued a medal to commemorate the massacre. But in THREE-AND-A-HALF YEARS, HENRY III, who succeeded his brother Charles IX, entered into a treaty with the HUGUENOTS, which was concluded and published on 14th of May, 1576, whereby all former sentences against them were revised, and free and open exercise of their religion was granted to them: they were to be admitted to all honours, dignities and offices, as well as the Papists; and the judges were to be half of one religion, and half of the other; with other articles greatly to their advantage." They were told "COME UP HERE."

Who were the German witnesses? In 1499, the BOHEMIAN BRETHREN sent representatives throughout Europe to find if there were any other witnesses with a similar testimony to their own, and found none, because of the Papal extermination. This is why they were clothed in SACKCLOTH. On December 16th, 1513, a Papal Bull was issued calling the remaining BOHEMIAN dissenters to present their case before the ninth session of the Fifth Lateran Council convened for May 5th, 1514, with the object of completing the extermination of all "heresies." That day came and the representatives from different "TONGUES and NATIONS" of the Church of Western Europe gathered in the Lateran Church at Rome to hear the famous proclamation of triumph, "Jam nemo reclamant, nullus obsistit." No witnesses appeared to testify to the truth. Their voices were all silent as if they were DEAD. The council orator exultingly declared: "Now, no one contradicts, no one opposes." To the Pope he said: "The whole body of Christendom is now seen to be subjected to its head, that is to thee." The same day, the Pope issued an edict, one purpose being "the perpetual elimination of all heretics from the Church Visible." Penalties were increased. One was the DENIAL of BURIAL to heretics, and that involved eternal damnation. When the Council was dissolved, a plenary indulgence was granted, and a Te Deum was sung. There were splendid banquets, general REJOICINGS and congratulations, and SENDING of GIFTS. When the General Council was dissolved in 1517, historians of the Papacy such as Roscoe in his Life of Pope Leo X confirm the remarkable accuracy of merry-making, banqueting and exchanging gifts among the leaders of the Church mentioned in verse 10.

In 1179, the third General Council of Lateran, under Alexander III, enjoined princes to make war upon "heretics," to take their possessions for a spoil, to reduce their persons to slavery, and to WITHHOLD from them Christian BURIAL. This was supposed to involve eternal damnation. The Council of the Roman Church also repeatedly issued edicts from 1514 to 1517 excommunicating the "heretics," ordering the SCRIPTURES in the common tongues to be BURNT, ordering the BONES of the Protestant martyrs to be DUG UP and burnt, and Christian BURIAL to be REFUSED to all "heretics."

Cyprian was the last champion of doctrinal independence from Rome. All rivalry after his time was confined to Rome versus Constantinople. Cyprian was the first to express the idea of the Roman Catholic Church having a monopoly on salvation in 257 A.D. This doctrine was not effectively challenged until Luther nailed up his ninety-five Theses on the Wittenburg Church door in 1517 A.D. In the year 257 A.D. Cyprian had a dream in which he was promised one day respite from impending martyrdom. He actually had one year exactly of respite. His deacon who records the story, remarks upon the symbolism of a day for a year as being scriptural (Pontius, Life of Cyprian, sec.13). Now if we add 1260 years to 257 A.D. we get 1517 A.D.

From 5th May, 1514 when the council orator of the 9th session officially declared: "Now no one contradicts, no one opposes," to 31st October, 1517 when LUTHER posted his theses to the Wittenburg Castle Church door in Germany, defying papal Rome and inaugurating the Reformation, are THREE-AND-A-HALF YEARS. Within a month, LUTHER'S protest, which he supported by Scriptures, aroused all Europe. Thus the witnesses figuratively "STOOD on their feet" after being as "dead bodies" for 3 1/2 years. In 1516 ERASMUS published his New Testament in Greek which made possible the translation of the Bible into the common tongues from 1517 onward. "ERASMUS laid the egg, and LUTHER hatched it." This shows us how interdependent the two witnesses were. ERASMUS the scholar of the Bible text and LUTHER the preacher who refused to grant absolution for purchased indulgences (1 Pet. 1:18-19). Prince FREDERICK in Germany protected Martin LUTHER after dreaming a dream of a monk who used a 100-year-old goose quill ("HUSS" means "goose" in Bohemian) to poke the Pope's ears. Then Germany in 1532 granted full toleration to Protestants with the Pacification Decree of Nuremberg. This was followed by more decrees; till at Augsburg in 1555, Protestants were put on an equal footing with Romanists and admitted as judges in the Supreme Imperial Chamber. Thus German witnesses ascended into the German political heaven after hearing the "COME UP HERE" decrees.

In 1523, in an address to the Diet of Nuremberg, Pope Adrian unconsciously testified to the fulfilment of this prophecy in verse 11 when he said, "The heretics HUSS and JEROME seem now to be alive again in the person of LUTHER." In 1528 LUTHER himself wrote the following: "We are not the first ones who applied the Antichristian kingdom to the Papacy: this many great men have dared to do many years before us and that frankly and openly under the greatest persecution. The old divinely-ordained WITNESSES confirm our doctrine, and the BODIES OF THESE SAINTS ARISE as it were among us with the NEWLY-VIVIFIED GOSPEL, and awaken much confidence." In 1530 the Reformers began to be known as "Protestants" which comes from the Latin word meaning "WITNESSES." LUTHER said in his Table Talk: "The Papists in Germany are filled with FEAR " (2:29).

What was the "great EARTHQUAKE"? Earthquakes in the Bible symbolize POLITICAL UPHEAVAL. The English REVOLT against the Papacy by King HENRY VIII, EDWARD VI, Queen ELIZABETH, JAMES I, and Parliament's Act of Supremacy in 1534 where the British monarch became head of the Church of England rather than the Pope, caused "the TENTH PART of the city" of Rome to fall. Ten nations had supported Rome for centuries. The adoption of the Book of Common Prayer, together with the ratification of the "Thirty-nine Articles" by Act of Parliament and Queen ELIZABETH in 1571, completely severed England from Rome (The "forty stripes save one" for law-breakers -- Deut. 25:3). Then in the Revolution of 1688 A.D. and the Settlement of 1697 A.D. (where the King must declare the adoration of the Virgin Mary, Saints and Mass to be idolatrous.) further distance was added. Since Denmark, Norway and Sweden were never part of the Roman territory to begin with, they don't count as one of the ten. But in a larger sense, the separation of the Protestant nations of Switzerland, Denmark, Norway, Sweden, England, Scotland (1518-1558) and the United Provinces of Holland (1581) from Papal Rome revealed these nations as the Lord's portion -- his TITHE or TENTH of the priesthood to serve God.

In the days of Elijah there were "SEVEN THOUSAND" who did not bow the knee to Baal images or KISS them (1 Kings 19:18) just as in the Protestant Reformation there were "SEVEN THOUSANDS" plural meaning seven tribal sub-divisions (cp. Ex. 18:21; Nu. 10:36) or SEVEN northern PROVINCES of HOLLAND that rebelled against the Spanish yoke and papal rule in 1579 who didn't KISS the toes of the bronze statue of Jupiter or Zeus (renamed Peter) in the Vatican. The toes of this graven image are almost worn away, having been KISSED by millions of Roman Catholics. The Netherlands were once composed of seventeen Provinces, under the cruel rule of Philip II of Spain. After a struggle lasting 37 years, their independence as a Protestant power was virtually acknowledged in 1609. They were Holland, Zealand, Utrecht, Friesland, Groningen, Overyssel and Guelderland forming the Dutch Republic. They were symbolically "SLAIN" in the eyes of Rome. It is significant that the remnant "gave glory to the GOD of heaven" rather than saints or the Virgin Mary, showing that the Protestant religion had arrived. It was from these same United Provinces, a century later, that God raised up the deliverer, William III, Prince of Orange (anti-type of Elijah), who defeated Popery in the British Isles on the banks of the River Boyne in July 1690, thereby preserving the Protestant character of the Royal Throne, so that even to this day the sovereign of the U.K. must swear at the Coronation to be a "faithful Protestant."

By means of the Counter-Reformation, the formation of the Jesuits (1540) and the Council of Trent (1545-1563), aided by the military might of Emperor Charles V and Philip of Spain and their successors, the Papacy halted and turned back the Reformation in non-Israelite European nations. In 1629, Emperor Ferdinand, by military might, restored all the ecclesiastical lands and offices in northern Germany to the Roman Catholic Church.

But Israel went into idolatry in Solomon's reign (958 to 918 B.C.), bringing "seven times" or 2520 years punishment which ran out in 1562 to 1602 A.D. We should therefore expect Israel to start coming out of idolatry in that same era.

The Treaty of Westphalia in 1648 was the end of the Reformation Era and Switzerland, Denmark, Norway, Iceland, Sweden, England, Scotland and Holland were established and recognized by international law as permanent Protestant nations.

The Treaty of Ryswick, in 1697 made peace between Papal and Protestant nations of Europe. The Treaty of Carlowitz in 1699 seriously diminished the Ottoman Power. From the time of these two treaties, the power of Rome and Turkey has waned.

"The second woe is past; and behold, the third woe cometh quickly. And the seventh angel sounded; and there were great voices in heaven, saying, The kingdoms of this world are become (lit. "are becoming") the kingdoms of Our Lord, and of His Christ; and He shall reign for ever and ever" (Rev. 11:14-15).

Throughout the seventeenth century the Turks attacked the Holy Roman Empire and besieged Vienna. At the close of the century the fourteenth Papal Crusade, with the united armies of Venice, Savoy, Germany, Austria and Poland turned the tide of battle. The second woe passed away in 1699 when Turkey signed the Treaty of Carlowitz with the Holy Roman Empire. Turkey gave up huge territories including Hungary, Transylvania, and the Ukraine. After that, there was no more fear of Turks invading central Europe. Turkey was again defeated in 1791 by Russia. All the events from Revelation 9:13 to 11:14 occurred during the era of the Sixth Trumpet or Second Woe. The third woe or the seventh trumpet came "quickly" in the eighteenth century. The growth of infidelity and atheistic Communism led to the French Revolution which began the final judgments on the Papacy. Revelation 11:14 therefore occupies 1699 to 1789 A.D.

"And the seventh angel sounded; and there were great voices in heaven, saying, The kingdoms of this world are become the kingdoms of our Lord, and of his Christ; and he shall reign for ever and ever. And the four and twenty elders, which sat before God on their seats, fell upon their faces, and worshipped God, Saying, We give thee thanks, O Lord God Almighty, which art, and wast, and art to come; because thou hast taken to thee thy great power, and hast reigned. And the nations were angry, and thy wrath is come, and the time of the dead, that they should be judged, and that thou shouldest give reward unto thy servants the prophets, and to the saints, and them that fear thy name, small and great; and shouldest destroy them which destroy the earth. And the temple of God was opened in heaven, and there was seen in his temple the ark of his testament: and there were lightnings, and voices, and thunderings, and an earthquake, and great hail" (Rev. 11:15-19).

Astronomically, the temple of God is the starry sky dome. The ark of the testament is Argo the Ark -- a wooden vessel with overshadowing wings of a sail. Historically the Protestant Reformation's triumph began the foundation of the Stone Kingdom (Dan. 2:44-45) and the mountain of the Lord's house (Isa. 2:1-5) manifested humanly and imperfectly by the British Empire and the United States. The Kingdoms of this world became the Kingdoms of God as "one third" of the earth came to be ruled by Anglo-Saxons by 1940. God also gave "reward" to Anglo-Saxondom as the British and Americans became wealthy and powerful. Here the temple scene in Revelation 11:19 dovetails into Revelation 15:5-8, linking the seventh trumpet with the seven vials.

"The fundamental benefit of the Monarchy is not the power it has, but the power it denies others" (Catholics) (Time, 12 April 1993).

The Protestant Throne Of Israel

The pope is the direct successor of the high priest of the Chaldean fish-god Dagon who became popular with the Philistines (Judges 16:21-30; 1 Sam. 5:5-6). This artist's composite representation (left) shows the origin of the papal mitre. From a bas-relief on the palace of Assur-nasir-pal, King of Assyria, circa 885 B.C. and a Mesopotamian sculpture from the same period (right). Bacchus was known as ICH-THUS (Hesychius p.179) and "Christians" still imitate pagans (top).

Constantine Defeats Paganism
& Christian Israel Flees to Britain
Chapter 12
(313 to 540 A.D.)
(The Other Side of the Scroll)

From chapter 6 to the end of chapter 11, the visions proceed in their chronological order; but now they turn back in time to the sixth seal corresponding to chapter 12. Chapters 12 through 22 give us what was written "on the backside" (Rev. 5:1) of the book. This outside series of visions,12 through 22, parallels and explains the series of visions from chapters 6 through 11.

"And there appeared a great wonder ("sign" -- of the zodiac) in heaven -- a WOMAN (Virgo) clothed with the SUN, and the MOON under her feet, and upon her head a crown of twelve STARS (twelve constellations or signs of the zodiac because each is represented by a star) And she being with child cried, travailing in birth, and pained to be delivered" (Rev. 12:1-2).

Who is the WOMAN? "I have likened the DAUGHTER of Zion ("my people -- Isa. 56:16) to a comely and delicate WOMAN" (Jer. 6:2), or a BRIDE (Isa. 62:5). "For the husband is the head of the WIFE, even as Christ is the head of the CHURCH" (Eph. 5:23) "in the wilderness" (Acts 7:38) which is "a chaste VIRGIN" (2 Cor. 11:2). (see also Isa. 50:1; 47:7-9; 54:1; Jer. 3:1-25; Hos. 2:1-23).

What does the SUN represent? Genesis 37:9-10 defines the SUN as Jacob or ISRAEL -- supreme kingly authority ruling the day; the MOON as RACHEL -- ruling the night with subordinate religious authority, and the twelve STARS as the 12 TRIBES of IS-RAEL (Gen. 37:9-10). The WOMAN is thoroughly clothed with ISRAELITE practices and customs and in supreme authority. Since CHRIST is the "SUN of Righteousness" (Mal. 4:2), the woman is clothed with CHRISTIANITY. The LUNAR "rulers of darkness" (Eph. 6:12) and the "power of darkness" (Col. 1:13) of PAGAN religion are now under her feet-- including the Mohammedan CRESCENT. "The WICKED ... shall be ashes under the soles of your feet" (Mal. 4:3).

"And there appeared another wonder in heaven; and, behold, a great RED DRAGON, having SEVEN HEADS and TEN HORNS, and seven crowns upon his heads" (Rev. 12:3).

Who is the RED DRAGON? Astronomically this is the constellation Serpens with seven heads in the red glow before sunrise. Corona Borealis has seven stars which are these seven crowned heads. Historically, Arrian mentioned DRAGONS as military standards among the Romans. Vegetius (about 386 A.D.) wrote, "The first standard of the whole legion is the eagle, which the aquilifer carries. DRAGONS are also borne to battle by the draconarii." Since one legion consisted of TEN cohorts, there wereTEN draconarii to every one aquilifer. The DRAGON-standards were painted RED. The pagan ROMAN EMPIRE was the fourth empire of Daniel 7:23-24 with "TEN HORNS" and since the "RED DRAGON" also has "TEN HORNS" (Rev. 12:3), they must be the same beast. The pagan ROMAN EMPIRE tried to "devour her (Christ) child" first using Herod in the reign of Augustus Caesar (Matt. 2:16) and second using Pilate in the reign of Tiberius. The "SEVEN" most significant Holy Roman Emperors or "HEADS" were Justinian (527-565 A.D.), Charlemagne (800-814 A.D.), Otto the Great, (962-973 A.D.), Frederick Barbarossa (1152-1190 A.D.), Charles V (1520-1556 A.D.), Louis XIV (1661-1715 A.D.) and Napoleon (1804-1814 A.D.). The seven forms of Roman government were: Kings (750-510- B.C.), Consuls (510-498 B.C.), Dictators (498-451 B.C.), Decimvirs (451-443 B.C.), Military Tribunes (443-27 B.C.), Military Emperors (Imperial Caesars) (27 B.C.-284 A.D.) and Despotic Emperors (Diocletian ignored his Senate, creating three other rulers with himself) (284-313 A.D.). Since the DIADEM ("crown") -- the badge of oriental royalty -- was not adopted earlier than 292 A.D. when Diocletian made his partition of the Empire, the vision cannot be dated before then. From that time the DIADEM became the imperial badge and subsequent emperors adopted it. Also, since the DRAGON is the ruler of PAGAN, not Christian, ROME, the vision must be dated BEFORE the Empire became CHRISTIAN in 324 A.D. The symbolism fits only the period of 292-324 A.D. That is why the "MAN-CHILD" must be CONSTANTINE. The "TEN HORNS" are Ostrogoths, Visigoths, Vandals, Sueves, Franks, Burgundians, Heruli, Huns, Lombards and Anglo-Saxons. These were the ten kingdoms that the Roman Empire split into after 476 A.D. The seven-headed serpent is even now worshipped in India. In Moor's Hindu Pantheon, p.171, is a plate of a seven-headed Buddha and against p.12 is a plate where a serpent is swimming and leaning his seven heads over Vishnu's (the man Noah's) head as he sleeps. The seven-headed serpent was also worshipped in Egypt. It has been traced back to Accad, one of the cities of Nimrod: "we read in a very ancient Accadian hymn, 'The thunderbolt of seven heads, like the huge serpent of seven heads (I bear)' (Records of the Past 3:128). M. Lenormant well compares the Accadian serpent with the seven-headed Indian serpent, Vasonki, which was doubtless derived from it" (Brown's Great Dionysiak Myth 1:120). The Indian seven-headed serpent is sometimes called Naga ... derived from Nagash, and the Accadian, Egyptian and Indian are doubtless the same as the Lernean Hydra, one of whose heads was supposed to be invulnerable till Hercules attacked it." (p.342, Computation of 666).

"His tail drew the THIRD part of the STARS of heaven and did cast them to the earth" (Rev. 12:4).

Astronomically, Hydra stretches about one third the circumference of the celestial heaven. Historically, who are the STARS? "They that turn many to RIGHTEOUSNESS" are like "the STARS" (Dan.12:3) or "ANGELS" (Rev. 1:20). When the He-goat's little horn "cast down some of the hosts of heaven, and of the STARS to the ground, and

stamped upon them ... the MIGHTY and the HOLY PEOPLE" (Dan. 8:9-24), one interpretation (besides Antiochus Epiphanes or the Moslems or the Eastern Orthodox
Church) is when the eastern Roman General Pompey conquered the Promised Land
in 63 B.C. and enslaved the RULERS of JUDAH. Likewise, in 313 the Roman Empire
was divided into three parts. In two of these the CHRISTIANS were granted toleration
by the Milan Decree of Constantine and Licinius; while in the third, Maximin preferred
paganism and made war against the CHRISTIANS under his jurisdiction. These are
RIGHTEOUS, HOLY PEOPLE cast to the earth in persecution. This "THIRD" of the
Empire also happened to be the GREEK, the THIRD empire of Daniel.

"The DRAGON stood before the woman who was ready to be delivered, to devour
her CHILD as soon as it was born" (12:4).

Astronomically, the constellation Serpens is right under Virgo's feet as she gives
birth to the SUN. Historically this symbolism represents the attitude of Galerius and
Maxentius towards Christianity and CONSTANTINE its champion. Maximin was
defeated. In 323, Licinius apostasized, and made war on Christianity. Constantine
defeated Licinius in 324 A.D. at the Battle of Adrianople and "ruled all." "Christianity" went on to become the dominant religion of the Empire. Constantine became
the sole ruler of the Empire in the symbolic "heaven" of political power. Constantine
himself in his epistle to Eusebius and other bishops concerning the re-edifying and
repairing of churches, said "that liberty being now restored, and that DRAGON being removed from the administration of public affairs, by the providence of the great
God" (Thomas Newton, Dissertations on the Prophecies pp. 523-524).

"And she brought forth a MAN CHILD, who was to RULE all nations with a rod of iron;
and her child was caught up unto God, and to his THRONE" (Rev. 12:5).

Who is her CHILD? Revelation 4:1 says, "I will show thee things which must be HERE-
AFTER." After 96 A.D. Therefore the primary meaning of the MAN-CHILD cannot be
Jesus the Messiah. "My little CHILDREN, of whom I travail in birth again, until Christ
be formed in you" (Ga. 4:19) defines the CHILD as a CHRISTIAN. CONSTANTINE the
Great became a CHRISTIAN and his mother was a British lady named Helena of York,
so he was a child of ISRAEL. Just as Jesus the Messiah and Titus the Roman general
both fulfilled Daniel 9:27 by causing "the sacrifice ... to cease," (31 A.D. and 70 A.D.),
so also Jesus the Messiah and CONSTANTINE the Great both fulfill Revelation 12:5
"to RULE all nations with a rod of IRON."

Four pagan Emperors ruled the Roman Empire co-jointly at the close of the third
century. CONSTANTINE'S father, Constantius, was one of them. He sympathized
with Christians. When he died at York in Britain, the army proclaimed CONSTANTINE
his successor whose dominion lay in Gaul and Britain. He also sympathized with
Christians. It was not the place of the army to appoint a successor. The power lay
with Galerius, the chief emperor, who hated Christians. He was filled with rage when
he heard of the army's action. However he accepted the nomination, intending later

to depose and destroy CONSTANTINE. He made secret arrangements to invade Gaul and Britain.

But CONSTANTINE realized what was taking place, and pre-empted him. He left Britain and marched his army across the Alps before Maxentius (who had taken the place of Galerius, who was deceased by this time) was aware of it. He defeated an army three times his own size and marched toward Rome. Another army, and another opposed him but both dispersed before his swift movements and powerful attacks. The Roman Senate, after his third victory at Saxa Rubra, threw open the gates of Rome, and proclaimed him Emperor of the Romans in 313 A.D. He was now a ruler of one third of the Roman Empire. He established the CHRISTIAN faith throughout his third. Christ was "caught up" to "God" and to his "throne" (12:5) just as CONSTANTINE was "caught up" to the Roman Empire's THRONE. "God ruleth in the kingdoms of men, and giveth it to whomsoever he will" (Dan. 4:32).

"And the woman fled into the wilderness, where she hath a PLACE PREPARED by God, that they should feed her there a thousand two hundred and threescore days" (12:6).

Where is the PREPARED PLACE? Israel left Palestine in 745, 721-718 and 677 B.C. Anglo-Saxons arrive in Britain but defeated by Britons at Mount Badon in 516 A.D; Anglo-Saxons arrive successfully in Britain in 540 A.D. (Gildas), and establish the Saxon Heptarchy in 582 A.D. (Gibbon), all 1260 years after migrating through the Near East and Europe. It "shall be for a time, times, and a half a time; and when he shall have accomplished to SCATTER the power of the holy people" (Dan. 12:7) just as Israel fled from pagan Egypt to the land of Palestine. Jews survived in a different way. They were an economic necessity. They became the merchants and bankers of Christendom. They were grudgingly fed or nourished by their "Christian" enemies.

"There was WAR in heaven. Michael and his angels fought against the dragon, and the dragon fought and his angels, and prevailed not, neither was their place found any more in heaven. And the great red DRAGON was CAST OUT, that old serpent, called the devil and Satan" (Rev. 12:7-9).

What is the WAR? This pictured the downfall of paganism and the establishment of Christianity in the fourth century (referred to twice before in the the the sixth seal -- Rev. 6 -- and the fifth trumpet -- Rev. 9). Diocletian caused thousands of Christians to perish from 303 until 313 A.D. When Constantine arrived in 313 A.D. the persecution stopped. Following the Edict of Toleration of Licinius in 313 A.D., the Roman Empire was divided into three parts -- Europe under Constantine, Africa under Licinius and Asia under Maximin. In two-thirds -- Europe and Africa -- Christians had toleration, but in the one-third, Asia, Maximin renewed persecution against them, until defeated by Licinius, when the Christians were restored to favor. Thus was the remaining third of paganism overthrown. Later, Licinius apostasized from the Christian faith, and began to persecute Christians again -- or devour the woman's offspring. Licinius, however, was finally defeated by Constantine, and Christianity made the State religion in 325 A.D. Astronomically, by precession of the equinox, the heel of the constellation Hercules (Michael) is gradually bruising the head of the constellation Drago as it moves uppermost more and more. Drago's first star Thuban no longer rules at the pole, as it had in early Chaldea, as the "Prince of the Powers of the Air." Also Orion (Michael) bruises Cetus. Jesus said, "I beheld Satan as lightning fall from heaven" (Luke 10:18). Hydra is like a long streak of lightning rotating down behind the red-sunset horizon.

"And I heard a loud voice saying in heaven, Now is come salvation, and strength, and the kingdom of our God, And they overcame him by the blood of the Lamb, and by the word of their testimony; and they loved not their lives unto the death. Therefore rejoice, ye heavens, and ye that dwell in them. Woe to the inhabiters of the earth and of the sea! for the devil is come down unto you, having great wrath, because he knoweth that he hath but a short time. And when the dragon saw that he was cast unto the earth, he persecuted the woman which brought forth the man child" (Rev. 12:10-13).

Many Christians believed at the time that the Millenium was beginning. But Emperor Constantine believed in Arianism which rejected the divinity of Christ. He also appointed a bishop who had renounced the scriptures under persecution to save his life. Thus Constantine's Christianity was imperfect, but it was a great improvement over polytheism. Barbaric customs such as branding humans, crucifixion, and gladiatorial combat were abolished. Christianity, even in a corrupt form, has a humanizing effect on society. Christ's rule, which Constantine only typified, will be perfect.

Then Julian the apostate took the throne and reigned two-and-a-half years (between 360 and 363 A.D.). Julian fought against Christianity and for heathenism. Then Theodosius (379 to 395 A.D.) with great severity suppressed heathen worship. The great dragon and his angels in the guise of heathen rulers and officials were finally cast down from the political "heaven" of the Roman Empire. Gibbon says "that, in a full meeting of the Senate, on a regular division, Jupiter was condemned and degraded by a large majority" in favor of Christ.

"And to the woman were given two wings of a great eagle that she might fly into the wilderness, into HER PLACE, where she is nourished for a time, times, and half a time FROM the face of the SERPENT" (12:14).

"Ye have seen what I did unto the Egyptians, and how I bare you on EAGLE'S WINGS, and brought you unto myself" (Ex. 19:4). "As an EAGLE stirreth up her nest, fluttereth over her young, spreadeth abroad her WINGS, taketh them, beareth them on her WINGS: so the Lord alone did lead him, and there was no strange god with him" (Deut. 32:11-12). The literal rendering of verse 14 is "The EAGLE, the GREAT ONE." Not only was Emperor Theodosius named "the GREAT," but his coins showed EAGLE'S WINGS protecting his eastern and western dominions. Because of the persecution of the Dragon, Theodosius representing the "TWO WINGS," East and West, of the EAGLE Empire, befriended the persecuted Church. In 381, the Council of Constantinople confirmed the decision of the Council of Nice, and upheld the divinity of Christ. His rule greatly aided the flight of Israel towards the BRITISH ISLES and the spread of Christianity.

"Moreover I will appoint a PLACE for my people Israel, and will plant them, that they may dwell in a PLACE of THEIR OWN and move no more" (2 Sam. 7:10). Where is it? The BRITISH ISLES. It could not be Palestine because Israel had moved out of that land. Isaiah 69:12 says Israel will come "from the NORTH and the WEST" (Isa. 49:5-12) meaning "the ISLES AFAR OFF" (Jer. 31:10) where this "virgin of Israel" (31:4) is "gathered" (31:10). The flight of the woman began with the fall of heathenism (313) and ended with the rise of the Papacy (533-610), a period of less than three centuries. From 516, 540, and 582 A.D. she was protected in BRITAIN from this Holy Roman Empire for 1260 years. Gathered. Verse 6 doesn't say "HER PLACE" or "FROM the SERPENT." Therefore two different 1260-year periods are mentioned in verses 6 and 14 making the "seven times" punishment complete. Then BRITAIN and the UNITED STATES rose to greatness (Isa. 41:1) from 1776 onward. Saxons, Danes, Jutes and Hibernians are really Isaac's sons, Danites, Jews and Hebrews. Just as John ate the Bible (John 10:10), so also the woman is fed and nourished with Scripture during this time. Moreover, the 2520 years ended in 1776 (American Independence), 1800-1803 (Louisiana Purchase) and 1844 A.D. (Texas a U.S. Territory).

"And the serpent cast out of his mouth water as a flood after the woman, that he might cause her to be carried away of the flood. And the earth helped the woman, and the earth opened her mouth, and swallowed up the flood which the dragon cast out of his mouth" (Rev. 12:15-16).

Astronomically Cetus, the aquatic dragon, casts forth the river Eridanus after Androm-eda to devour her according to Chaldaeo-Greek legend but the river is swallowed up by the horizon as it rotates toward the earth. Aquila is the "great eagle." Biologically, dragons and alligators spout out water to overcome their enemies. "The Egyptian account of (the crocodile) ... was that sixty days elapsed before its eggs were laid, that the eggs were ... sixty, that sixty days passed ere they were hatched, that the animal had sixty vertebrae ... sixty nerves, that their teeth amounted to sixty, that ... their annual ... fasting lasted sixty days, and ... they obtained the age of sixty years" (Wilkinson's Egypt 5:237). Historically, when the Dragon could no longer use State persecution against the Christian Church, he attempted to overwhelm it and corrupt it by the inrush of unconverted pagans who brought with them heathen beliefs and practices. These are the "waters" defined as "peoples, multitudes, nations, and tongues" (17:15) which became a flood into the church after Christianity was made the state religion in 325 A.D. They corrupted the visible Roman Church but by then the true church was long gone. Later military expeditions ("floods") were despatched by the Catholic government against "heretics" in the Roman Empire but lovers of liberty used violence to defend the true Christians.

Also, another "flood" that Satan stirred up was the Goths, Vandals and Huns from Mongolia to overwhelm the now Christianized Roman Empire and obliterate Christians and Israel through miscegenation and mass immigration to gain political and religious control. But the Huns, Vandals and Goths submitted to the religion of the conquered Christians and also absorbed Roman laws, manners, language and customs (Gibbon 4:37:20-24). They settled down to farming and herding. In 410 A.D. Rome had to recall her legions from Britain to defend Rome itself from the Goths under Alaric. This left Britain wide open for the Jutes in 449. Attila the Hun attacked the Roman Empire from 433 to 450 A.D. But eventually "Christianity was embraced by almost all the barbarians" (Gibbon ch.37). Just as the Red Sea swallowed Pharaoh's army, so also the English Channel or "earth's open mouth" provided a separation between the true Christian Israel and the pagan Roman Catholic Church as well as the barbarian hordes. Jutes, Angles, and Saxons built ships and escaped to Scandinavia and the British Isles.

"And the dragon was wroth with the woman, and went to make war with the remnant of her seed, who keep the commandments of God, and have the testimony of Jesus Christ" (Rev. 12:17).

The remnants who remained behind on the continent were victimized. The true Christian church has no idols or images of Jesus, Mary or the saints; doesn't worship a wafer host; doesn't pray to statues; rests on the Sabbath rather than Sunday; doesn't keep the Scriptures in Latin; rejects the confessional and the cross symbol; believes in tithing ten percent of wages; avoids eating pork and celebrates the festivals of Passover, Pentecost and Sukkot.

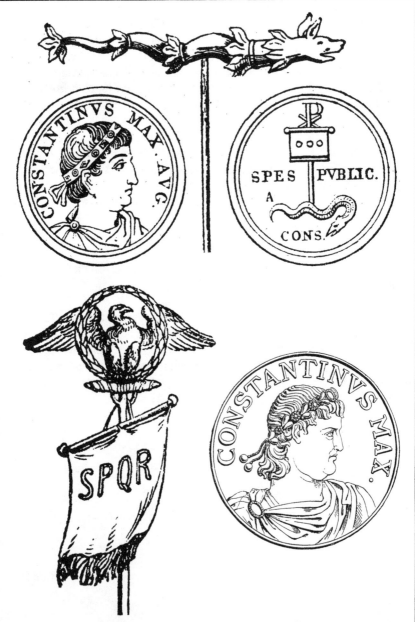

Top: Roman Dragon Standard. Middle: Coin with Constantine on one side and the Chi-Rho sign triumphing over the Dragon of paganism on the other. Lower Left: Roman Eagle Standard. Lower Right: Coin with Constantine's image.

The Beast & The False Prophet (42 Months)
(Chapter 13)

John wrote, "And I stood upon the sand of the sea, and saw a beast rise up out of the sea, having seven heads and ten horns, and upon his horns ten crowns, and upon his heads the name of blasphemy" (Rev. 13:1).

The "sand" is Abraham's "seed" (Gen. 22:17; 32:12) so John in vision is standing in the midst of Abraham's seed in Britain and viewing European developments. The Sea is the Mediterranean "peoples" (Rev. 17:15). The beast is a "kingdom" (Dan. 7:17,23). Historically and astronomically, the seven heads are the Babylonian lion (Leo), Medo-Persian bear (Ursa Major), Greek leopard with four heads (Ursa Minor -- anciently considered a leopard) and Roman dragon (Hydra rising from the celestial sea). The "ten horns" or "kings"(Dan. 7:24) (on the dragon's head -- Rev. 12:3) are the same as the "ten toes" of Daniel 2 and represented the ten kingdoms into which the Western half of the Roman Empire was divided after its fall in 476 A.D. "Horns" are lesser world powers that spring from greater world powers or "beasts" (Dan. 8:21-22). "Crowns" go from heads (12:3) to horns (13:1) to non-existence except for a woman rider (17:3). The horns were the Ostrogoths (Hungary & Yugoslavia), Visigoths (Spain), Vandals (N. Africa), Sueves (Portugal), Franks (France), Burgundians (Switzerland & S. Gaul), Heruli (Italy), Huns (Alemani) Lombards (Austria & Czechoslovakia) and Anglo-Saxons (England). Three separate authors all testify that these were the ten Gothic kingdoms -- Gibbon, Procopius and Machiavelli (Hist. Floe. i).

"And the beast which I saw was like unto a leopard, and his feet were as the feet of a bear, and his mouth as the mouth of a lion: and the dragon gave him his power, and his seat, and great authority" (Rev. 13:2).

Who is this BEAST? A mixture of all four world empires from 604 B.C. to 1917 A.D. rolled into one. "The (seven) times of the Gentiles" (Dan. 4:32; 7:17; Luke 21:24) (2520 years) portrayed in one animal instead of four in Daniel. A condensed version of World History. Also an end-time Gentile world government for seven literal years where the Nebuchadnezzar-Darius-Alexander-Caesar will be assassinated by a "deadly wound" after a 3 1/2 year "ministry" (Dan. 9:27; Rev. 13:3-5) and then be "resurrected," stop the sacrifice and claim to be the Messiah -- having taken captive the British Empire, the United States and the Jews just as his anti-types did.

"The dragon (Drago at the celestial north pole) gave him his ... seat (throne)" (Rev. 13:2). The high priest of the old Babylonish religion was the original Pontifex Maximus. Nimrod the king of ancient Babylon had been both king and High Priest, or Pontifex Maximus. When Belshazzar was slain (Dan. 5:30), and the Chaldeans were defeated by Darius the Mede, the Babylonian priests were expelled. Some fled east to Tibet where they introduced "LAMAISM" which bears a striking similarity to Roman Catholicism. Others moved their Central College to Pergamos -- "Satan's seat" (Rev. 2:13) where the serpent-worship of Aesculapius the "child of the incarnate sun" continued. The King of Pergamos dressed in scarlet and purple, wore the mitre of Dagon the Fish-god, held the crozier of Nimrod and the keys of Cybele and Janus (whose sacred bird was the cock). The last of the original Babylonian priests was King Attalus III, Pontifex Maximus of Pergamos. At his death, he bequeathed the priestly title and his dominions to the Roman people in 133 B.C. Thus Phrygia became part of the Roman Empire in 133 B.C. As Roman Emperor, Julius Caesar accepted the title about 63 B.C., and Roman Emperors from that time were called "Pontifex Maximus" up to 375 A.D., when Emperor Gratian, being a nominal Christian, renounced it, and transferred the title and paganism to the Bishop of Rome, Pope Damasus, who accepted it and to the present time calls himself Pontifex Maximus (see Hislop's Two Babylons, pp. 240-241, 279). Therefore Augustine wrote that "Rome was founded as the second Babylon and as the daughter of the former Babylon" (City of God 5:439). Babylon is another name for Rome (Sybilline Oracles 5:159; Apoc. of Baruch 2:1 & 4 Esdras 3:1).

"And I saw one of his heads as it were wounded to death; and his deadly wound was healed: and all the world wondered after the beast" (Rev. 13:3).

Astronomically Hercules smites Drago's head. Historically, Heruli king Odoacer deposed Romulus Augustulus -- the Roman head -- on 22nd August, 476 A.D. In 2 Thessalonians 2:3-8 Paul said that the pagan Roman Emperor "who now letteth (restraineth) will let (restrain), until he be taken out of the way." "Then shall the wicked one (Pontifex Maximus of Papal Rome) be revealed." The Pope causes the "falling away" because he is the "son of perdition" who "exalteth himself"

"And there was given unto him a mouth speaking great things and blasphemies; and power was given unto him to continue forty and two months. And he opened his mouth in blasphemy against God, to blaspheme his name, and his tabernacle, and them that dwell in heaven" (Rev. 13:5-6).

The "great voice" of Babylon (Jer. 51:55) and "a mouth speaking great things ... great words against the Most High" (Dan. 7:8,25) both belong to the Pope who claims he can forgive sins past and future; claims to be the Universal Bishop who is able to open and shut the doors of heaven and hell at will; claims to be above all law -- human or Divine -- above Scripture. The Doctrine of Papal Infallibility issued July 18, 1870, teaches that when the Pope speaks "ex cathedra" (from his chair of authority) his utterances are infallible. Judgment came with loss of Temporal Power three months later. Alphonsus Liguori wrote, "When they pronounce the words of consecration 'Hoc est Corpus Meum,' God himself descends on the altar; He comes whenever they call Him and as often as they call Him and places Himself in their hands even though they should be His enemies; having once come He remains entirely at their disposal ... Mary conceived Jesus Christ only once ... but by consecrating the Eucharist, the priest as it were conceives Him as often as he wishes ... hence priests are called

The Beast From The Sea
(Rev. 13)

the parents of Jesus.... Thus the priest may ... be called the creator of his Creator; since by saying the words of consecration, he creates ... Jesus in the sacrament ... the power of the priest is ... of a divine person; the transubstantiation of the bread requires as much power as the creation of the world" (Dignity and Duty of Priests). "Them that dwell in HEAVEN" refers to "Israel" in Revelation, so the Pope attacks the British church. Jesus told his disciples "their names were written in HEAVEN" (Luke 10:20).

AFTER his deadly wound was healed he continued 42 months or 1,260 days. But how long did he exist BEFORE receiving the wound? The first king of Babylon was Nabonassar who ascended the throne Feb. 26, 747 B.C. (Ptolemy's Almagest). If we add 1222.5 solar years (1260 lunar years x 354.37/365.24 = 1222.48), we arrive at the fall of Romulus Augustulus, Aug. 22nd, 476 A.D. Adding 1260 lunar years more brings us to 1698 when the two treaties that limit the two "little horns" are bisected: the completion of the Protestant Revolution at the Peace of Ryswick Sept. 20, 1697 and the Peace of Carlowitz Jan. 26th, 1699 A.D. If we add 1260 solar years to 747 B.C., we arrive at the accession of Hormisdas in 514 A.D., the first pope to speak of Papal supremacy. Adding 1260 solar years more brings us to 1774 -- the royal accession of Louis XVI who lost his life in the French Revolution; the defeat of the Turkish army by Russia resulting in the Peace of Kainarge; and the Jesuits banished by Clement.

The 2520 years is the "(seven) Times of the Gentiles" (Luke 21:24) or "seven times" punishment (Lev. 26:28) or "Mene [1000 gerahs], Mene [1000 gerahs], Tekel [20 gerahs], Upharsin [500 gerahs]" (Dan. 5:25; Ez. 45:12) divided in half by a "deadly wound" in 476 A.D. (Rev. 13:4-5) symbolized by an angel dividing a river at mid-point (Dan. 12:5-7). In 496 A.D. Clovis, King of France, subjected his sovereignty to the Bishop of Rome; and his example was followed by the other nine kingdoms. Popes wore the tiara (triple crown) as well as the mitre. They were emperors as well as bishops. This is synonymous with the "little horn" of Daniel 7:8. Justinian subdued (or plucked up) three of the ten kingdoms (horns) which were established in the Roman Empire after its fall -- Alemanni, Vandals and Ostrogoths. From 533 when Justinian recognized the Roman Bishop as head of all the churches to 1793 A.D. when the Pope was arrested in French Revolution equals 1,260 years. In 607 A.D. Phocas gave Pope Boniface III supremacy over Church and State. In 610 A.D. Emperor Phocas died. Then from 1867-1870 A.D., the Pope lost temporal power after 1,260 years. In 1866 Italy crowned its first king, Victor Emmanuel. (If another "deadly wound" was "healed" by Mussolini's Lateran Treaty in 1929 which gave Vatican City to the Pope, then perhaps we should add 1260 months to that date (1260 / 12 = 105) to arrive at 2034 A.D.)

"It was given unto him to make war with the saints, and to overcome them" (Rev. 13:7).
1208 -- Tens of thousands of Albigenses massacred.
1237 to 1342 -- Tens of thousands of Vaudois massacred in N. Italy, by order of Pope.
1300 and 1413 -- Terrible persecution of Lollards in England by order of Pope.
1421 -- Thousands of Bohemian Hussites killed by order of Pope.
1481 to 1808 -- Spanish Inquisition burnt alive 31,912 and tortured 300,000.
1484 -- Persecution of the Waldenses in northern Italy.
1488 -- In Piedmont, 3,000 Vaudois burnt & suffocated to death in cave.

1546 -- Emperor Charles V caused 50,000 Fleming and German Protestants to be hanged, burned or buried alive.

1555 -- In England, some 300 burned alive under Catholic "Bloody" Mary.

1567 -- Duke of Alva in Netherlands executed 36,000 Protestants, and thousands more fled to England.

1572 -- Massacre of St. Bartholemew's Day; 60,000 butchered in France in one day.

1631 -- Some 20,000 Protestants massacred at Magdeburg in Germany.

1641 -- In Ireland, the Roman Catholic bishops proclaimed a "war of religion" in which 40,000 Protestants were martyred without mercy.

1655 -- Waldensians massacred in Piedmont.

1666 -- Great Fire of London started by five Jesuits.

1685 -- The French Dragoons butchered 400,000 Huguenots, while 500,000 escaped to Britain.

1686 -- Some 11,000 Vaudois put to death in northern Italy.

When the Waldenses, Albigenses, Vaudois, Wycliffites, Hussites, Lutherans, Bohemian Brethren and Calvin's Huguenots realized and taught that the Papal dynasty was none other than the prophesied "man of sin" and "Antichrist," the result was war. Pope Urban II stated: "We judge that they are not murderers who ... should happen to kill any of them." In the oath administered to Bishops they vow that: "Heretics, schismatics and rebels against the same our Lord (the Pope) or his appointed successors, I will to the utmost of my power persecute and fight against." And St. Thomas Aquinas, whose writings are expressly recommended to the clergy, declared that: "Heretics immediately after they are condemned of heresy deserve not only to be excommunicated, but justly to be put to death." In the First Crusade (1096 A.D.), Second Crusade (1147 A.D.) and Third Crusade (1190 A.D.), thousands of Jews were massacred throughout Europe. The Rindfleisch massacres of Rottingen Germany killed 100,000 Jews from 1298 to 1303 A.D. Another 6,000 Jews were killed in Navarre Spain in 1328 A.D. In 1391, the massacre of 50,000 Jews in Spain and Portugal occurred. In 1492, 200,000 Jews were expelled from Spain and Sicily. In Poland-Lithuania in 1648, 76,000 Jews were massacred. In Russia from 1918 to 1920 over 60,000 Jews were killed in pogroms. In some Catholic countries, Jews were expelled. In others, they were forced to wear yellow hats (Poland -- 1266 A.D.; France -- 1525 A.D.; Lithuania -- 1556 A.D.; Rome -- 1555 A.D.) or a yellow badge (Rome -- 1257 A.D.; Venice -- 1393 A.D.; Germany -- 1530 A.D.; Austria -- 1551 A.D.).

"He that leadeth into captivity shall go into captivity; he that killeth with the sword must be killed with the sword. Here is the patience and the faith of the saints" (Rev. 13:10).

"Vengeance is Mine; I will repay, saith the Lord" (Rom. 12:19). From the victory of Constantine at the Milvian Bridge, October 28th 312 A.D., the Papal Era of Indictions began because Constantine was a Catholic "Christian" and persecuted all other Christians as "heretics." To see the vengeance we must add 1,260 years. Notice:

312 + 1,260 lunar years = 1536 when the "Act Against the Pope's Authority" was made law. This Act removed the last traces of Papal power in England, including the Pope's right to decide disputed points of Scripture. The passing of this Act, together with the Act in Restraint of Appeals (1533) and the Act of Supremacy (1534) made it unacceptable for monastic communities, who owed allegiance to parent institutions outside England, to remain. 312 + 1,260 prophetic years = 1555 when the Religious Peace of Augsburg between the Catholics and Protestants in Germany occurred which was a victory for the Lutheran cause in Germany. From 1555 to 1773 Jesuits suffered no less than 37 expulsions from nations on account of their intrigues, immoral doctrines and evil practices. Pope Clement XIV in July 21, 1773, banished the Jesuits from the Church and world. He was poisoned a few months later. 312 + 1,260 solar years = 1572 when the massacre of St. Bartholemew occurred which began 24th of August 1572 and continued through September 1572, when Huguenots were massacred without mercy and survivors fled to England.

From 533 A.D. when Emperor Justinian recognized the Bishop of Rome as "head of all the holy churches and all the holy priests of God," we add 1,260 years to see the vengeance. Notice:

533 + 1260 lunar years = 1755 when the outbreak of infidelity against religion occurred (Voltaire, Rousseau) -- 1st vial (Rev. 16). 533 + 1260 prophetic years = 1774 Accession of Louis XVI which was the starting point of the French Revolution. Jesuit Order suppressed by Pope Clement also in 1774. 533 + 1260 solar years = 1793 France's "Reign of Terror" when the French Revolution began. Catholic King Louis XVI and Queen Marie Antoinette executed.

From 607 A.D. when Eastern Roman Emperor Phocas conceded to Boniface III headship over all the Churches of Christendom (This decree has been confirmed by two Latin historians: Paulus Diaconus and Anastasius quoted in Elliot's Horae Apoc.3:163) and 610 A.D. when Emperor Phocas was "taken out of the way" (he died) we add 1,260 years to see the vengeance.

607 + 1,260 lunar years = 1830 French people compelled their Roman Catholic King Charles X to abdicate. 607 + 1,260 prophetic years = 1848 when Karl Marx published the first Communist Manifesto. The so-called "Year of Revolutions." In 1848-1849 the French people compelled their Roman Catholic King Louis Philippe to abdicate. The Roman National Assembly divested the Pope of all temporal power Feb. 8th, 1849. Then the Pope fled from Rome Nov. 24, 1849. One of the Pope's last acts before being made a prisoner was to emancipate the Jews from the degrading Ghetto. On the 17th April, 1848, the walls of the Ghetto were broken down and the 5,000 Jews given the rights of citizenship. Austria also emancipated the Jews at this time. 607 + 1,260 solar years = 1,866 when the Battle of Sadowa occurred 3rd July 1866. Also Papal Austria was overthrown by non-Roman Catholic Prussia. Also France, Spain, Austria, and other Roman Catholic countries were overthrown. The temporal power of the Papacy ended when Garibaldi overthrew the Papal kingdom of Italy in stages: Venetia fell October 1866; then Tuscany fell on

Fall Of Papal States. From A History Of Europe by Fisher, p.960

October 1870. Garibaldi, that great man of God, said, "The Bible is the canon that must liberate Italy." He paved the way for the complete overthrow of the Papal Kingdom of Italy, in preparation for the general acceptance of Victor Emmanuel as king of Italy. By A.D. 1866-1870, before the victorious armies of Victor Emmanuel, all Papal States had incorporated into the Italian Kingdom. Italy had come into the hands of its first king since the Caesars. From this time on, the Popes have been confined to the "Vatican City," powerless to stop the free circulation of the Bible, which has never before been allowed in Rome during the 1260 years.

"And I beheld another beast coming up out of the earth; and he had two horns like a lamb, and he spoke like a dragon" (Rev. 13:11).

Whereas the sea represents the general mass of humanity, the earth represents the citizens of the Roman Empire. The first beast is a political power or king, the second beast is a religious power or "false prophet" (Rev. 16:13; 19:20; 20:10). Jesus said, "Beware of false prophets, which come unto you in sheep's clothing, but inwardly are ravening wolves" (Matt. 7:15). This "false prophet" looks Christian ("lamb of God"

[Aries] is Christ -- John 1:29) but sounds Satanic ("dragon" [Cetus] is "Satan" -- Rev. 12:9). His two horns signify two kinds of "Christian" clergy in Europe: the Eastern Greek Orthodox and Western Roman Catholic churches -- the two "little horns" of Daniel 7 and 8. A lamb's horns must be "little horns." The Eastern Greek Orthodox Church based in Constantinople being a continuation of the Greek leopard while the Western Roman Catholic Church in Rome is a continuation of the Roman dragon. In 606 A.D. Constantinople's Emperor Phocas decreed the right of Roman Pope Boniface III to headship of all the churches, Eastern as well as Western. This joined the two "little horns" of Daniel 7 and Daniel 8 into one lamb-dragon (Rev. 13:11). When Constantinople was conquered in 1453 A.D., the Greek Orthodox scholars moved west and gave their help to the Roman Catholic Church in the Counter-Reformation causing "them that dwell therein (the earth) to worship the first beast whose deadly wound was healed" (Rev. 13:12). That is why the two "little horns" are no longer separated as in Daniel. "Two horns" also refer to Roman Archbishop's, Bishop's or Abbot's mitre, from Dagon the fish-god, which was anciently cleft from front to back, giving the appearance of horns; whence they used to be called in the Middle Ages, "Goruti" or "Cornuti" meaning "horned ones." Since the time of Pope Gregory (590 A.D.) all Archbishops and Bishops wore a pallium -- a strip of specially-blessed lamb's wool -- "like a lamb." "Vestments" were worn by Baal's priests (2 Ki. 10:22) while Israel's priests wore linen, not wool.

"And he exerciseth all the power of the first beast before him, and causeth the earth and them who dwell on it to worship the first beast, whose deadly wound was healed" (Rev. 13:12).

The paganism of Babylon, Medo-Persia, Greece and Rome is now being worshipped in the "Christian" Eastern Orthodox and Roman Catholic churches. At the time of the Reformation, the Papal claims were in great danger. To save the Papacy, the Society of Jesus was founded. Jesuits exercise the power of the Papacy, without morals. Members actively enter worldly affairs. The Jesuit Order (Society of Jesus) founded in 1540 by Ignatius Loyola, caused Europe to return to Papal worship. Its formula was (and still is) "the end justifies the means." It stood for (and still stands for) hypocrisy, deception and murder. The real force behind the Papal throne is the "Black Pope" or head of the Jesuits.

"And he doeth great wonders, so that he maketh fire come down from heaven on the earth in the sight of men, And deceiveth them that dwell on the earth by the means of those miracles which he had power to do in the sight of the beast, saying to them that dwell on the earth, that they should make an image to the beast, that had the wound by the sword, and did live. And he had power to give life unto the image of the beast, that the image of the beast should both speak, and cause that as many as would not worship the image of the beast should be killed" (Rev. 13:13-15).

Rome has thrown down anathemas, interdicts, persecutions, wars and cursed and excommunicated those who do not believe her false teachings and has called these

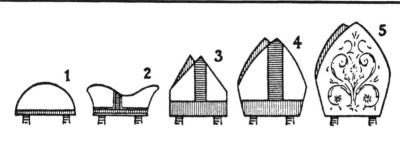

Papal Miters: 1. 11th century, 2. 12th century, 3. 15th century, 4. 18th century, 5. 20th century

curses "thunder and lightning" and pretended they came down from God himself. Images wept artificial tears and idols sweated blood. Statues raised their wooden arms in blessing if enough gold were laid at their feet. The greatest "miracle" is Transubstantiation, which means turning wine into blood and turning a wafer made of bread into the literal flesh of our Lord by the words, "This is my body." In 2 Thessalonians 2 it is called a "lying wonder." When our Lord said those words, he meant "This bread represents my body."

The religious image of the beast of paganism created in "Christianity" involved Mary-worship taking the place of goddess-worship; veneration of saints taking the place of worshipping many gods; Halos, monstrances, and tonsures replacing the sun's disk. Sunday church services replacing blatant sun-worship; steeples replacing obelisks ("Baal's phallus"); Nuns replacing temple prostitutes; Christmas replacing Saturnalia; the host ("hostage") replacing cannibalism; Lent (weeping for Christ) replacing 40 days of weeping for Tammuz. The priest's Pallium or Surplice replacing the Egyptian Ankh symbolizing sexual intercourse. Semiramis had commanded her priests to dress in female attire. The priest's stole (embroidered scarf) representing the astrological zodiac. Burning candles in daytime, holy water, the cross symbol (on forehead of Isis; on hand of Sphinx; suspended from necks of Vestal Virgins) and the title Pontifex Maximus were borrowed from the heathen. The pontiff's and prelate's mitre, crozier and mantle all taken from Osiris. Rosaries are symbols of the stars and planets. Hot Cross buns came from Egyptian Collyris Cakes which came from Persian dough cakes marked with a blood cross. The initials I.H.S. on the wafer were originally the pagan trinity of Isis, Horus, and Serapis and the letters I.N.R.I. originally formed the pagan symbol that by fire, nature will be renewed in its entirety (Igne Natura Renovetur Integra). The Roman Catholic crucifix says, "I.N.R.I." from the classical Latin "Iustum Necar Reges Impios" or "Carnage against Impious Kings is Justified" (Library of Congress Catalog Card #66-43354 -- under "Ceremony of Induction and Extreme Oath of the Jesuits"). The words on the stake said, "Jesus of Nazareth, King of the Jews." The sign was in Hebrew, Greek and Latin. In Latin the sign said, "Iesvs Nazarenvs Rex Ivdaeorvm" -- once again I.N.R.I. In Hebrew the sign said, "Yeshua HaNotri V'Melech HaYehudim." This was an acronym in which the first letter of each of the words formed YHVH -- God's name.

A verbal "image of the (Papal Roman) beast" was Rome's answer to the Reformation called the Council of Trent (1545), which was managed by the Jesuits, and passed the decrees they dictated. It has been said that Papal doctrine "was then completely articulated for the first time." The decrees of the Council have been Rome's test of orthodoxy ever since; effective agents in the hands of the Jesuits and the Inquisition. In them we have the verbal image, made at the suggestion of the second beast. Jesuits kill those who won't worship the Pope. In 1822 a Roman priest, Rev. L. Morissey, asserted that in Ireland, where he was priest, the priests have to swear to their bishops to "become ministers of the Holy Inquisition as well as of the Holy Gospel" (A Development of the Cruel and Inquisitorial System).

The political "image of the beast" (13:15) was a likeness of the Roman Empire. As Myers Medieval and Modern History says, "Long before the fall of Rome there had begun to grow up within the Roman Empire an ecclesiastical state, which in its constitution and its administrative system was shaping itself upon the imperial model. This spiritual empire, like the secular empire, possessed a hierarchy of officers" (p.27). "The Roman Church in this way privily pushed itself into the place of the Roman World-empire, of which it is the actual continuation; the empire has not perished, but has only undergone a transformation." (Harnack, What is Christianity?, p.216). "The Church was compelled to continue the process on which she had already entered of framing her government upon the model of the secular administration ... to reproduce for her own ecclesiastical purposes, the imperial system." (Bryce, The Holy Roman Empire, p.10). "In many ways, indeed, the Church was comparable to the Roman Empire of old, whose territorial and administrative organization it had taken over, and whose official language, Latin, it still maintained in its services, records and literature. Both were international in character. Everyone recognized the Pope as everyone had worshipped the Emperor. The Church had its legal system and courts ... It's missionaries and crusaders on the frontiers of Christendom were like the ancient legionaries on the Roman borders." (Thorndyke, Medieval Europe, p.414). "The Roman church began the process of imitating imperial patterns ... On the imperial model a chancery was established, and papal registers of incoming and outgoing mail were kept in the Lateran archives" (p.8). "The papacy as a legal and governmental institution readily borrowed a number of administrative features from the highly sophisticated imperial practice. Particularly conspicuous among these was the medium of communication with the authorities outside Rome ... The so-called decretal letter of the papacy was modeled on the "decrees" or "responses" of the emperor dispatched to principal governors which decided controversial legal matters" (p.12). Like the Roman Senate, "the College of Cardinals was a body specifically charged with the election of the pope ... on the model of the imperial court in Constantinople, the official meetings of the pope with the cardinals were called consisteries ... The College of Cardinals became the senate of the pope, similar in function to the ancient Roman senatorial body" (p.136).

"And he causeth all, both small and great, rich and poor, free and bond, to receive a mark in their right hand, or in their foreheads: And that no man might buy or sell,

1. Confessional: Where unmarried priests talk for hours to your wives and daughters about indecent sex. 2. Crosier (Lituus) used by augurs for divination in ancient Rome. 3. Triple crown ("three horns uprooted") adds up to 666. 4. Rosary for "vain repetitions" in prayer. 5. Host or hostage from days of human sacrifice and cannibalism. Wafer "sun-god." 6. Nun: "Attire of a (temple) harlot" 7. Priest wearing Egyptian Ankh (Crux Ansata) symbolizing Tammuz sun-god and Dagon fish-cap. 8. Steeple: obelisk (Baal's phallus).

save he that had the mark, or the name of the beast, or the number of his name" (Rev. 13:16-17).

What does this MARK mean? Astronomically Canis Minor is small and Ursa Major is great, Cepheus is rich and Bootes poor, Cygnus free and Andromeda and Pisces bound. All are identified by unique stars with names: "Natik" ("Wounded") is in the forehead of Aries which is composed of 66 stars. "Ras al Hagus" ("Head of Him who Holds") is in the forehead of Ophiuchus and "Ras al Gethi" ("Head of Him who Bruises") is in the forehead of Hercules. Many constellations have stars in their hands. Historically two small black boxes called Tefillin or Phylacteries are worn by an observant Jew: one on his left arm and the other between his eyes. Each box contains four scripture passages to represent all of God's laws. Eating unleavened bread seven days "shall be for a SIGN unto thee upon thine HAND, and for a memorial between thine eyes (FOREHEAD), that the Eternal's law may be in thy mouth" (Ex.13:9). Redeeming the first-born "shall be for a TOKEN upon thine HAND, and for frontlets between thine eyes" (FOREHEAD) (Ex. 13:16). To love God with all your might "shall be in thine heart ... And thou shalt bind them for a SIGN upon thine HAND, and they shall be as frontlets between thine eyes (FOREHEAD)" (Deut.6:6-8). Love and serve God and " lay up these my words in your heart and in your soul, and bind them for a SIGN upon your HAND, that they may be as frontlets between your eyes" (FOREHEAD) (Deut.11:18). (See also Pr.7:2-3; Rev.7:3-4 & 14:1) But most people will not accept God's law. Our THOUGHTS (agreeing with God's ways) and ACTIONS (obeying God) must surrender to God and obey him. What we BELIEVE and who we OBEY determine whether we have God's SIGN or Satan's MARK.

The practice, common in John's day, and for long afterwards, of slaves and soldiers being branded or punctured as an outward sign of subjection to their master or ruler, generally on the hand or forehead, a practice also followed by the devotees of certain religions as a mark of their god, is still common among Hindus in India and elsewhere (see Lev. 19:28; 21:5; Deut. 14:1; Ez. 9:4; 3 Macc. 2:29; Rev. 14:1; 7:2; 9:4) and supposed to be protective. This explains the use of the word in Galatians 6:17 where Paul regarded his SCARS as marks of servitude to God and of being protected by God. The number 6 in Greek is the letter "s" called "stigma" -- whence our word "stigmatize" meaning to "BRAND" cattle, slaves or soldiers.

Just as the SIGN is obedience to God's law, specifically the SABBATH "for it is a SIGN between me and you" (Ex. 31:13-17), and generally symbolized by PHYLACTERIES with a Hebrew Shin (ש) on them for "Shaddai," so the MARK is obedience to the teaching of Rome, specifically SUNDAY-keeping instituted by emperor Constantine in 321 A.D. ("the beast") who said, "On the venerable day of the Sun let the magistrates and people residing in cities rest, and let all workshops be closed." (Codex Justinianus 3:12:3) and generally symbolized by a Latin CROSS. Three Hebrew Vavs (ווו)look like a Shin (ש) but add up to 666. It is also remarkable that χρς is the Greek abbreviation for the Greek word "anointed" (Christ: χριστος) while χξς is the Greek number 666. Notice that the middle letter looks like a serpent springing up between Christ

(χ) and man (ς). Once again they are very similar. The MARK of the cross is put on the FOREHEADS of all baptised in the Roman faith; and on the HANDS of all who become priests and monks. "The Sacrament of Confirmation is also known by the name of Chrism, because the FOREHEAD of the person confirmed is anointed with chrism in the form of a CROSS" (Faith of Our Fathers by James Cardinal Gibbons, 1897, P.320). The priest "draws with his right hand the sign of the CROSS upon the HANDS of him whom he ordains" (Roman Catholic Rubric). On Ash Wednesday, the first day of Lent, Catholics put the Latin CROSS on their FOREHEADS in oil and ashes. Jews were prevented from BUYING or RENTING real estate from Catholics at the Synod of Ofen in 1279. Protestants were prevented from BUYING and SELLING at Rome's third Lateran Council in 1178 A.D. when Pope Alexander III issued an order that "no man presume to entertain or cherish them in his house, or land, to exercise TRAFFIC with them." In 1184 the same Pope passed a law against the Protestant Waldenses and Albigenses "that no man should presume to receive or assist them in SELLING or BUYING, that, being deprived of the comfort of humanity, they may be compelled to repent of the error of their way." Pope Martin V, in his decree sent out after the Council of Constance, commanded that "they permit not the heretics (Jews & Protestants) to have houses in their districts, or enter into contracts, or carry on COMMERCE, or enjoy the comforts of humanity with (Catholic) Christians." (Diocletian published an edict that Christians should not have the power of buying or selling any thing, nor be allowed the liberty of drawing water itself, before they had offered incense to idols.) This has occurred in recent times in Ireland -- and is called "BOYCOTTING." The Papal Bull "Unum Sanctum" declares it to be "essential to every man's salvation that he should be subject to the Roman See." Accordingly, the Papal clergy first take the vow of obedience, then impose it on their laity, then brand as "heretics" those who refuse allegiance.

"Here is wisdom. Let him that hath understanding count the number of the beast: for it is the number of a man; and his number is Six hundred threescore and six" (Rev. 13:18).

Goliath was SIX cubits high, his spear's head weighed SIX hundred shekels and he had SIX pieces of armour (1 Sam. 17:1-7). Nebuchadnezzar's image was SIXTY cubits high, and SIX cubits wide; and SIX instruments summoned worshippers (Dan.3:1-5). Irenaeus (155-202 A.D.) was a pupil of Polycarp who was a disciple of John. His solution was "Lateinos," meaning "Latin man," which in Greek adds up to 666 -- the first king of Latium in Italy (but figuratively the Pope). $\Lambda\alpha\tau\epsilon\iota\nu\sigma\varsigma$: L = 30, a = 1, t = 300, e = 5, i = 10, n = 50, o = 70, s = 200. In A.D. 663, Pope Vitallian -- 666 years after the birth of Jesus -- ordered exclusive use of Latin in all edicts, proclamations and services of the Church throughout Christendom. Mass, prayers, hymns, Litanies, Paternosters, Ave Maria, Canons, Decretals, Papal Bulls -- all are in Latin. The Latin Vulgate Bible was declared by the Council of Trent to be the only authentic version and is still used in purely Catholic countries. In Protestant England, where Catholics have access to Protestant Bibles, the Douay Version has been allowed for English-speaking Catholics. Latin was the language of all educated classes, of law, of medicine, of commerce. The founder and first king of Rome was Romulus. In Hebrew the word "Romiti" -- a Roman Man -- adds up to 666: רׁתׁיׁמׁסׁר: R=200, o=6, m=40, i=10, t=400, i=10. Also the fourth or Roman Kingdom in Hebrew is Romiith which adds up to 666. הׁתׁיׁיׁמׁסׁר: R=200, o=6, m=40, i=10, i=10, th=400. But it is feminine and so not "the name of a man." The name "Pope Sixtus III" (432-440 A.D.) literally means "Three Sixes." In 2 Thessalonians 2:3 Paul mentioned a "falling away" or apostasy. The word "apostates" in Greek is αποϛτατεϛ: a=1, p=80, o=70, st=6, a=1, t=300, e=8, s=200 which totals 666. There were 666 descendants of Adonikam who returned to Jerusalem from Babylonian exile (Ezra 2:13). In the Old Testament each year King Solomon received 666 talents of gold (1 Ki.10:14). In the New Testament the letters of the Greek word "euphoria," from which the word "wealth" is translated, total 666. Another New Testament word which has the value of 666 in Greek is "paradosis" meaning "tradition" (Acts 19:25; Matt. 15:2). Παραδοϛιϛ: P=80, a=1, r=100, a=1, d=4, o=70, s=200, i=10, s=200. Wealth and tradition are the two great corrupters of people and institutions. Catholic traditions have "equal authority" with scripture. The five Greek words which add up to 666 in the Bible are "euphoria" -- wealth, "paradosis" -- tradition, "appolumetha" -- we perish (Matt. 8:25), "diasporas" -- scattered, and "pleuran" -- side. The Roman Catholic Church in Greek is called Italika Ekklesia which means "Italian church" and this adds up to 666: Ιταλικα Εκκλεϛια: I=10, t=300, a=1,l=30, i=10, k=20, a=1, E=5, k=20, k=20, l=30, e=8, s=200, i=10, a=1. Elliott tried every other national church without similar results. The Latin Kingdom or He Latine Basileia in Greek adds up to 666. Ηε Λατινε Βαϛιλεια: H=0, e=8, L=30, a=1, t=300, i=10, n=50, e=8, B=2, a=1, s=200, i=10, l=30, e=5, i=10, a=1. Clarke illustrates the remarkable nature of this solution by listing more than 400 other kingdoms similarly expressed in Greek, without one other kingdom adding up to 666. In the Council of Trent, the Pope was given the Latin title, "Vicarius Generalis Dei In Terris" which adds up to 666: V=5, i=1, c=100, i=1, v=5, l=50, i=1, D=500, i=1, i=1, i=1. Pope Paul V was given a title "Pavlo V Vice Deo" which Bishop Bedell discovered added up to 666. v=5, l=50, V=5, V=5, i=1, c=100, D=500. Residents of Venice, Italy concluded the Pope was Antichrist. In Latin the Pope's official title is "Vicarius Filii Dei" meaning "Vicar of the Son of God." It was inscribed by one of the Popes over the Vatican door. This is synonymous with the original meaning of the Greek word "Antichrist" which meant a "Vice-Christ" or one in the place of Christ, which is the Pope's claim -- not "against Christ." This title also adds up to 666: V=5, i=1, c=100, a=0, r=0, i=1, u=5, s=0, F=0, i=1, l=50, i=1, i=1, D=500, e=0, i=1. Notice that the five letters which have no numerical value add up to "farse." One of the greatest persecutors of Christians was the Roman Emperor Nero Caesar, who's name when written in Hebrew adds up to 666. נׁסׁרׁ נ קׁשׁר: "Neron Caesar" is N=50, r=200, o=6, n=50, K=100, s=60, r=200. Another persecutor was "Diocletian Augustus" whose name in Latin adds up to 667. D=500, i=1, c=100, l=50, i=1, v=5, v=5, v=5. Louis XIV, King of France, had the Latin title "Ludovicus" which adds up to 666 (L=50, v=5, d=500, v=5, i=1, c=100, v=5). The two letters in his name having no value are the "o" (sun-seed) and "s" (serpent). Another Roman Emperor who fought against the British was "Napoleon" whose name in Greek, using the dative or dedicatory case, adds up to 666. Notice: N=50, α=1, π=80 , o=70, λ=30, ε=5, o=70 , v=50, τ=300, ι=10. The name means "the lion from the thicket" and is suggestive of Jeremiah 4:7. The Pope has a number of titles. Here are two in Latin with their meanings: "Captain of the Clergy" is "Dux Cleri" which adds up to 666: D=500, v=5, x=10, C=100, l=50, e=0, r=0, i=1 and "Chief Vicar of the Court of Rome" is "Ludo Vicus" which adds up to 666 as we've already seen. The ancient name of Rome was "Saturnia"-- the city of Saturn (Pliny's Natural History 3:5). Hislop states that Saturn is known in Chaldee (Babylonian language) as Satur (Two Babylons, p.269) or Satyr -- the goat-legged god. In Chaldee it is spelled with four letters: Stur. In this language S=60, t=400, u=6, and r=200 making a total of 666 (Num. 13:9). Jacob Grimm mentions the possibility that the name Saturn is related to the name Satan (Teutonic Mythology, translated by J. Stallybrass, pp. 247-248, 1601). The "Azazel" "Scapegoat" of Leviticus 16 taken to an "uninhabited wilderness" (Lev. 16:22) is a type of Satan and reminds us of "satyrs" who dance in Babylon -- a place that "shall never be inhabited" (Isa. 13:19-21). These same "satyrs" are translated "demons" in Leviticus 17:7 (see also 2 Chr. 25:14-15). Our Lord described the Vatican as "the habitation of demons" (Rev. 18:2). Yes, Satan is worshipped as the "Holy Ghost" -- a counterfeit evil Spirit of the Holy Spirit. In Masonic and Occult Symbols Illustrated by Burns, pp.50-51, the he-goat is associated with the Devil also known as "Goat of Mendes" or "Baphomet" or "Pan." The Greek name for Satan is Teitan (Τειταν) which adds up to 666 in Greek: T=300, e=5, i=10, t=300, a=1, n=50. Titus, the Roman general who overthrew Jerusalem in 70 A.D. inflicting horrible wrath upon the land and people, and who later became Caesar, in the Greek language was known as Teitan. Antiochus IV , a Syrian, sacrificed a pig on Jerusalem's altar. He forbade circumcision and destroyed all Old Testament books he could find. He placed an idol of Jupiter in the Holy of Holies and took the title "God Manifest" or EPIPHANEIA (7 (ε) + 80 (π) + 10 (ι) + 500 (φ) + 1 (α) + 50 (ν) + 7 (ε) + 10 (ι) + 1 (α) = 666). America's first Catholic J. F. Kennedy received 666 votes for President at the 1956 DNC. He received a deadly wound.

The Universal Product Code barcodes found on most commercial products are characterized by guard bars at the beginning (101), middle (01010) and end (101) made up of two thin lines. Numbers 0-9 on the left have a white-black-white-black order while numbers 0-9 on the right have a black-white-black-white order. Two thin lines also appear in the UPC encoding for the digit 6 (1010000 -- the last four zeros being merely placeholders), and so to human eyes (but not to an electronic barcode reader) the guard bars appear to read 666. There is only one number in twenty that contains the "101" pattern and that number is the RIGHT code SIX used for all three guard bars. This fulfills the prophecy that no man will be able to "BUY or SELL" without this mark on the RIGHT hand (side) (Rev. 13:16-17). The inventor of the UPC barcode is George J. Laurer. In 1971 while an employee with IBM, he was assigned the task "to design the best code and symbol suitable for the grocery industry." In 1973 the UPC barcode was finished. When he was asked about the apparent 666 phenomenon, he replied, "It is simply a coincidence like the fact that my first, middle, and last name all have six letters." Perhaps he designed the guard bars this way to be like a metaphor for his name. This fulfills the prophecy that 666 would be the "number of a man."

In Chinese culture, 666 sounds alot like the words "Things going smoothly." It is considered one of the luckiest numbers in Chinese culture. It can be seen prominently in many shop windows across the country, and people there often pay extra to get a mobile phone number including this string of digits. In Hebrew, 666 is "Waw, Waw, Waw" or "WWW" as in World Wide Web -- the internet. Also, if A=6, B=12, C=18, etcetera, then the word "COMPUTER" adds up to 666. ASCII stands for American Standard Code for Information Interchange -- the language of computers. Using ASCII, the name "Bill Gates 3" adds up to 666. Notice: 66 (B) + 73 (i) + 76 (l) + 76 (l) + 71 (G) + 65 (a) + 84 (t) + 69 (e) + 83 (s) + 3 = 666 (Also "Windows 95" and "MS-DOS 6.21" both add up to 666 using ASCII.) If A=6, B=12, C=18, etc., then the word "VAC-CINATION" also adds up to 666. Vaccinations are live viruses and germs mixed with formaldehyde and Thimersol (a mercury derivative) injected into healthy babies to cause autism, asthma, diabetes, etcetera -- "SORCERIES" (drugs) (Rev. 9:21). The Washington Monument (Obelisk) is 555 feet high which is exactly 6660 inches tall. It goes down 111 feet for a total of 666 feet in length. When Boy Scouts of America end their motto they say: "Everything is A-okay in the Boy Scouts." Then they each do the OK sign with their right hand and place it on their forehead. The hand unconsciously forms 666. The name "George Bush" adds up to 666 in Hebrew. Notice: G (ג) 3 + e (ע) 5 + o (ם) 70 + r (ר) 200 + g (ג) 3 + e (ע) 5 + B (ב) 2 + u (צ) 70 + s (ש) 300 + h (ה) 8 = 666. "William J. Clinton" adds up to 666 in Hebrew and Greek. Notice: W (ו) 6 + i (n/a) + l (ל) 30 + l (ל) 30 + i (n/a) + a (n/a) + m (מ) 40 + J. (י) 10 + C (כ) 20 + l (ל) 30 + i (n/a) + n (נ) 50 + t (ת) 400 + o (n/a) + n (נ) 50 = 666 and W (ς) 6 + i (ι) 10 + l (λ) 30 + l (λ) 30 + i (ι) 10 + a (α) + m (μ) 40 + J. (ι) 10 + C (κ) 20 + l (λ) 30 + i (ι) 10 + n (ν) 50 + t (τ) 300 + o (o) 70 + n (ν) 50 = 666. Both "William Jefferson Clinton" and "Hillary Rodham Clinton" add up to 666 using A=6, B=12, C=18, etc. So does "Kissinger." The names "Saddam" and "Hussein" both add up to 666 in Hebrew. Notice: S (ם) 60 + a (א) 1 + dd (ד) 4 + a (א) 1 + m (ם) 600 = 666 and H (ה) 5 + u (ו) 6 + s (ש) 300 + s (ש) 300 + e (ה) 5 + in (נ) 50 = 666. The New Age messiah called "Maitreya" was expected in 1998 (3 x 666) and would be recognized by 216 (6 x 6 x 6) marks on his body. Transcribed into Hebrew the name becomes Maithrie and adds up to 666. Notice: M (ם) 40 + a (א) 1 + i (י) 10 + th (ת) 400 + r (ר) 200 + i (י) 10 + e (ה) 5 = 666

RFID implants and Verichip implants are placed "in" (KJV) the hand or forehead and also fulfill the "grievous sore" (Rev. 16:2). "Wherefore, if thy hand (or "all-seeing eye" in your forehead) ... offend thee, cut it off, and cast it from thee; it is better for thee to enter into life lame or maimed, rather than ... cast into everlasting fire" (Matt. 18:8). The Greek word for "mark" is "charagma" meaning "a scratch or etching," "graven" (Strong's). A microchip is etched or engraved, creating an integrated circuit/PCB, capacitor and antenna coil, encapsulated in glass, then injected using a syringe. "Charagma" refers to the bite of a snake's fangs in Soph. Phil. 267. Yes, the "Day of the Lord" is like "a serpent" biting a man's "hand" (Amos 5:18-19). In fact the Greek letter stigma (ς) in 666 (χξς) also means "a mark incised or punched (for recognition of ownership)" (Strong's). It looks like a snake slithering. The Xi looks like a snake striking. The Chi is a cross. Many eastern traditions hold that Chi is an internal energy flow. Verichip will run on an internal energy source. RFID chips come in Swastika or Maltese Cross shapes as well as the Lozenge shape.

From Henry VIII
to the Peace of Ryswick
(Chapter 14)
(1534 to 1697 A.D.)

John wrote, "And I looked, and, lo, a Lamb stood on the mount Sion, and with him an hundred forty and four thousand, having his Father's name written in their foreheads" (Rev. 14:1).

Who is the LAMB? Jesus ... the LAMB of God" (John 1:29). Astronomically it is Aries the Ram.

Where is Mount ZION? Mount Zion is in worldly Jerusalem. To Jesus belongs the throne of David, who ruled on Mount Zion (Luke 1:32). But the throne of David today is the Coronation Chair in Westminster Abbey, London, England. "Ye are come unto mount Sion, and unto the city of the living God, the HEAVENLY JERUSALEM, and to an innumerable company of angels, To the general assembly and church of the firstborn, and to God the judge of all, and to the spirits of just men made perfect. And to Jesus the mediator of the new covenant" (Heb. 12:22-24). This "HEAVENLY JERUSALEM" is wherever the 144,000 Christian Israelite saints are who migrated to the British Isles in chapter 7. Only Jews dwell in earthly Mount Zion today. "The Lord hath chosen Zion: he hath desired it for his habitation. This is my rest for ever: here will I dwell" (London in type; Jerusalem in anti-type) (Psalm 132:13-14). (See also Isaiah 9:6, Micah 4:7, Isaiah 24:23.). Yes "the LORD, my God, shall come, and all the saints with thee" (to London in type; Jerusalem in anti-type) (Zech. 14:5; cp. 1 Thess. 4:16-17). He "hast made us ... kings and priests" (Rev. 5:10) and "judgment was given to the saints ... and ... the saints possessed the kingdom" (Dan. 7:22). "Let the saints be joyful in glory ... Let the high praises of God be in their mouth, and a two-edged sword in their hand, To execute vengeance upon the heathen, and punishments upon the peoples; To bind their kings with chains, and their nobles with fetters of iron; To execute upon them the judgment written. This honor have all his saints" (from London in type; Jerusalem in anti-type) (Ps.149:5-9; Rev. 2:26-27).

In type this occurred in 1534 with the Act of Supremacy when Henry VIII destroyed Papal supremacy in England. Henry had married his deceased brother's wife (Catherine of Aragon) in obedience to Deuteronomy 25:5. But five of her six children had died, causing Henry to wonder if God was displeased (cp. Lev. 20:21; Matt. 14:4). But the Pope wouldn't grant a divorce. Henry divorced anyway and married Ann Bolyn. In 1535, Henry VIII found countless convents served by 'lewd confessors' full of illegitimate children and clergy having sex with whores and married women (de Rosa's Vicars of Christ, pp.579-580). In 1539, all Catholic monasteries were dissolved and Henry VIII ordered copies of the Great Bible to be printed and placed in every English church by Royal command (secured by a chain to a reading desk). This enabled the

LAMB to begin ruling in English lives. It enabled "HEAVENLY JERUSALEM" to be built in England. Henry also was the first to build battleships with cast iron cannons (1/5 cost of bronze). He consented before his death in January 1547, to abandon the Roman Catholic Mass for the Communion service, to confiscate Rome's land and money in England, and to allow the clergy to marry. The formulation of the 39 Articles in the Convocation of 1563 under Queen Elizabeth completed the separation from the Pope. Then in 1611 the King James Authorized Version was produced.

"And I heard a voice from heaven, as the voice of many waters, and as the voice of a great thunder: and I heard the voice of harpers harping with their harps: And they sung as it were a new song before the throne, and before the four beasts, and the elders: and no man could learn that song but the hundred and forty and four thousand, which were redeemed from the earth" (Rev. 14:2-3).

Astronomically, Gemini and Lyra are the harpers. Taurus has an alternate image of a harp too. There are 24 stars in Ursa Minor (the Little Flock). Historically, the FOUR BEASTS symbolize the FOUR CAMPS of ISRAEL in the British Isles. The 24 elders (Rev. 4:4) denote 12 sons of Jacob (Old Covenant) and 12 apostles of Jesus (New Covenant). After David had been "brought ... up ... out of an horrible pit," he said that God "hath put a NEW SONG in my mouth" (Ps. 40:3). David also said, "I will sing a NEW SONG unto thee, O God ... who delivereth David, his servant, from the hurtful sword" (Ps. 144:9-10; cp. 33:3; 96:1; 98:1; 149:1). Therefore, a "NEW SONG" means "a new DELIVERANCE" from some kind of trouble. The DELIVERANCE of the 144,000 is DELIVERANCE from Papal Rome in 1534 and from the feebleness of mortal human nature at Christ's second coming. "For the Eternal ... will beautify the meek with salvation" (Ps. 149:4). They "shall shine like the brightness of the firma-ment" (Dan. 12:3). "Arise, shine" (Isa. 60:1). But in type the "NEW SONG" was the British NATIONAL ANTHEM -- "God Save The King" composed in 1652. By the Act of Settlement in 1689, it was once and for all determined that the British monarch must be a Protestant. That was something to SING about. At succeeding coronations, the monarch was required to take the Oath that he will defend the Protestant Faith and maintain the Act of Settlement. In 1910 the Declaration was "watered down."

"These are they which were not defiled with women; for they are virgins. These are they which follow the Lamb whithersoever he goeth. These were redeemed from among men, being the firstfruits unto God and to the Lamb" (Rev. 14:4).

This must be taken figuratively because "Marriage is honorable" (Heb. 13:4) and wives are "heirs together" with their husbands of the grace of life (1 Pet. 3:7) and the bulk of the apostles were married men (1 Cor. 9:5; cp. Luke 10:42; Acts 8:12). If the Roman Catholic Church is the "mother of HARLOTS" (Rev. 17:5) (she is often called the "mother church"), the DAUGHTERS must be recognized in her OFFSHOOTS -- all sects and denominations that recognize her as their "mother." These "HARLOT" churches are the "WOMEN" that have not defiled the 144,000. The 144,000 have been outside popular "Christianity" which is just a "refuge of lies" (Isa.

28:17). True Christians obey the Bible. They follow Jesus into suffering and then into glory. "Our light affliction which is but for a moment, worketh for us a far more exceeding and eternal weight of glory" (2 Cor. 16:17). "Them who honor me I will honor, and they who despise me shall be lightly esteemed" (1 Sam. 2:30). "If ... we suffer with him ... we may be also glorified together" with him (Rom. 8:17). "But he that denieth me before men shall be denied before the angels of God" (Luke 12:9).

Redeemed Israel is a "VIRGIN" (Eph. 5:25-27; 2 Cor. 6:14-18; 7:1; 11:2). All Protestant European Israel nations are "VIRGINS" -- England, Holland, Switzerland, Denmark, Norway, Iceland, Sweden and Scotland. Sir Walter Raleigh asked Queen Elizabeth if he could name the eastern United States "VIRGINIA" -- after her. She consented. It was colonized by English Puritans and Separatists (Pilgrims) who rejected everything Roman Catholic. As the daughter of Henry VIII and Ann Bolyn, Queen Elizabeth, as England personified, entertained Catholic suitors from Catholic countries, among whom were King Philip II of Spain, Archduke Charles (Hapsburg) of Austria, and the French Duke of Anjou to buy time, but remained a Protestant VIRGIN till death. She caused the Bible to be distributed throughout the kingdom and read in English and forbade the elevation of the host. The Pope excommunicated her as a heretic.

Why are they "FIRSTFRUITS"? "Every man in his own order: Christ the firstfruits; afterward they that are Christ's at His coming" (1 Cor. 15:23). The main, great harvest will be at the end of the Millenium as the result of the work of Christ and the saints in ruling the world for a thousand years. Multitudes will ripen for immortality under their reign. The first resurrection is "the twelve tribes ... FIRSTFRUITS" (James 1:1,18). The "two wave loaves" of wheat (144,000 & innumerable multitude -- Rev. 7) (Lev. 23:17) due to the "former rain" (Joel 2:23) before the Millenium (Rev. 20:4-6); the second resurrection is "fruit of a citron, an unopened palm frond, myrtle branches and willows" (Lev. 23:40) due to the "latter rain" (Joel 2:23; James 5:7) after the Millenium (Rev. 20:11-15).

"And in their mouth was found no guile: for they are without fault before the throne of God" (Rev. 14:5).

Psalm 32:2 says, "Blessed is he whose transgression is forgiven, whose sin is covered. Blessed is the man unto whom the Lord imputeth not iniquity, and in whose spirit there is no guile." Every man is saved by grace (Eph. 2:8) but rewarded "according to his works" (Matt. 16:27). In order to be saved by grace we must have good works since "The unrighteous shall not inherit the kingdom of God" (1 Cor. 6:9).

"And I saw another angel fly in the midst of heaven, having the everlasting gospel to preach unto them that dwell on the earth, and to every nation, and kindred, and tongue, and people" (Rev. 14:6).

"And this GOSPEL of the kingdom shall be preached in all the world for a witness unto all nations; and then shall the end come" (Matt. 24:14). Gutenberg's printing press was invented in 1454. In 1476 Caxton introduced printing into England. In

Babylon's "Mother and Child" were worshipped as Semiramis and Tammuz. Then in Egypt as Isis and Horus. Then in Ephesus as Diana (Acts 19:27) -- the goddess by herself. But at the Council of Ephesus in 431 A.D., Diana was renamed "Mary" and Mary-worship became official Catholic doctrine. The solar disk of Isis became Mary's halo. Diana's necklace became Mary's rosary. The titles of Semiramis ("Mediatrix," "Queen of Heaven," etc.) were transferred to Mary.

1526 Tyndale's English New Testament was printed. In 1535 Coverdale's Complete English Bible was printed. In 1539 the "Great Bible" was printed under Coverdale's supervision and placed by Royal Command in every church for the use of parishoners. In 1611 the King James Authorized version was printed. The British and Foreign Bible Society founded in 1804 and the American Bible Society founded in 1816 both print millions of Bibles per year in over 1000 different languages to the countries of the world. This establishes the Anglo-Saxon nations as being Israel "my witnesses, my servant" (Isa. 43:10). "The Lord gave the word: great was the company of those that published it" (Ps. 68:11).

"Saying with a loud voice, Fear God, and give glory to him; for the hour of his judgment is come: and worship him that made heaven, and earth, and the sea, and the fountains of waters, And there followed another angel, saying, Babylon is fallen, is fallen, that great city, because she made all nations drink of the wine of the wrath of her fornication" (Rev. 14:7-8).

"Babylon" caused all nations to toast her idol-gods with her wine of false doctrines poured into, and drunk out of, God's HOLY VESSELS stolen from His Temple (Dan. 5:1-4; cp. Jer. 50:28; 51:7; Rev. 9:20-21; 17:2; 18:2-3). The wine of this spiritual fornication -- the worship of images, holy pictures, holy relics, holy medals, and demons, through the medium or channel of BIBLICAL names, characters and associations such as Jesus, Mary, angels, saints -- has deceived and stupefied all nations. The false SACRIFICE of the Mass, the false "ISRAEL" of ten Latin-German nations and the false MILLENIUM of the Dark Ages (533 to 1534 A.D.) have all made the world drunk. This prophecy is repeated in Revelation 16:19 and 18:2. Babylon fell once in 539 B.C. and fell again in 1527 A.D., so "is fallen, is fallen." In 1527 A.D., a Protestant army consisting of Spaniards, Italians and Germans under Charles the Fifth took the city of Rome and for nine months sacked the city and insulted the pope (Gibbon's Decline and Fall, ch.31). This was a token pledge of the complete fall just like the transfiguration was a foretaste of the kingdom (Matt. 16:28; Mark 9:1; Luke 9:27). Just as JERICHO had to fall before Israel could possess the Promised Land, so ROME must fall before British and Americans can possess the worldwide Kingdom of God.

"And the third angel followed them, saying with a loud voice, If any man worship the beast and his image, and receive his mark in his forehead, or in his hand, The same shall drink of the wine of the wrath of God, which is poured out without mixture into the cup of his indignation; and he shall be tormented with fire and brimstone in the presence of the holy angels, and in the presence of the Lamb, And the smoke of their torment ascendeth up for ever and ever: and they have no rest day nor night, who worship the beast and his image, and whosoever receiveth the mark of his name. Here is the patience of the saints: here are they that keep the commandments of God, and the faith of Jesus" (Rev. 14:9-12).

Astronomically, the three angels who fly "in the midst of heaven" are the three bird constellations Aquila (eagle), Cygnus (swan) and Lyra (vulture). The smoke of tor-

"Pharaoh's chariots (the Pope's Spanish Armada) and his host hath he cast into the sea; his chosen captains also are drowned in the Red Sea (North Sea) ... Thou didst blow with thy wind" (Ex. 15:4, 10).

ment is the Milky Way. Historically, Jesus will be "revealed from heaven in flaming fire, taking vengeance on them that know not God, and that obey not the gospel of our Lord Jesus Christ: who shall be punished with everlasting destruction" (2 Thess. 1:7). Paul describes it as "a fearful looking for of judgment and fiery indignation, which shall devour the adversaries" (Heb. 10:27). Malachi says it is "a day that will burn up the wicked, that it shall leave them neither root nor branch" (Mal. 4:1). Sodom and Gomorrah also suffered "the vengeance of eternal fire" (Jude 7) though "overthrown as in a moment" (Lam. 4:6).

In 1588 the Pope and Philip of Spain assembled their great fleets in Spain and a large army in the Netherlands, in an effort to conquer the "heretical" Island and end England's Reformation. Just as it set sail, the Chief Commander, Marquis Santa Cruz, died. On the first day of battle, the Spanish lost two flag ships, 450 men, the paymaster of the fleet and 100,000 ducats of gold. The Protestant Dutch blocked the harbor at Dunkirk thereby making it impossible for the great army of the Duke of Parma to be transported across the Channel. At the same time Drake and his fire ships spread havoc in the Spanish galleons. Then the enforced passage around the coast of the British Isles completed the destruction of the Armada. 8,000 Spaniards perished along the Irish coast, murdered for their clothing and jewelry by Irish Catholics. From the year Constantine named the capital Constantinople in 328 A.D., thereby fulfilling 2 Thess.2:7, till the defeat of the Spanish Armada in 1588 A.D., is 1260 years.

From 1572 to 1609 Protestant Holland's William of Orange fought for independence from Catholic Spain's Philip II and his Duke of Alva. From 1562 to 1629 the Huguenot Wars in France were fought between Protestant and Catholic France. From 1618 to 1648 the Thirty Years' War was fought between Catholic and Protestant princes of Germany, but gradually involved almost all the nations of the continent. From 1649 to 1652 Cromwell's English Protestants defeated Catholic Irish Royalists. In 1660, Charles II, and in 1688 James II, in turn allied themselves with Louis XIV of France in an endeavour to restore Roman Catholicism to Britain with French troops and money. The people revolted in 1688 and offered Protestant William Prince of Orange the Crown. The outcome of this Protestant Revolution was the separation from the Catholic church of north Germany, Denmark, Norway, Sweden, England and Scotland along with parts of Switzerland and the Netherlands. These Nordic peoples transferred their allegiance from the Church to the Bible.

"And I heard a voice from heaven saying unto me, Write, Blessed are the dead which die in the Lord from henceforth: Yea, saith the Spirit, that they may rest from their labours; and their works do follow them" (Rev. 14:13).

"And I looked, and behold a white cloud, and upon the cloud one sat like unto the Son of man, having on his head a golden crown, and in his hand a sharp sickle, And another angel came out of the temple, crying with a loud voice to him that sat on the cloud, Thrust in thy sickle, and reap: for the time is come for thee to reap; for the harvest of the earth is ripe. And he that sat on the cloud thrust in his sickle on the earth; and the earth was reaped. And another angel came out of the temple which is in heaven, he also having a sharp sickle. And another angel came out from the altar, which had power over fire; and cried with a loud cry to him that had the sharp sickle, saying, Thrust in thy sharp sickle, and gather the clusters of the vine of the earth; for her grapes are fully ripe. And the angel thrust in his sickle into the earth, and gathered the vine of the earth, and cast it into the great winepress of the wrath of God. And the winepress was trodden without the city, and blood came out of the winepress, even unto the horse bridles, by the space of a thousand and six hundred furlongs" (Rev. 14:14-20).

The constellation Bootes (meaning "He Cometh") depicts the Coming Judge -- a man with a SICKLE in his hand (Ps. 96:13)-- sitting on a cloud. One of the bright stars is called Arcturus ("He Cometh") (Job 9:9). "Behold, the Lord cometh with ten thousands of his saints, To execute judgment upon all" (Jude 14, 15). "And before him (Jesus) shall be gathered all nations: and he shall separate them one from another, as a shepherd divides his SHEEP from the goats: And he shall set the SHEEP on his right hand, but the goats on the left" (Matt. 25:32-33). The "lost SHEEP of the house of ISRAEL" (Matt. 15:24) are the "SHEEP" nations. The "goat" nations are everyone else. The "TEMPLE" is the heavenly vault of the SKY. Verse 17 may be referring to the constellation Perseus who has a pruning knife in hand. He has wings on his feet so may be coming "out of the temple" of the starry sky-dome. The other two angels could be almost any of the constellations. The "vine of the earth" is Hydra who is "trodden" by Leo "without" the ecliptic. The red glow of sunset rises to the level of the horse's bridal and bit in Auriga's right hand an equal distance inside the ecliptic.

Yes, in type the SICKLE was the CRESCENT of ISLAM which was an instrument used by God to gather and slaughter wicked Roman Catholic forces of Europe. Suleiman the Magnificent captured Belgrade in 1521 after several assaults. In succeeding years Turks regularly raided Hungary (1526-1566) and Austria (1529-1691), creating panic throughout central Europe. Moslem Turks also battled Sicily and southern Italy (1534), Spain (1554-1585), Venice (1537-1684), Malta (1565), Russia (1677-1702) and Poland (1672-1676). Finally the united armies of Venice, Savoy, Germany, Austria and Poland in the Fourteenth Papal Crusade turned the tide. In 1699 the Treaty of Karlowitz ended the fighting. Turkey yielded up huge territories including Hungary, Transylvania and Ukraine.   "He will thoroughly purge his floor, and gather His wheat into the garner; but He will burn up the chaff with unquenchable fire" (Matt. 3:12).

What is the WHITE CLOUD? "So great a CLOUD of witnesses" (Heb. 12:1). The CLOUD that helps the Turkish Islamic reaper cut down Roman Catholics in eastern Europe stands for a MULTITUDE and the color WHITE stands for RIGHTEOUSNESS, so a WHITE CLOUD is a RIGHTEOUS MULTITUDE of Protestant witnesses who are fighting Roman Catholics in western Europe.

What are the VINE CLUSTERS? "The righteous shall rejoice when he seeth the vengeance; he shall wash his feet in the blood of the WICKED. So that a man shall say,

Verily there is a reward for the righteous; verily he is a God that judgeth in the earth" (Ps. 58:10). "The slain of the Lord shall be in that day from one end of the (Roman) earth even to the other end of the (Roman) earth; they shall not be lamented, neither gathered, nor buried: they shall be dung upon the face of the ground" (Jer. 25:33). "The indignation of the Lord is upon all nations, and his fury upon all their armies: he hath utterly destroyed them, he hath delivered them to the slaughter" (Isa. 34:2).

What is the WINEPRESS? In type it is western Roman Catholic Europe -- particularly France where grape wines are famous. But in anti-type it may be western Washington State where grape wines are also famous. "Let the heathen be wakened, and come up to the Valley of JEHOSHAPHAT (Kidron Valley); for there will I sit to judge all the heathen round about. Put in the sickle; for the harvest is ripe; come, get down; for the press is full, the fats (vats) overflow; for their WICKEDNESS is great" (Joel 3:12-13). Also Armageddon (Megiddo) (Rev. 16:16). Then will be "a time of trouble, such as never was" (Matt. 24:21). A day when "the haughtiness of man will be humbled, and the Lord alone exalted" (Isa. 2:17). Palestine is between 150 and 200 miles in length and will be a battleground for the overflowing winepress (Joel 3:12-14). Therefore it is interesting that 1600 furlongs equal 184 miles (607 feet per furlong x 1600 furlongs = 971200 feet / 5280 feet per mile = 184 miles.). The Seine-Marne River valley in France is about 184 miles long -- the site of bloody fighting in World War 2. The equivalent location in America would be from Everett to Portland in the Pacific NW -- 184 miles.

What are the "HORSE BRIDLES" and "1600 FURLONGS? In anti-type we learned in Revelation 6 that a HORSE symbolized the ROMAN EMPIRE. Therefore, a HORSE BRIDLE must be the place where the HORSE is controlled -- the PAPACY. Pagan and Papal Rome received her fill of blood after 1600 years. If each FURLONG represents a YEAR (just as seven ears of corn and seven cattle stood for seven years -- Gen. 41:26-27), and if we begin counting in 96 A.D. (when John wrote the Book of Revelation), we arrive at 1697 A.D. when the Peace of Ryswick was signed ending Christian religious wars between Catholic and Protestant. Then the Treaty of Carlowitz in 1699 was signed ending Christian religious wars between Moslems and Christians. Furthermore, the mid-date of these two treaties is 1698 which was 1,260 lunar years from the end of the Western Roman Empire in 476 A.D., and 2,520 lunar years or "seven times" from Nabonassar (747 B.C.) -- the starting point of Babylon's chronology. In the early days of the Reformation, when Protestantism was weak and divided, the Moslem Turks kept the papal forces pre-occupied with Moslem diversionary wars. Once Protestants were safe, Moslems made peace.

Also 1600 furlongs are exactly 200 Italian miles -- the extent of the Pope's Roman States, namely of the Provinces in Italy which specially belonged to the Pope, and which extended from Rome to the River Po and were called "Peter's Patrimony." Napoleon deprived the Pope of these Papal States, and they were finally taken from him in 1870 and his temporal power abolished. But many believe the city of Rome will be destroyed by earthquake and volcanic eruptions to accomplish another fulfillment.

Chapter 14 encourages the martyrs of papal Rome foreseen in chapter 13, just as chapter 7 encourages the martyrs of pagan Rome foreseen in chapter 6.

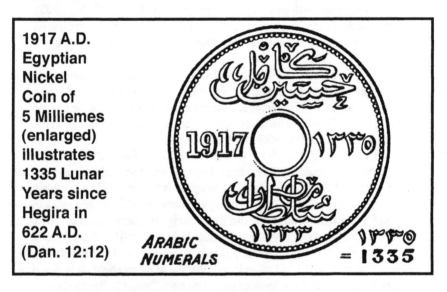

1917 A.D. Egyptian Nickel Coin of 5 Milliemes (enlarged) illustrates 1335 Lunar Years since Hegira in 622 A.D. (Dan. 12:12)

ARABIC NUMERALS

Protestant Martyrs branded with "Mark of the Beast" Before Execution as this old woodcut by H. Crisp (recently enhanced) shows.

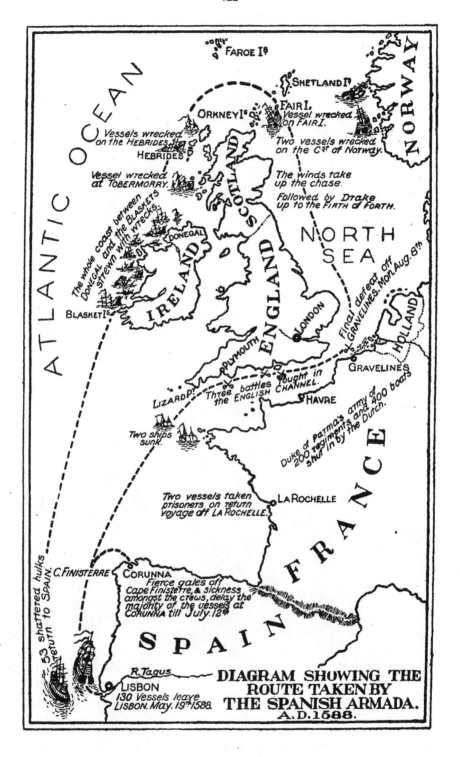

DIAGRAM SHOWING THE
ROUTE TAKEN BY
THE SPANISH ARMADA.
A.D. 1588.

From the Treaty of Carlowitz
to the French Revolution
(1699 to 1793 A.D.)
(Chapter 15)

Chapter 15 resumes the theme which was broken off at the end of chapter 11:14 by the supplementary visions (chapters 12, 13 & 14). All the events from Revelation 9:13 to 11:14 occurred during the era of the Sixth Trumpet or Second Turkish Woe. The Reformation (Rev. 10 & 11) still belongs to the Sixth Trumpet era. Even the Treaty of Carlowitz in 1699 A.D. (chapter 14) belongs to the Sixth Trumpet. The Seventh Trumpet or Third Woe comes "quickly" and encompasses everything from the French Revolution in 1793 A.D. forward to today.

"And I saw another sign in heaven, great and marvellous, seven angels having the seven last plagues; for in them is filled up the wrath of God. And I saw as it were a sea of glass mingled with fire: and them that had gotten the victory over the beast, and over his image, and over his mark, and over the number of his name, stand on the sea of glass, having the harps of God" (Rev. 15:1-2).

What is the "SEA of GLASS"? This "SEA of GLASS" represents the North Sea surrounding most of the Protestant nations of Europe like a moat. They have made their "stand" on it. "Glass" is clear, reflective, green and flat just like water. Also a "SEA" is "PEOPLES" (Rev. 17:15) before the Throne of God (Rev. 4:6) and "mingled with FIRE" -- going through "fiery TRIALS" (1 Pet. 4:12). Papal Europe is the SEA of GLASS that Protestant saints "stand" over -- rule over -- now that the "Times of the Gentiles" are completed. Papal Europe failed to repent under the Turkish "Sixth Trumpet" that passed away in 1699 A.D. by the Treaty of Carlowitz. Papal Europe also rejected the Reformation. Therefore, God's wrath was expressed through the "Third Woe" or "Seventh Trumpet" which followed "quickly." "Shall not God avenge his own elect, which cry day and night unto him, though he bear long with them?" (Luke 18:7).

In the eighteenth century the growth of infidelity and atheistic Communism led to the French Revolution -- a judgement on Papal Christendom. The anti-Papal French "Reign of Terror" began in 1793 A.D., exactly 1,260 years (Rev. 13:5-10) after Justinian's Imperial Decree in 533 A.D. acknowledging the Pope as head of Christendom. These plagues are the "last" and in them is "filled up" God's wrath. Israel's taskmasters are about to be destroyed so that Israel can enter into her promised inheritance. Israel is the Protestant nations of Switzerland, Denmark, Norway, Sweden, Iceland, England, Scotland and Holland. To these chosen must be added the overseas British Dominions which are also Protestant: Canada, Australia, New Zealand and South Africa. Finally, the "great people" of the United States form the largest single Protestant nation. More and more of God's people have politically "come out of Babylon" and emigrated overseas to this "multitude of nations" (Gen. 17:5-8) promised to Abraham.

"And they sing the song of Moses the servant of God, and the song of the Lamb, saying, Great and marvellous are thy works, Lord God Almighty; just and true are thy ways, thou King of saints. Who shall not fear thee, O Lord, and glorify thy name? for thou only art holy: for all nations shall come and worship before thee; for thy judgments are made manifest" (Rev. 15:3-4).

Israel sings the song of their deliverance from Papal bondage. There were actually two "Songs of MOSES." Moses and Israel sang the first, after God, through the priestly ministry of Moses and Aaron, had poured out the plagues on idolatrous Egypt which led to Israel's exodus and to the drowning of their Egyptian pursuers in the Red Sea. The second song was sung after Moses had led Israel through the wilderness period of trial and sanctification, and after Jericho had fallen, and when Israel stood on the edge of the Promised Land ready to enter God's Kingdom in Canaan (Ex. 15:1-21 and Deut. 31:30; 32:1-43). This proves that the story of Israel in Egypt, the Exodus, the wilderness journey, and the entry into the Promised Land, is an allegory of the Protestant Reformation, of the outpouring of the seven plagues of Revelation on Continental Europe, and of the deliverance of the Protestant Anglo-Saxon Israel nations and their establishing God's Kingdom on earth -- in type known as the BRITISH EMPIRE. This is confirmed by the similarity of the Apocalyptic plagues to those of ancient Egypt.

God's people sang the "Song of the Lamb" which indicates that they accepted the "PASSOVER Lamb" rather than the Roman Catholic MASS of "Transubstantiation." The Protestant nations accept Jesus Christ's sacrifice for their sins. These three songs show that the time of the seven vials, the nineteenth and twentieth centuries, is the national EXODUS of Protestant Israel from "EGYPTIAN-Babylonian" idolatry, false doctrines, spiritual slavery and oppression and of Israel becoming God's servant.

Let's now translate these songs into their latter-day counterparts using the recent history of Protestant nations. The first "Song of MOSES" (Exodus 15:1-21) has an obvious fulfillment. Yes, the SPANISH ARMADA was "thrown into the sea" (15:1) and the Spanish soldiers were "cast into the sea" (15:4). "His chosen (Spanish) captains also are drowned" (15:4) "The depths have covered them; they sank into the bottom as a stone" (15:5). The Armada's total weight was 60,000 tons. "Thy wrath ... consumed them as stubble" (15:7), not only from broadsides, but because Drake and his fire ships spread havoc in the Spanish galleons. "And with the blast of thy nostrils ... Thou didst blow with thy wind; the sea covered them; they sank as lead in the mighty waters" (15:8-10). Winds blew the Armada off her course and smashed many ships on the rocky coasts of France, Norway, Scotland and Ireland (cp. Ps. 48:7). "With his chariots ... The horse and his rider hath he thrown into the sea" (15:19-21). We are sure the Spanish took "wagons" with them in their ships (p.20, Defeat of the Spanish

Armada by Close) and this implies also horses to pull them. Of the 30,000 Spanish soldiers and sailors who had sailed in the Armada, scarcely 10,000 returned home. Of the 130 Spanish ships that set sail, only 53 returned home. No more than 100 English sailors were killed and none of the English ships were lost. In acknowledgment of the Providence of God, numerous medals were struck illustrating the deliverance and with the words inscribed "He blew with his winds and they were scattered." Thus England sang the "Song of MOSES" literally.

The second "Song of Moses" (Deut. 32:1-43) has anti-type fulfillments in British and American history. "Remember the days of old ... When the Most High divided to the nations their inheritance, when He separated the sons of Adam, He set the bounds of the people according to the number of the children of Israel. For the lord's portion is His people; Jacob is the lot of his inheritance" (Deut. 32:7-9). In the fifteenth and sixteenth centuries, the Papacy divided the New World of North and South America among Latin nations of Spain and Portugal (Treaty of Tordesillas -- 1494) as if the pope were God. It seemed as if Spain, Portugal and France were to become mighty Catholic empires in contradiction to God's limit for the "times of the Gentiles" as well as his limit of their territorial "bounds." Then came the amazing and miraculous expansion of Protestant England. Victory after victory of her navies and armies, often against ridiculous odds, which represented nothing less than Yahweh's protection, led to the defeat of Latin colonialism. At the end of the eighteenth century, Spain had lost her West Indian possessions while her South American colonies revolted from her. France was defeated in both India and Canada by the victories of Clive at Plassey, 1757, and Wolfe at Quebec, 1759. Although a French explorer discovered Australia first, it became British. The French were beaten to New Zealand by a British Frigate only one day before the French arrived. The "times of the Gentiles" were over. The "bounds" of their "inheritance" had been set. God had set aside certain lands for Israelites to become a "Company of Nations" and a "Great People" (Gen. 35:10,11; 48:19). This Providence of God was recognized by British armies, navies, merchants, colonists and missionaries. They were the "Lord's Portion" of the earth, "Jacob, the lot of His inheritance" and "His servant nation." The pulpits and press of Britain resounded with this portion of Moses' second song.

"As an eagle stirreth up her nest, fluttereth over her young, spreadeth abroad her wings, taketh them, beareth them on her wings, So the Eternal alone did lead him ... He made him ride on the high places of the earth, that he might eat the increase of the fields; and he made him to suck honey out of the rock, and oil out of the flinty rock; Butter of kine (cows), and milk of sheep, with fat of lambs, and rams of the breed of Bashan, and goats, with the fat of kidneys of wheat; and thou didst drink the pure blood of the grape" (Deut. 32:11-14).

This portion of the "Song of Moses" refers to God as our EAGLE who has led us to a BOUNTIFUL land and taught us to fly. This foretells the United States of AMERICA which was colonized in 1620 by Holland's Pilgrims at Plymouth and in 1629 by Puritans at Boston who wanted to be purified of "popish taints" in the Anglican Church and build a "new Zion." It is no accident that the city of "Boston" and counties of "Norfolk," "Suffolk" and "Essex" became names of Massachusetts brought over from England. The United States declared its independence (1776) and expanded by declaring its "Manifest Destiny" to spread the ideas of liberty, republican institutions and the Protestant Church. When we sing "America the Beautiful" and "Battle Hymn of the Republic" we are repeating these Biblical themes. Thomas Jefferson purchased the Louisiana Territory (827,987 square miles of land) for about $15 million from Napoleon in 1803. That's less than four cents per acre. Florida was purchased from Spain for $5 million in 1819. Americans were invited into Texas by Mexico's Santa Anna in 1821. Within ten years there were about 30,000 Americans and 3,500 Mexicans in Texas and the Americans demanded greater representation. Instead they got independence. After defeating Mexico in1848, America paid Mexico $15 million for California, Nevada, Arizona, Utah, New Mexico and parts of Colorado and Wyoming (525,000 square miles of land). Russia sold Alaska to America in 1867 for $7,200,000 -- about two cents per acre. Joseph's "branches" ran "over the wall" (Gen. 49:22).

The "Song of the Lamb" sung by Protestant nations of Britain, America and Scandinavia during this time was the spiritual revivals that took place and the hymn-writing during this era. For example, Charles Wesley wrote some 6,500 hymns. Missionary and Bible Societies sprang up. The British and Foreign Bible Society was formed in 1804 and the American Bible Society in 1816. The American Declaration of Independence was in itself a song of deliverance and liberty.

"And after that I looked, and, behold, the temple of the tabernacle of the testimony in heaven was opened: And the seven angels came out of the temple, having the seven plagues, clothed in pure and white linen, and having their breasts girded with golden girdles. And one of the four beasts gave unto the seven angels seven golden vials full of the wrath of God, who liveth for ever and ever. And the temple was filled with smoke from the glory of God, and from his power; and no man was able to enter into the temple, till the seven plagues of the seven angels were fulfilled" (Rev. 15:5-8).

The temple scenes in Revelation 15:5-8 and in Revelation 11:19 link the seventh trumpet with the seven vials. What does the "TEMPLE in HEAVEN" mean? Astronomically, Aquarius gives a full bucket or Cup to each of the seven stars (angels) in "Crater" who pour out an army flood from each Cup of Wrath. The smoke in this astronomical Temple is the Milky Way. Historically, during the New Covenant age, the ISRAELITES themselves become "a TEMPLE of living stones" (1 Cor. 3:16; 6:19; 2 Cor. 6:16; 1 Pet. 2:5-9) in the political heaven and are no longer under the feet of Gentiles. "Pure and WHITE LINEN" is the "RIGHTEOUSNESS of saints" (Rev. 19:8). Not being able to enter the Temple (15:8) is taken from Exodus 40:35-37 and means that Papal Europeans were not able to emigrate to Protestant Anglo-Saxon nations, or convert to Protestantism, while the French Revolution, Napoleonic Wars, and other crises were occurring. The ARK of GOD in the midst of the Temple (Rev. 11:19) means the "GLORY of GOD" has RETURNED to the Protestant Anglo-Saxon nations (1 Sam. 4:21). This is truly a picture of the British Empire and the United States in the nineteenth and twentieth centuries (a type of the Kingdom of God), who have been used by God to punish disobedient nations. British arms played a part in the first vials (cups) in the Napoleonic era. Both British and Americans destroyed Germany, Austro-Hungary and Turkey in 1914-1918. Again, both British and Americans destroyed the Nazi-Fascist powers in 1939-1945.

"It is a sin and even an insanity to hold that men have inalienable right to Liberty of Conscience and Worship, or to deny that Rome has the right to repress by all force all religious observance save her own, or to teach that Protestants in a Catholic country should be allowed the exercise of their religion." -- Roman Cardinal Manning "If Catholics ever gain sufficient numerical majority in this country, religious freedom is at an end." -- Catholic Bishop of St. Louis, 1851

128

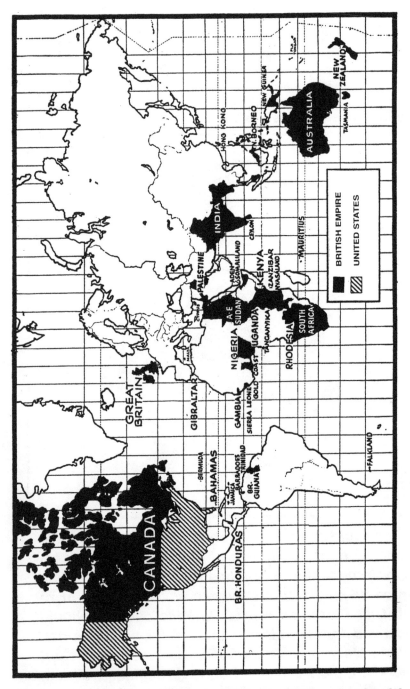

"The kingdoms of this world are become the kingdom of our Lord, and of his Christ" (Rev. 11:15).

From the French Revolution
to World War Three
(Chapter 16)
(1789 to present)

At Passover the Jews recite the ten plagues while dropping ten drops of wine onto their seder plates from the second "cup of freedom" (a.k.a. "cup of wrath" -- Rev. 14:10; 16:19; 17:4; 18:6). All of these seven cups are symbolically that second "cup of freedom" pouring out the Egyptian plagues. "For in the hand of the Eternal there is a cup, and the wine is red; it is fully mixed, and he poureth out of the same; but the dregs thereof all the wicked of the earth shall drain them, and drink them" (Ps. 75:8; Ps. 11:6). The first four Vials (Cups) here judge PAPAL Rome (16:2-8) like the first four Trumpets of chapter 8 that judged PAGAN Rome. Both are poured out respectively on 1. the "earth" 2. "sea" 3. "rivers" and 4. the "sun." The sixth Trumpet and sixth Vial (Cup) both concern the "EUPHRATES."

"And I heard a great voice out of the temple saying to the seven angels, Go your ways, and pour out the vials (cups) of the wrath of God upon the earth. And the first went, and poured out his vial (cup) upon the earth; and there fell a noisome and grievous sore upon the men which had the mark of the beast, and upon them which worshipped his image" (Rev. 16:1-2).

Astronomically, there are seven main stars (angels) in Crater (the Cup of Wrath). The cup is turned upside down as the earth rotates on its axis causing the sun and/or moon to "drop out." The stars also drop out of the cup and cover or dot the bodies of the celestial constellations giving the appearance of "sores." Historically, from 1758 to 1770, infidel, atheistic literature flooded France. The "voices" (Rev. 11:19) of Voltaire, Diderot, Boyle and Rousseau originated and led a school of ATHEISTIC philosophers who waged a literary war agitating for APOSTASY against Roman Catholicism leading to massacres and confiscations against Catholics as well as the aristocrats and Royalty that supported them -- and later against eachother. Why? Divine retribution for two past crimes.

The first occurred about 200 years before in France. Catholics had massacred innocent Protestants in the St. Bartholemew Massacre. It is estimated that 100 thousand Huguenots were murdered. Rome was filled with great joy and a Te Deum was sung. Pope Gregory XIII called it a "glorious and joyful victory." Rome taught the people that they had the right to depose or murder Protestant rulers, close Protestant churches, and kill and confiscate their property. Papal clergy seized Protestant property and thus held one fifth of the land of France prior to the Revolution. The industry and skill of the Huguenots had contributed to the greatness of France. Without these who were the "salt of the earth," Roman Catholic France went "putrid" in infidelity and immorality. At least one million Huguenots fled France and took their skills with them. Nobody was left to restrain the people or check the faults in government.

The second occurred about 100 years before the French Revolution in 1685, Louis XIV, the Sun King, revoked the Edict of Nantes and trampled under foot civil and religious liberty of his Huguenot subjects. Their children were kidnapped. Their property confiscated. Their churches demolished and their ministers banished. The King's soldiers were billeted in their houses and used those houses as horse stables and raped their wives and daughters. Huguenot men were made galley slaves. The women imprisoned in Rome's convents. Bibles were burned. Libraries closed. Protestant universities suppressed. Rome celebrated, sang Te Deums, and a special Papal medal was struck celebrating the Revocation. The martyrs had asked, "How long, O Lord ... do you not ... avenge our blood?" (Rev. 6:10). The French Revolution was the reply.

What was the "noisome and grievous SORE"? The sixth plague against Egypt was literal "BOILS ... upon the magicians and upon all the house of Pharaoh" (Ex. 9:10) and from 1770 to 1800, a literal plague of SMALLPOX afflicted the French Royal Family. Louis XV died from the disease, while Louis XVI caught the malady on ascending the throne, and it spread to and affected many other members of the Royal Family and the Court of Versailles. The Revolutionary leader, Marat, had "open sores, often running" that pitted his countenance because he was in the last stages of Syphilis. Danton's face was "pockmarked, hideous, his mouth distorted by a scar" and Robespierre was shot in the jaw while being arrested, so had a wound. Since the Papacy is called "spiritual Egypt" (Rev. 11:8), there is also a spiritual symbolic SORE. Isaiah likens a variety of SINS to "wounds, and bruises, and putrefying SORES: they have not been closed, neither bound up, neither mollified with ointment" (Isaiah 1:6). Then he specifically defines the SORES as a "country ... desolate ... cities ... burned with fire ... land ... overthrown by strangers ... a besieged city ... like Sodom and ... Gomorrah ... incense is an abomination ... your appointed feasts my soul hateth ... your hands are full of blood.... How is the faithful city become an harlot ... murderers ... Thy silver has become dross ... Thy princes are rebellious, and companions of thieves; every one loveth bribes" (Isa. 1:7-23), etcetera. This is a description of the French Revolution (1789-1793) which began within the French political body and spread to all other Roman Catholic nations by means of the printing press and revolutionary agents. In 529 A.D. Justinian's Imperial Code confirmed Papal supremacy. Adding 1260 years (Dan. 7:25; Rev. 11:2-3; 13:5-7) we come to 1789 A.D. when the French Revolution occurred. In 533 A.D. a Decretal letter recognized the Pope as "Head of all the Churches." Adding 1260 years to this date we come to 1793 A.D. when the Reign of Terror occurred in France. Roman Catholic Churches were burned and thousands of priests, monks and nuns were slain. It was the plague of INFIDELS. In other words, general LAWLESSNESS which ran wild and unrestrained into APOSTASY. The Sunday-Sabbath was abolished. Scriptures were trampled under foot. God and Christianity renounced publicly. A donkey was made to drink the wine out of the Communion Cup. A prostitute was worshiped as the Goddess of Reason, with all its subsequent orgies. King Louis XVI (of the French Royalty who had initiated the Bartholemew Massacre and Revocation of the Edict of Nantes and Dragonnades against Protestants) and Queen Marie Antoinette (of the Hapsburgs who had persecuted Bohemian and Netherlands Protestants) were guillotined. It is estimated by historians that in five years 2,000,000 people were roasted alive, drowned, guillotined or shot; that 24,000 priests (like the magicians of Egypt who were afflicted) were murdered, and 40,000 churches turned into stables and 4,000 monasteries and nunneries were suppressed. Church and State were separated and the Pope stripped of his temporal sovereignty. The atheistic Revolutionaries cried "Ecrasez l'infame" or "Crush the Wretch" (Roman Catholicism). The purchasing power of the money in circulation was diluted by printing unlimited amounts of currency known as "assignats" causing inflation. Many contemporary historians likened the French Revolution to a DISEASE. Edmunde Burke described it as "An infectious PLAGUE requiring the most severe quarantine." Sir Walter Scott in his "Life of Napoleon" described French affairs during this time as "wasting SORES." Lambert, the French Dominican monk, described it as "A sick man covered with ULCERS." The great historian Niebuhr, who was ambassador at one time to the Papal Church, said, "The Revolution of 1789 was the breaking out of a local DISEASE peculiar to the Roman Catholic nations and governments of southern Europe.... owing to the despair created by an effete aristocracy and a hypocritical priesthood." Britain, like ancient Israel, was spared this plague of Egypt because of the open Bible as antidote. Voltaire once boasted that "It took twelve ignorant fishermen to establish Christianity, I will show the world how one Frenchman can destroy it." But within thirty years of his death, his home was purchased by the Geneva Bible Society and became a Bible storage building, while his infidel printing press was used to print an entire edition of the Bible.

"And the second angel poured out his vial (cup) upon the sea; and it became as the blood of a dead man: and every living soul died in the sea" (Rev. 16:3).

How does the sea become like the "BLOOD of a DEAD man"? We know that the sea would have to CONGEAL and STOP CIRCULATING. Britain STOPPED all TRADE by SEA. The first plague against Egypt was also "waters ... turned to blood" (Ex. 7:20). In 1793 France declared war on Great Britain, the strongest naval power in history. Truly the years 1793-1813 saw terrible naval warfare in which hundreds of ships and their crews, belonging to France and Spain, were destroyed. To mention a few of the sea battles, in 1793 almost the whole of the French Fleet at Toulon was destroyed by Lord Hood. In 1794, Lord Howe defeated the French off Ushant. In 1797 the Spanish Fleet was beaten by the British off Cape Saint Vincent. Then came Lord Nelson's mighty victories such as the Nile (1798) and Trafalgar (1805), against Spain and France. At Trafalgar the French fleet was nearly annihilated, and England was rescued from all chance of invasion. It was a period of naval warfare and bloodshed unique in history. The maritime powers of the Papal nations were SWEPT OFF the seas by the British victories. This was God's retribution. Huguenots were persecuted as galley-slaves in these Papal ships. Therefore, these Papal fleets were "persecuted" by the British. Also the spirit of the French Revolution spread to the Latin colonies overseas resulting in Spain and Portugal LOSING their South American possessions which REVOLTED and finally became INDEPENDENT. For instance, the island of San Domingo experienced a bloody civil war from 1792-1804 where 60,000 blacks were killed and all white French colonials were exterminated. Then it became lost to France and was known as the Republic of Haiti. This, coupled with Britain's victories in the colonial warfare, is probably the meaning of the symbolism in the prophecy that "every living soul died in the sea" -- it was the death of the sea-power and overseas colonies of Papal Europe. This is when Britannia began to rule the waves.

"And the third angel poured out his vial (cup) upon the rivers and fountains of waters; and they became blood. And I heard the angel of the waters say, Thou art righteous, O Lord, which art, and wast, and shalt be, because thou hast judged thus. For they have shed the blood of saints and prophets, and thou hast given them blood to drink; for they are worthy. And I heard another out of the altar say, Even so, Lord God Almighty, true and righteous are thy judgments" (Rev. 16:4-7).

Just as the third trumpet was Attila the Hun, so the third vial was Napoleon Bonaparte. Napoleon, who was unaware of this type and anti-type, exclaimed, "I will prove to be an Attila to Venice." In 1795 France declared war against the ruling classes of the other nations. The revolutionary armies carried the revolution everywhere by military force. Europe was then plunged into the bloodiest war history records since the fall of Rome. The Revolutionary Wars merged into the Napoleonic Wars. From 1796-1799, the revolutionary armies invaded and fought Germany, Piedmont, Sardinia, Lombardy and Austria -- all persecutors of Waldensians. The rivers separating these countries became the natural positions around which the battles raged. In the whole history of Papal Europe there has never been any one war in which the valleys of the Rhine, Danube and the Poe were so filled with bloodshed. These same lands which witnessed such carnage were also the "fountains" or sources of the rivers of Europe. John heard two angels testify that these disastrous battles were the judgments of a righteous God on these Papal nations because they had shed the blood of his saints.

The children deserved the penalty for their parents' sin because they supported their parents' deeds. God visits "the iniquity of the fathers upon the children unto the third and fourth generation of them that hate me" (Ex. 20:5). In the same way, Jesus told the Jews of his generation that upon them would come all the righteous blood shed upon earth from "the blood of righteous Abel" to that day (Matt. 23:35), because "ye allow the deeds of your fathers" (Luke 11:48). Therefore "The fathers have eaten a sour grape, and the children's teeth are set on edge" (Jer. 31:29) when they approve. "Whatsoever a man soweth, that shall he also reap" (Gal.6:7) immediately individually (Judges 1:6-7; Job 15:31; Matt.10:10) and delayed nationally as here shown.

"The waters ("peoples" -- Rev. 17:15) became blood." Truly the valleys of the Rhine, Danube and Alpine streams of Italy had witnessed the martyrdom of hundreds of thousands of Waldensians, Albigenses, Vaudois, Hussites, Moravians, Lutherans, Reformers and Hugenots. Thus the "altar" of martyrs sacrificed under the fifth Seal (Rev. 6:10) is now mentioned again as being satisfied with the vengeance. An estimated ten million men fell on all sides or died of wounds or disease between 1792 and 1815.

"And the fourth angel poured out his vial (cup) upon the sun; and power was given unto him to scorch men with fire. And men were scorched with great heat, and blasphemed the name of God, which hath power over these plagues: and they repented not to give him glory" (Rev. 16:8-9).

Who is the "SUN"? The SUN represents the head of the family (Gen. 37:9-10) or Byzantine ruler (Rev. 9:2) or Holy Roman Emperor (Rev. 8:12) and this imagery was commonly used in the Middle Ages. A halo behind the head of these leaders emphasized this point. Those who REIGN "SHINE as the brightness of the firmament" (Dan. 12:3). After the tribulation "shall the sun be darkened" (Matt. 24:29) as all human government collapses. In 1799 a young artillery officer named Napoleon, already famous as a military leader, overthrew the revolutionary government and established himself as a military DICTATOR or "SUN." Thenceforth the French "liberating" armies became, under Napoleon, the scourge of Europe. In 1801 his armies defeated the imperial armies in Germany and northern Italy. Napoleon then replaced the Imperial Code of Justinian, which had given legal recognition to the Papal supremacy of Christendom with his own Code. In 1804 Napoleon was crowned EMPEROR of the Holy Roman Empire, and was "sanctified" by the presence of the Pope. During his Egyptian campaign, Napoleon earned the title "Sultan of Fire" due to his aggressive use of artillery in warfare. Within the space of eight years, the Napoleonic "SUN" SCORCHED every kingdom in Europe, from Naples to Berlin, and from Lisbon to Moscow by means of oppressive wars and grinding taxation. Ancient kingdoms withered before the intense BLAZE of his power. Plagues accompanied his progress. He established a system of spoilation, extortion and oppression to enslave subjected nations to the will of one man. Like the sun, there was nothing hidden from his great HEAT; and the exercise of his power caused misery to millions (Keith's Signs of the Times p.191).

Great Britain, as Protestant Israel, was never invaded. She alone feared God. Norway, Sweden, Holland and Denmark were all either allies or part of Napoleon's Empire. Moreover, Britain's navies helped in this judgment on the Papal nations by blockading Europe's trade. Britain's armies under the Duke of Wellington finally defeated Napoleon at Waterloo in 1815. In spite of all these judgments, the hearts of the Latin-German nations were only further hardened and they refused to repent of the Papal sorceries and infidelity. At the Congress of Vienna the Papal kingdom was restored, the Church of Rome reinstated, and the wicked Roman Catholic kings of France, Spain and Naples returned to their thrones. The Papacy continued to boast that it was "Semper Eadem" or never changes.

"And the fifth angel poured out his vial (cup) upon the seat of the beast; and his king-dom was full of darkness; and they gnawed their tongues for pain, And blasphemed the God of heaven because of their pains and their sores, and repented not of their deeds" (Rev. 16:10-11).

Where was the "SEAT of the BEAST"? The VATICAN in ROME. The Pope's "king-dom" consisted of the Papal States. Progressive disintegration began in 1789 when all Church property was confiscated in defiance of its legal guardian, the Pope. The tithes due to the Pope were seized by the State, and the clergy, appointed by and subject to the Pope, were popularly elected, and made pensioners and servants of the State. In 1793, the Roman Catholic religion was officially abolished in France. In 1797 Napoleon defeated Austria, the chief supporter of the Papal "THRONE," defeated the Papal army in Italy and by the Treaty of Tolentino the Pope surrendered almost all his political SOVEREIGNTY, paid heavy tribute to Napoleon, and handed over most of the art treasures of the Vatican to enrich Paris. This was retribution for the Papal robberies over the centuries. In 1798 the French Revolutionary army invaded the Papal States, captured ROME February 10th, and on February 15th, General Haller, a Swiss Calvinist, with a band of French soldiers, broke down the doors of the Sistine Chapel with axes and proclaimed the Pope's reign to be at an end. On the 18th, Haller took the Pope's so-called "Ring of the Fisherman" from his finger. As the Vatican was being stripped to the bare walls, the actual Chair of St. Peter was found by the French to bear the Arabic inscription, "There is no God but Allah and Mohammed is his prophet." February 20th, Pope Pius VI was arrested and escorted out of Rome by French soldiers. He was taken first to an Augustinian Convent at Sienna, but this was damaged by an earthquake during his stay and he was taken to Florence. Finally he was escorted to the French fortress of Valence where he died July 28th, 1798. The regalia robes of the Pope and his Cardinals were burnt to melt down the gold in them. Gold, precious stones, silver and valuable relics were taken from the VATICAN palaces. The new Pope was forced to watch while Napoleon took the crown from his hands and crowned himself Emperor in Notre Dame Cathedral in 1804. Then in 1809 the new Pope Pius VII rebelled. Napoleon launched against him the Decrees of Schonbrunn and Vienna. These revoked the Donations of Charlemagne to the Papacy, annexed the Papal States to Italy, abolished the Pope's temporal POWER and reduced the Pope to a salaried official of the State. At the same time he removed the Pope and the Papal Offices to Paris where the Pope remained a prisoner of Napoleon till 1814. The Congress of Vienna in 1815 restored the status quo of the Papacy and the Papal States. In the next European Revolution in 1848, the French overthrew King Louis Philippe and the ruling House of Orleans and Pope Pius IX was divested of all his temporal authority and forced to flee from ROME, but restored by Napoleon III. In 1854 the Pope taught the doctrine of Immaculate Conception, that Mary the mother of Jesus was born without sin (cp. Rom. 3:23). In 1860 the Sardinians under Victor Emmanuel invaded the Papal States and defeated the Papal troops. By 1861 the Papal territory had been reduced to the city of Rome and the surrounding area known as the Patrimony of Saint Peter. In 1870 the Pope assembled the Vatican Council to declare him "infallible" when seated on the "chair of St. Peter." A contrivance was set up in the Church of St. Peter to surround the Pope with dazzling light, so that the assembled crowd would see the Pope in a blaze of glory. But it depended on the sunshine which never came. Instead "his kingdom was full of DARKNESS" just as the ninth plague of Egypt was "thick DARKNESS" (Ex. 10:22). A terrible, DARK storm broke over Rome -- the thunder roared, the lightning flashed and terrified them all. Loud thunder frequently interrupted the voting. Including the Pope (Pius IX), there were 754 present. Of them, 533 voted for Infallibility; 62 were for it with reservations; 71 were neutral (including Pius IX) and 88 voted against this blasphemy. Thus, 754 - 88 = 666. Then the next day war was declared between France and Germany. All the French troops who had defended the Pope had to leave Rome to join the war. So the Pope was left DEFENSELESS and 60,000 Italian soldiers marched to ROME. When they had made a hole in the wall surrounding the city, one of the first to enter was a dog named "Pius" pulling a cart full of Bibles that England had sent over. It was the first time the Bible -- burned and hated by Catholics -- could be publicly carried into ROME. In October 1870 the people of ROME were asked if they would have the Pope or the King of Italy as their ruler. They almost unanimously (133,681 vs.1,507) replied they preferred the king. ROME was incorporated into the Kingdom of Italy, thus ENDING the rule of the Pope as a temporal POWER. During all those years of decline, the Papal powers "gnawed their tongues for pain," and hurled anathemas and curses at those forces instrumental in their decline. Instead of repenting of their idolatry which had brought this plague, the Popes continued to blaspheme God just as "Pharaoh's heart was hardened" (Ex. 7:22).

In 533 A.D. Justinian's Imperial decree recognized the Pope as the only head of Christendom. Then in 606 A.D. Phocas also recognized the Pope as the only head of Christendom. In 610 A.D. he was "taken out of the way." Then 1260 years from these dates (Rev. 13:5) we reach 1793, 1848 (using 360-day years) and 1866-1870, all of which witnessed the overthrow of the Papal States and Rome. The 1335 years (Dan. 12:12) from 1870 bring us to 1945 -- the end of World War Two -- Rome's latest attempt to create a Holy Roman Empire.

"And the sixth angel poured out his vial (cup) upon the great river Euphrates; and the water thereof was dried up, that the way of the kings of the east might be prepared" (Rev. 16:12).

Astronomically, the kings east of the Eridanus (Euphrates) are Cepheus, Perseus and Bootes. Historically, the Sixth Trumpet or Second Woe (Rev. 9:13-21) was the rise and growth of the Turkish empire beginning in 1062 A.D. when the Turks crossed the Euphrates symbolized by conquering horsemen from the Euphrates Valley, as if the river itself had overflowed its banks and flooded Asia Minor and S.E. Europe. This sixth vial (cup) now reverses that process by the destruction and "drying up" of the Turkish Empire and Islam. In 1683 the Turkish army was defeated at the unsuccessful siege of Vienna and the final end of Turkish aggression westward was marked by the Treaty of Passarowitz in 1718 which removed the Turks from Hungary. In 1826 the Sultan massacred the flower of his army -- the Janizaries -- because of their complaining, dictatorial attitude. The Janissaries were the children of slaughtered Christian parents, brought up to renounce their faith and to work for the advance of Islam. Bureaucrats replaced them leading to internal decay. In 1829 Greece obtained independence from Turkish rule with help from both Britain and Russia. In 1844 Great Britain compelled Turkey to grant religious rights to minorities. The Crimean War (1853-1856) resulted in Moldavia and Wallachia becoming independent. The Turkish Empire was now known as the "sick man of Europe." In the Russo-Turkish War of 1878, England took Cyprus, Russia claimed parts of Asia, Greece took Thessaly, France grasped Algiers and Tunis, and Austria annexed Bosnia and Herzegovina. Serbia, Montenegro, Romania and part of Bulgaria were made independent. Just four years later in 1882, Egypt became a British Protectorate and in 1896 the followers of the Islamic prophet, the Mahdi, were defeated by Kitchener and the Sudan came under British control. Both had been Turkish provinces. In 1911 Italy declared war on the Turks and by the peace treaty of October 1912 modern Libya and some of the Aegean Islands passed into Italian control. Then the Balkan War of 1912-1913 resulted in an independent Albania and caused Turkey to shrink almost out of Europe with the spoils divided by Greece, Serbia and Bulgaria. In 1914-1918, British Imperial troops completed the drying-up process by driving the Turks out of Egypt, Palestine, Syria and Mesopotamia which included the actual valley of the Euphrates itself. On December 11th, 1917 Jerusalem was liberated by British General Allenby. "The mighty men of Edom shall be as the heart of a woman in her pangs" (Jer. 49:22). "I will lay my vengeance upon Edom by the hand of my people Israel" (Ez. 25:14). These Turkish losses were formalized at the Treaty of Sevres (August 10, 1920). In November 1922 the Sultan of Turkey abdicated and fled his empire. In October 1923, Mustapha Kemal became president of the Turkish Republic. On March 6, 1924, the expulsion of the whole House of Ottoman occurred and the Turkish Caliphate was abolished. By constitutional amendment in 1928, Turkey ceased to have a state religion. Modern Turkey, a small republic in Asia Minor, possesses only the source of the Euphrates.

This cleared the way for certain "kings of the east" to move across and then destroy "Babylonian" civilization under the final seventh vial (cup). Ancient Babylon fell when the Medo-Persian "kings of the east," Cyrus and Darius, diverted the Euphrates River from its course "by a canal into the basin ... a marsh" (Her. 1:191). As Jeremiah 50:38 says, "They must be dried up." Then Cyrus entered underneath Babylon's walls along its dried-up river-bed and conquered the city. In the anti-type, the way has been prepared for the advance of modern "kings of the east," Soviet Russia (the Medes) into Papal Europe (Babylon) to destroy its civilization (Jer. 50--51). October 1917 Communism appeared in Russia just after Turkey receded from eastern Europe. We await their full invasion. Perhaps the United States will be defeated by cheap labor costs in China drying up our lifeblood economy of debt and usury.

"And I saw three unclean spirits like frogs come out of the mouth of the dragon (pagan Roman Empire), and out of the mouth of the beast (Papal Roman Empire), and out of the mouth of the false prophet (Papacy). For they are the spirits of devils, working miracles, which go forth unto the kings of the earth (Roman Catholic Europe) and of the whole world (worldwide), to gather them to the battle of that great

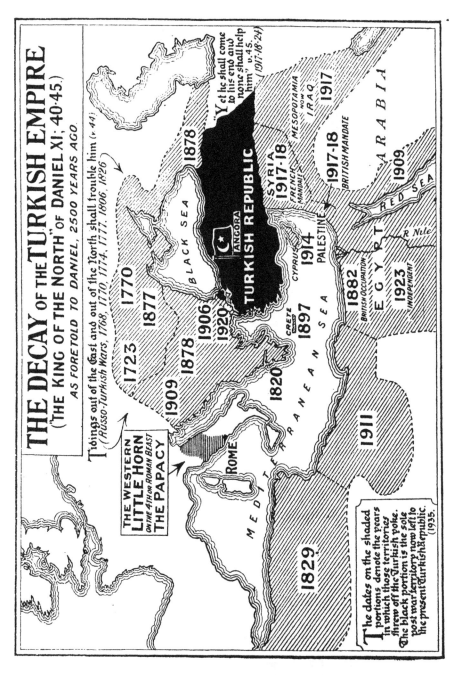

The Turkish flag portrays a star (angel) "having ... in his hand a sharp sickle" (Rev. 14:14) because Moslems were used to cut down idolatrous Christians.

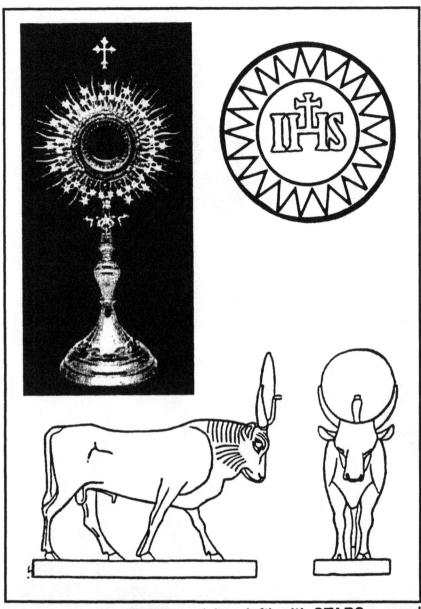

The monstrance (<u>SUN</u>burst) (top left) with <u>STARS</u> around the circumference. The <u>LUNETTE</u> in the center holds the round, wafer host (top right). The golden calf or Apis bull (Ex. 32:4) also has <u>LUNAR</u> horns holding the <u>SOLAR</u> disc (bottom) in the <u>STARRY</u> constellation Taurus. Notice the similarity. Both devices receive worship. Good King Josiah destroyed "<u>SUN</u> images" (2 Chr. 34:4).

What is the "Abomination of Desolation" that stands "in the holy place" (Dan. 9:27; 11:31; 12:11; Matt. 24:15)? In 2 Maccabees 6:2 he is called "<u>ZEUS</u> Olympios." The guides at the Vatican commonly tell visitors that the bronze statue of "Saint Peter" in Saint Peter's Bascilica in Rome is the ancient statue of Jupiter (<u>ZEUS</u>) which was adopted, "canonized" and sanctified. His one big toe is regularly kissed at certain ceremonies. A round <u>SUN</u>-wheel sits above his head. He is certainly in the holy (separated) place. He holds the keys of Janus and Cybele -- not Peter.

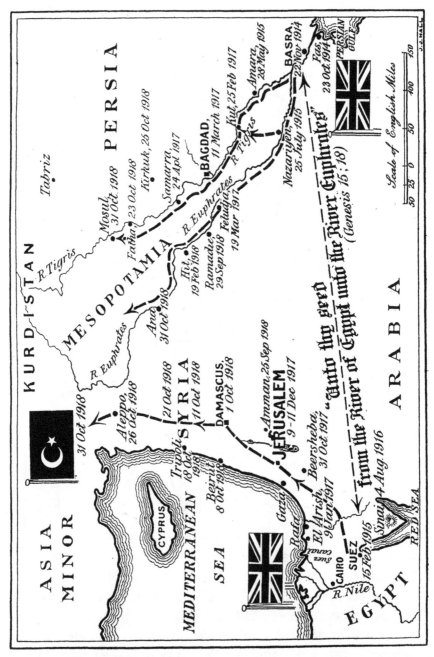

After World War One in 1919 the League of Nations mandated to Great Britain Palestine, Trans-Jordan and Iraq. This "Promised Land" was given "from ... the river Euphrates even unto the uttermost sea shall your coast be" (Deut. 11:24; Gen. 15:18). By 1921 Faisal was ruling Iraq.

day of God Almighty (1945). Behold, I come as a thief. Blessed is he that watcheth, and keepeth his garments, lest he walk naked, and they see his shame. And he (lit. "they") gathered them together into a place called in the Hebrew tongue Armageddon" (Rev. 16:13-16).

Who are the three "FROGS"? Astronomically, Khan Cer (Arabic "Place of Holding") was interpreted as a "Crab" because "Cancer" is Latin for Crab. Better ancient choices have been a Cattlefold (Denderah, Egypt) or Frog (Tibetan). This Constellation hops out of Hydra's mouth (dragon) and Leo's mouth (beast) and Aries/Cetus' mouth (false prophet). Biologically frogs are camoflaged, carnivorous PREDATORS with very big mouths (appetites) who haunt stagnant pools. Therefore the "drying up" of the Euphrates is appropriate imagery for frogs to start appearing. Historically, the second plague against Egypt was frogs (Ex. 8:3) so Pharaoh, the god-king, would "Let my people go." In the same way, the SECOND World War against Europe was NAZI-FASCISM which gobbled up and devastated all Europe, particularly the ROMAN CATHOLIC nations of Poland, Austria, Hungary, Germany, France and Italy, whose cities were bombed and their lands turned into battlegrounds. The slaughter of millions upon millions of both civilians and soldiers, the millions of homeless and refugees, the disintegration of the nations was so the Pope, the god-king, would "Let my people go" across the Red Sea (English Channel) to obey God. The frogs could swim under water (submarines), on the surface (ships), walk on land (tanks) or hop through the air (planes) -- just like the armies of Hitler and Mussolini. The frog SWELLS while it croaks. Therefore, its a familiar symbol of ARROGANT claims put forth with NOISY PERSISTENCY. EVIL PROPAGANDA is therefore the persistent croakings of frogs all night long. It is what comes "out of the mouth." "FALSE teachers ... speak great SWELLING words of vanity ... they promise ... liberty" but they themselves "are the servants of CORRUPTION" (2 Pet. 2:1-19). The three demon-inspired ideologies were represented by frogs.

The first frog came from the "dragon" of Satanic PAGANISM -- German NAZISM -- which began in 1923 represented by the swastika. In Egypt, Tibet, China, India and Japan the OCCULT swastika was used as a MAGIC charm to protect from harm. Hitler's NAZISM advocated restoring the worship of ancient gods and the destruction of Christianity. After Chamberlain appeased Hitler's desire for Czech territory, Hitler said, "Ich bin von himmel gefallen" meaning "I have fallen from heaven." Christ said, "I beheld SATAN as lightning FALL from HEAVEN" (Luke 10:18). "How art thou FALLEN from HEAVEN, O LUCIFER" (Isa. 14:12-15). This indicates Hitler may have been demon-possessed. Hitler, Goering, Himmler, Goebbels and others were attached to black magic and the occult. Several authors testify that Hitler was a "medium" and "possessed" (Ascent to Greatness by McNair, p.351; Hitler and the New Age by Rosio, p.66). Hitler probably borrowed from the German philosopher Nietzsche (born 1844), who, after writing several books, became mad. He called Christianity "the one great curse," taught that "might is right" and declared himself "God." He claimed "Odin is greater than Jehovah." German "Higher Criticism" of the Bible also PAGANIZED Germany. In fact DEUTSCHLAND adds up to 666 if A=6, B=12, C=18, etcetera. The aim of Hitler and the Nazis was to restore the Holy Roman Empire. Franz von Papen, co-signer with Pope Pius XII of the Vatican's Concordat with Hitler's Reich said, "The Third Reich is the first power which not only recognizes, but puts into practice, the high principles of the Papacy." (Jan.14, 1934) Hitler's name "Schicklegruber" actually adds up to 667 in the following manner: S=100, C=3, H=8, I=9, C=3, K=20, L=30, G=7, R=90, U=300, B=2, E=5, R=90. The second frog came from the beast or Roman Empire -- Italian FASCISM -- which began in 1922. Mussolini's Italian FASCES symbol was identical with the Imperial Roman Fasces (sticks bound around an axe), the symbol

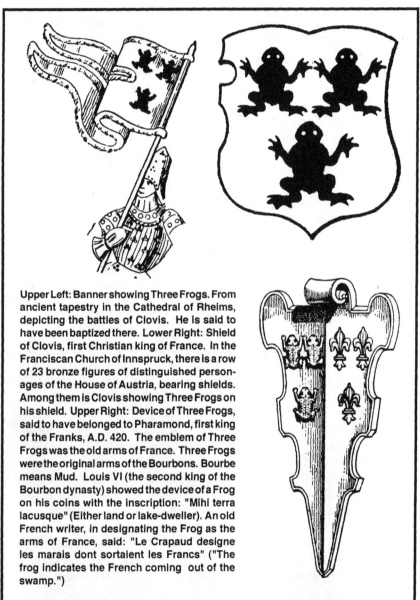

Upper Left: Banner showing Three Frogs. From ancient tapestry in the Cathedral of Rheims, depicting the battles of Clovis. He is said to have been baptized there. Lower Right: Shield of Clovis, first Christian king of France. In the Franciscan Church of Innspruck, there is a row of 23 bronze figures of distinguished personages of the House of Austria, bearing shields. Among them is Clovis showing Three Frogs on his shield. Upper Right: Device of Three Frogs, said to have belonged to Pharamond, first king of the Franks, A.D. 420. The emblem of Three Frogs was the old arms of France. Three Frogs were the original arms of the Bourbons. Bourbe means Mud. Louis VI (the second king of the Bourbon dynasty) showed the device of a Frog on his coins with the inscription: "Mihi terra lacusque" (Either land or lake-dweller). An old French writer, in designating the Frog as the arms of France, said: "Le Crapaud designe les marais dont sortaient les Francs" ("The frog indicates the French coming out of the swamp.")

of power in the ancient Roman Empire that Mussolini was trying to restore. A common poster in Italy in World War Two was "VV IL DVCE" or "Viva II Duce" which adds up to 666 in Latin. (5 + 5 + 1 + 50 + 500 + 5 + 100 = 666) The third frog came from the "false prophet" of Roman CATHOLICISM -- the Pope -- whose temporal power was partially restored by the Lateran Treaty or Concordat of February 1929 with Mussolini through the creation of the Vatican City within Rome. The Pope gave his blessing to Fascism whose aim was the revival of the Papal Roman Empire in Europe. The Pope's official title is "Vicarius Filii Dei" meaning "Vicar of the Son of God." This title adds up to 666. V=5, i=1, c=100, a=0, r=0, i=1, v=5, s=0, F=0, i=1, l=50, i=1, i=1, D=500, e=0, i=1. These three frogs gathered the armies of the world to "Armageddon" where they met their doom. In World War Two, France was conquered by all three frogs and was the location of "Armageddon." In southwestern France we find the province of "Armagnac." Ancient coins and banners of France show three frogs. Three frogs are the old arms of France from the wars of Clovis in the tapestry of Rheims. In A.D. 496, Clovis, King of the Franks, was styled by the Pope, "the eldest son of the Church." Franks came from Phrygians or Fraggoi, hence the nickname "frogs."Even the name "Charles DeGaulle" adds up to 666 in Hebrew. Ch (שׁ) 300 + a (א) 1 + r (ר) 200 + le (ל)30 + s (ם) 60 + D (ד) 4 + e (א) 1 + G (ג) 3 + a (א) 1 + u (ו) 6 + I (ל) 30 + le (ל) 30 = 666. Their propaganda went forth by radio, printing press, mass meetings and parades. In 1 Kings 22:20-38 a "lying spirit" was sent by God to convince King Ahab to go to war and meet his doom also.

Where was "ARMAGEDDON"? World War Two was not fought in Megiddo, but in western Europe. That is the prophetic location of "Armageddon" just as the prophetic location of "Babylon" is western Europe -- not a city in the Middleast. Not ancient literal Babylon, but "The daughter of Babylon is like a threshing floor; it is time to thresh her" (Jer. 51:33). Two of Israel's greatest victories were at Megiddo: Barak defeated the Canaanites there and Gideon defeated the Midianites there, so "Megiddo" is any "theater of battle" where Israel defeats her enemies. These verses also refer to Temple watchmen not knowing at what hour their overseer would come. If he found any watchman sleeping at his post, the penalty was that the offender should be stripped of his garments and turned out, to his shame. "And if he come in the second watch (midnight: 9-12 p.m.), or come in the third watch (cock-crow:12-3 a.m.), and find them so (watching), blessed are those servants" (Luke 12:37-38). Jews were stripped at"Auschwitz" which adds up to 666 if A=6, B=12, C=18, etcetera.

"And the seventh angel poured out his vial (cup) into the air; and there came a great voice out of the temple of heaven, from the throne, saying, It is done. And there were voices, and thunders, and lightnings; and there was a great earthquake, such as was not since men were upon the earth, so mighty an earthquake, and so great. And the great city was divided into three parts (atheistic Communists; Protestant Anglo-Americans; Catholic Europeans), and the cities of the nations fell (Vienna, Prague, Budapest, Warsaw, Rome, Paris, Brussels, Berlin): and great Babylon came in remembrance before God, to give unto her the cup of the wine of the fierceness of his wrath. And every island fled away, and the mountains (nations) were not found. And there fell upon men a great hail out of heaven (allied bombing of Europe), every stone about the weight of a talent: and men blasphemed God because of the plague of the hail; for the plague thereof was exceeding great" (Rev. 16:17-21).

The "voices, thunders and great earthquake" are a repetition of Rev. 11:19 and show that the 7th vial is the final phase of the 7th trumpet woe. The 1st and 2nd World Wars began the 7th vial (cup) of wrath. This is the first time God's wrath falls on the "AIR" because ZEPPELINS, AIRPLANES, and MISSILES (Hitler's V-2 rockets) have now been invented. In 1917, Germany, Austro-Hungary, Italy, Bulgaria, Turkey and Czarist Russia suffered devastation and revolutions proving they were the 2520-year gentile succession that had ended -- not Israelite nations. World War 2 has indeed proven to be the greatest "earthquake" the civilized world has ever experienced. The War ravaged all Europe, particularly the Roman Catholic nations of Poland, Austria, Hungary, Germany, France and Italy, whose cities were bombed and their lands turned into battlegrounds. The slaughter of millions of both civilians and soldiers, of homeless and refugees, the disintegration of the nations all became a "great earthquake."

August 23, 1939 a Nazi-Soviet nonaggression pact was signed. Then in June 22, 1941 "Operation Barbarossa" began exactly 666 days later. (See Their Days Are Numbered by Nicklin for many more Divine timetables in recent history.) But just as ancient Babylon was conquered by Medo-Persia symbolized by a "BEAR," so also western Nazi Europe (Papal Babylon) was conquered by Russia (the Medes -- Ukraine; the Persians -- East and West Prussia) whose national emblem is a BEAR. Stalin ordered Russian troops to move into the territory of the former "Euphrates" power called Turkey in order to defeat the Nazi-Fascist "Babylon." Then Romania, Yugoslavia, Albania, Bulgaria and Hungary were made atheistic and Communist, preparatory to the final onslaught on western Europe when "Babylon comes to remembrance before God." The "cities" of the "nations" fell both literally by being bombed, and, in the Baltic States, the Balkan States and Eastern Europe, by forsaking Roman Catholic civilization and accepting atheistic Soviet Communism. The fall of China with its 450,000,000 to Communism and the millions who have followed suit in south-east Asia since 1945, all helped to make "a great and mighty earthquake, such as never was."

Verse 19 may refer to World War 3 against western Europe. The following is one possible scenario: When Russians sweep across Europe, the "islands and mountains" (nations and kingdoms) will "not be found" rather than just be "moved" as in the fall of Pagan Rome (6th Seal). Modern planes and missiles have put an end to such barriers. The "hail" of Rev. 16:21 or "great hail" of Rev. 11:19, may be Russian missiles just as natural hail storms sweep over Europe from the north. Each "stone" or missile weighs about a "talent." That is 158 pounds 10 ounces Troy Weight or 130 pounds Avoirdupois Weight. But the Latin-German nations will not repent of their idolatries by recognizing God's Russian punishment. Instead they will blaspheme. The walls of Jericho-Egypt-Babylon will "fall" flat and the "city" will be burnt with fire by "the kings of the east" -- Russia. Just as ancient Babylon was conquered by Medo-Persia symbolized by a "bear," so also western Europe (Papal Babylon) will be conquered by the Russian bear (the Medes -- Ukraine) as well as other Eastern European countries (the Persians -- East and West Prussia). Russia in World War Two only partially conquered Europe. It will finish the job in the future.

But where does Imperial Japan fit into prophecy? Japan was also one of the "kings of the east" (literally "rising sun") (Rev. 16:12) even though on the opposite side in the war and on the opposite side of the globe (nowhere near the Turkish Empire) because unintentionally Japan really did wake up the United States by means of Pearl Harbor so that Catholic Europe could be punished by America. Also Japan did punish the Roman Catholic Philippines -- a similar "Babylon" to Europe but on a smaller scale. Indonesia and Malaysia were the "Euphrates" that dried up in this case since they are 90% Moslem. Another way of looking at Japan's role is to say that she also punished North American's for our toleration of Roman Catholics just as Russia punished European Catholics. But Japan also got punished for her sins.

The part played by the British Empire and the United States in defeating FASCISM and NAZISM (the PAPAL "Babylon"), identifies these nations as ISRAEL just as the ancient defeat of Babylon involved the active participation of the "MEDES" who were partly composed of the lost ten tribes of ISRAEL who had been taken captive to "the cities of the MEDES" (2 Ki. 17:6). Thus Churchill and Roosevelt and others were used by God to fulfill prophecy. A sobering thought is that in World War Two both the British (at Singapore) and the Americans (at Pearl Harbor and the Philippines) suffered serious losses and defeats at the hands of the "kings of the east" or rising sun. If World War Three is merely a repeat of World War Two with slight changes (as we think will be the case since the prophecy hasn't been completely fulfilled yet) then we could expect North Korea or Communist China (both "kings of the east") to launch missiles at us this time (the "hail" -- Rev. 11:19; 16:21) causing serious losses or even worse.

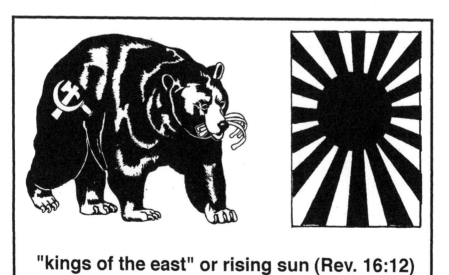

"kings of the east" or rising sun (Rev. 16:12)

146

The Seven Cups

Rev.	Cup	A.D.	Historical Events
16:1-2	First	1755-1793	Outbreak of Continental Infidelity leading to the French Revolution, July 14th, 1789 and Reign of Terror. Infidel Calendar adopted, Nov. 24, 1793.
16:3	Second	1793-1815	Naval Warfare. France declares war against England: ended by banishment of Napoleon to St. Helena. French maritime power destroyed.
16:4-7	Third	1793-1804	Land Warfare. Napoleon fights Austria and Italy: dethrones Pope (1798). Peace of Luneville, Feb. 9, 1801. Papal religion re-established in France. Napoleon declared Emperor of the French.
16:8-9	Fourth	1804-1814	Height of Napoleon's career to his abdication (April 5, 1814) and removal to Elba (escapes following year). Inquisition and Jesuits revived, Aug. 7, 1814 proving "Men ... repented not."
16:10-11	Fifth	1866-1870	Papacy Loses Temporal Power. Papal Austria overthrown by Protestant Prussia (Sadowa, July 3, 1866). Ecumenical Council at Rome, Dec. 8, 1869 -- Nov. 11, 1870. Rome and Papal States incorporated into Italy, Oct. 9.
16:12-16	Sixth	1917- today	"Drying-up" of Turkish Woe ("Euphrates"). Loss of Palestine, Mesopotamia, etc., followed by Third Woe, Bolshevism.
16:17-21	Seventh	1917- today	Bombs and missiles, the "great hail" that falls, of World War One, Two and Three.

The "Holy Roman Empire" Defeated
(Chapter 17)
(1789 A.D. to present)

The 17th and 18th chapters supplement the Vials just as the 12th, 13th and 14th chapters supplement the Trumpets and the 7th chapter supplements the Seals. The time frame is now the Seventh Vial since that is when "Babylon comes to remembrance before God, to receive the cup of the fierceness of his wrath" (Rev. 16:19). Therefore, the 17th chapter may be that "remembrance" elaborating on Revelation 16:19.

"And there came one of the seven angels which had the seven vials, and talked with me, saying unto me, Come hither; I will shew unto thee the judgment of the great whore that sitteth upon many waters: With whom the kings of the earth have committed fornication, and the inhabitants of the earth have been made drunk with the wine of her fornication" (Rev. 17:1-2).

Who is the "great WHORE"? Astronomically, Virgo who sits upon the seven-headed Hydra that comes out of Crater -- the cup of darkness, tohu-bohu, the bottomless pit. God's TRUE CHURCH is like a PURE WOMAN: "I have likened the daughter of Zion ("my people" -- Isa. 51:16) to a comely and delicate WOMAN" (Jer. 6:2; cp. Isa. 62:5; Rev. 19:7-8; Eph. 5:23; 2 Cor. 11:2). Therefore, when John "saw" a "GREAT WHORE," we know she is a FALSE CHURCH. Idolatrous Israel was called a "WHORE" (Isa. 1:21; Ez. 16:28-33; Jer. 3:3; 13:27). Spiritual "HARLOTRY" is idolatry which is the worship of demons (1 Cor. 8:1-5; 10:20-21; 1 Tim. 4:1; Ps. 96:5). Even the name VATICAN means "place of Divinations" (Ancient Monuments of Rome, p.75). The Roman Catholic Church is a drunk, domineering woman. She has many images and idols. In 1564 Pius IV, in the 8th Article of his New Creed, stated, "I most firmly assert that the images of Christ, or the Mother of God, ever Virgin, and also of other saints, may be had and retained: and that due honour and veneration are to be given to them." But far from taking the place of Christ in worship, Mary herself said, "Whatsoever he (Jesus) says unto you, do it" (John 2:5). The second commandment is omitted from Roman Catechisms. But God says, "Thou shalt not make unto thee a graven image (which would include possessing)... thou shalt not bow down thyself unto them (which would include honoring and respecting), nor serve them" (Ex. 20:4-6). To even set up a cross as a religious sign is to "serve" it. But men become addicted to power and a paycheck and will preach whatever is required to get it -- even idolatry. John identified this woman as a HARLOT because she was dressed like a temple prostitute --with a special religious uniform that only temple prostitutes wore. Speaking plainly, she was dressed like a NUN. "Witchcraft" adds up to 666 if A=6, B=12, C=18, etcetera.

What are the "many WATERS"? Jer. 51:13 says, "O thou (Babylon) that dwellest upon many WATERS, abundant in treasures, thine end is come." "The WATERS ...

are PEOPLES... and NATIONS" (Rev. 17:15). Recall that the EUPHRATES (Tiber, Hudson) ran through BABYLON (Rome, New York) and sometimes overflowed its banks becoming a SWAMP. Rome (Babylon, New York) boasts of being "CATHOLIC" or "Worldwide" just as the true church is a "nation and company of nations" of one stock with Gentiles grafted in. A medal of Pope Leo XII, issued in a Jubilee Year, 1825, shows a woman sitting on a GLOBE, her right arm extended holding a cup of the Mass, by which Transubstantiation is taught, which fatally intoxicates adherents. Around the figure is the legend: Sedet super Universum -- "She sits over the whole EARTH." This image bears a striking resemblance to the Statue of Liberty. Both wear a long flowing robe, have seven horns coming from their heads and hold a golden "cup."

"So he carried me away in the spirit into the wilderness: and I saw a woman sit upon a scarlet coloured beast, full of names of blasphemy, having seven heads and ten horns. And the woman was arrayed in purple and scarlet colour, and decked with gold and precious stones and pearls, having a golden cup in her hand full of abominations and filthiness of her fornication" (Rev. 17:3-4).

Astronomically, Virgo sits on Hydra with Crater in her hand. Stars are the "precious stones and pearls." But where is this "WILDERNESS"? Historically, the "wilderness" is the desolate Campagna of Rome. This wilderness condition was brought about by barbarian raids upon Imperial Rome in the fifth and sixth centuries when they spoiled, desolated and burned Rome and the regions surrounding it. "About the close of the sixth century ... the Campagna of Rome was speedily reduced to the state of a dreary wilderness, in which the land is barren, the waters impure, and the air infectious ... In a season of excessive rains, the Tiber swelled above its banks, and rushed into the valleys of the Seven Hills. A pestilential disease arose from the stagnation of the deluge" (Gibbon ch. 45). When Papal Rome supplanted Imperial Rome, the Campagna of Rome continued in this condition all through the 1,260 year period of her temporal supremacy. In times of flooding, such as Gibbon described above, and which still occurred in the twentieth century, Rome viewed from a distance would literally appear as if sitting upon many waters.

What are the "names of BLASPHEMY"? The "names of blasphemy" are "Holy Reverend Father," "Vicar of Christ," and "Infallible," when referring to the Pope since "Holy and reverend is His (God's) name" (Ps. 111:9) and "Call no man your Father" (Matt. 23:9). "Mother of God," "Mary the Co-Mediatrix" and "Assumption of Mary" are blasphemous when referring to Mary (This is why Jesus called her "woman," never "mother"); also "Kingdom of God" when referring to the "Holy Roman Empire." "The Lord alone shall be exalted in that day" (Isa. 2:17). When the Pope is crowned in St. Peter's, a triple crown, called a tiara, is placed on his head with the words, "Receive this tiara, adorned with three crowns, and know thyself to be the father of princes and of kings, and the ruler of the world." The Vandals, Ostrogoths and Lombards were in dangerous proximity to Rome, so the Papacy "plucked up (these) three ... by the roots" (Dan. 7:8, 24). Some writers believe this is the original meaning of the triple crown. When the Papacy got its temporal power at the expense of these three

neighboring states, the triple crown became the permanent memorial of this event. The Messiah will have "many crowns" upon his head. Pope Gregory VIII declared, "We desire to show to the world that we can give or take away at our will, kingdoms, duchies, earldoms, in a word the possessions of all men we can bind or loose." Boniface VIII said, "The Pope alone is called Most Holy, Divine Monarch, Supreme Emperor, the King of Kings."

Who is the "SCARLET-colored BEAST"? This dragon is the Roman Empire (Rev. 12:3-4). "Though your sins be as SCARLET" (Isa. 1:18) shows that the "Holy Roman Empire" is very sinful. Its IRON teeth and BRONZE nails (Dan.7:19) indicate that it occupies Roman and Greek territory -- the two legs (Rome and Constantinople) of Nebuchadnezzar's statute. But all ten toes are in the western half because they are IRON or CLAY -- not BRASS. The "SEVEN HEADS" are Justinian (527-565 A.D.), Charlemagne (800-814 A.D.), Otto the Great, (962-973 A.D.), Frederick Barbarossa (1152-1190 A.D.), Charles V (1520-1556 A.D.), Louis XIV (1661-1715 A.D.) and Napoleon (1804-1814 A.D.) The "TEN HORNS" are Ostrogoths (Hungary & Yugoslavia), Visigoths (Spain), Vandals (N. Africa), Sueves (Portugal), Franks (France), Burgundians (Switzerland & South Gaul), Heruli (Italy), Huns (Alemani), Lombards (Austria & Czechoslovakia) and Anglo-Saxons (England). These were the ten kingdoms that the Roman Empire split into after 476 A.D. Three separate authors all testify that these were the ten Gothic kingdoms -- Gibbon, Procopius and Machiavelli (Hist. Floe.i). The Roman Catholic

Church controls and directs the ten-nation Roman Empire -- she rides it. Anciently, the ten-nation Hittite Confederacy (Gen.15:19-21), composed mainly of Canaanites or Phoenicians (Φενεχ), a name which adds up to 666 in Greek (Φ=6, ε=5, ν=50, ε=5, χ=600), opposed Israel and was a type of Roman Catholic Europe. Just as three horns were "plucked up" from one, so we read about the "seven" nations of Canaan later composing the other (Josh.24:11; Acts 13:19). In fact, Jezebel, a type of the Papacy, was a "Phoenician woman" or φοινικεα which in Greek adds up to 666. φ=500, ο=70, ι=10, ν=50, ι=10, κ=20, ε=5, α=1. Moses and Elijah opposed the ten nations of Canaan. Wycliffe and Luther (and many others) opposed the ten nations of Catholic Europe. Later and more strongly, William of Orange and Henry VIII opposed the ten nations of Catholic Europe. Two more witnesses will oppose ten future kings

"Purple" is worn by Roman Bishops. "Scarlet" is worn by Roman Cardinals. Now compare ancient Babylon's rulers who were "clothed with scarlet" (Dan. 5:16) and Chaldeans portrayed "in bright red" (Ez. 23:14). Scarlet, pearls, gold and precious stones are mentioned three times (17:4; 18:4,16) in chapters 17 and 18 and are the precise adornments of the Papal robes, the altars, the vessels, the images and the furnishings of the Church of Rome. They are the pomp of Papal Rome. The Church of Rome decks her bishops and cardinals and principal images with gold and jewels. The Bambino or image of the infant Christ in Rome, for example, is loaded with jewels. The regular priests are black-robed Baal worshippers because Zephaniah 1:4 mentions "Chemarim" from the Hebrew root "kamar" (Strong's #3648) meaning "to be black" because they wore black robes. They wear "vestments" (2 Kings 10:22). The cross combined with the oval (or yoni) forms the Crux Ansata or Ankh -- an old Egyptian symbol indicating the conjunction of the two sexes. Worn as part of the Papal religious dress, it is called the priest's PALLIUM or SURPLICE. The prelate's head is passed through the yoni. Today's Roman priests more often wear the ancient sistrum of Isis or the yoni of Hindus (no cross). It is symbolic of the celestial virgin. When donned by a Christian priest, he resembles pagan male worshippers, who wore a female dress when they performed sacred rites before the altar or shrine of the goddess. This is PHALLIC and YONIC worship. A man shall not "put on a woman's garment." This is an "abomination" (Deut. 22:5). Contrast all this with the plain "white robes" of the saints who are "clothed with humility."

What is the "GOLDEN CUP"? Astronomically Crater is the cup. Historically, "BABYLON hath been a GOLDEN CUP in the Lord's hand, that made all the earth drunken: the nations have drunken of her wine; therefore the nations are mad" (Jer. 51:7). The ancient queen Semiramis, who ruled over the city of Babylon, as well as the later nation of Babylon, poured out "wine" of false BABYLONIAN DOCTRINES (Jer. 51:7; Isa. 47:12-15) through the medium of a "GOLDEN CUP" -- one of God's holy vessels stolen from His Temple -- through which she toasted her gods (Dan. 5:1-4; Jer. 50:28; 51:7) and made the nations "drunken" (Jer. 51:7). The CUP of Semiramis was huge and weighed 1200 pounds (Pliny Nat. Hist. 33:15). In the Roman Catholic anti-type, the Bible and its ordinances are used as the medium to convey spiritual harlotry to the world. An idolatrous church deceptively pretends to worship God. "Abominations" refer to "idolatry" (2 Ki. 23:13; Isa. 44:19; Ez. 16:36) and other doctrines that came from Babylon such as weeping, bleeding, nodding, and winking images, indulgences (not rated according to the seriousness of the crime pardoned, but according to the income of the criminal), the confessional, extreme unction, incense, holy water, candles, host, monstrance, mass, flowers, bones, relics, enforced celibacy, infallibility, the rosary, penance, the tonsure, halo, purgatory, the cross, Christmas (Tammuz' birthday), Easter (Lady Day, March 25), Lent (Tammuz' death), Assumption (Isis' resurrection into heaven, Sept. 8), fan of Buddha, processions, steeples, the miter (from "Mithra"), crosier, nunneries, and monasteries, etcetera. All of these practices were borrowed from the religion of heathen Rome which came from Babylon. God said, "Ye shall break down their altars ... thou shalt not bring an abomination into thine house" (Deut. 7:5,26). We need only contrast the intellectual, moral, social and political conditions of Portugal, Spain, Italy and France with those of Great Britain to see the effects of drinking this intoxicating wine.

The chalice is the most important of the sacred vessels ... (It) may be of gold or of silver" (Catholic Encyclopedia pp.103-104). But this cup is "full of ABOMINATIONS and filthiness of her FORNICATION" (Rev. 17:4). Why? Because she demands her priests to be CELIBATE. This leads to fornication and homosexuality which are abominations, or to priests molesting choir boys. Paul wrote that a bishop should be "the husband of one wife" (1 Tim. 3:2; Titus 1:5-6). The Bible defines itself in Leviticus 20:13 which says, "If a man also lie with mankind, as he lieth with a woman, both of them have committed an ABOMINATION."

"And upon her forehead was a name written, MYSTERY, BABYLON THE GREAT, THE MOTHER OF HARLOTS AND ABOMINATIONS OF THE EARTH. And I saw the woman drunken with the blood of the saints, and with the blood of the martyrs of Jesus: and when I saw her, I wondered with great admiration" (Rev. 17:5-6).

Papal Rome's "forehead" is her history of beliefs and doctines. "Babylon" refers to the continuity of Papal Rome with the Babylon of Daniel and Isaiah 14 and 47. In fact, Isaiah 47 uses identical language with these two chapters of Revelation. "Pontifex Maximus" was the title of the High Priest of ancient Babylon. A custom common in St. John's day in Rome was for prostitutes to carry their name written on a label on their foreheads, where everyone but themselves could see and read it. "Babylon is another name for Rome" (Sibylline Oracles 5:159f; the Apocalypse of Baruch ii,1 and 4 Esdras 3:1). Tertullian wrote, "Babylon ... is a figure of the city of ROME" (Against the Jews). Augustine wrote that "ROME was founded as the second Babylon and as the daughter of the former Babylon" (City of God 5:439). In the same book Augustine again said, "Babylonia as the first ROME ... ROME itself is like a second Babylon" (ibid. p.371).

Why is she called "MYSTERY" ("of iniquity" -- 2 Th. 2:7-9) and why was John astonished? Because she is not what she seems. She is wearing a disguise. Claiming to be "Christian," but really Satanic. The Pope's tiara had a gold plate engraved with the title "MYSTERY" in Latin until 1553-1555 A.D., when Pope Julius III removed it because the Reformers identified it with Revelation 17:5. The Chaldean MYSTERIES were maintained by an oath of secrecy because IDOLATRY was forbidden by law (p.5, Hislop's Two Babylons). The Chaldean Mystery Cult baptized converts and traced a cross on their foreheads using saliva and salt. They worshipped a mother goddess (Semiramis) with a child (Tammuz) in her arms. They made round wafers or sun images to honor this "Queen of Heaven" (Jer.44:17-19; Jer. 7:18) with a cross on each standing for "Tammuz."

Why "the MOTHER of Harlots"? Anciently because Babylon had a bad reputation for sacred PROSTITUTION (Herodotus' History 1:199; Quintus Curtis v.1). Semiramis the Queen of Babylon committed harlotry with all the kings of the earth. More recently because nuns and priests must be CELIBATE leading them to immorality. Figuratively, the Lutherans, Anglicans, Baptists and Methodists all came from the Roman Catholic Mother and so they are DAUGHTER harlots to the extent they conform to Rome's rituals and doctrines. She has always called herself the "Mother" church. Convents have their "Mother Superior."

What "Abominations"? Anciently Freemasonry was founded on the mysteries of Isis and Osiris in the pantheon of Egypt which came directly from Babylon. "Freemason" in Hebrew adds up to 666. (נסשסמרו) ו=6, ר=200, מ=40, ש=300, ס=70, נ=50. The name "Osiris" (lit. "Seed man") adds up to 666 in Hebrew also. (צוראש) ש=300, א=70, ר=200, ו=6, צ=90). Another Egyptian god called "Amoun-Re" (Ham the Sun-god, son of Noah) also adds up to 666. (αμουν-ρε) α=1, μ=40, o=70, υ=400, ν=50, ρ=100, ε=5. The Hindu pantheon came directly from Babylon. The god Vishnu adds up to 666 also in Greek. (Φισνυ) Φ=6, ι=10 σ=200, ν=50, υ=400. The Greek pantheon came from Babylon. The god Dianus adds up to 666 in Greek. (Διανανσ) Δ=4, ι=10, α=1, ν=50, α=1, υ=400, σ=200. Also known as Janus (Yenes) which adds up to 666. (υηνησ) υ=400, η=8, ν=50, η=8, σ =200. Furthermore, one of Buddha's names was Jaines from where we got Janus or Yenes (p.337, Computation of 666). The religious philosophy of China known as Tao or Zadkiel Tao Sze (Zadkiel was the Chaldean name for Jupiter) also adds up to 666 in Greek. (Ζαδκιελ Ταο Σζη) Z=7, α=1, δ=4, κ=20, ι=10, ε=8, λ=30, T=300, α=1, o=70, Σ=200, ζ=7, η=8. In a more modern sense, Catholic dealings with the Bolsheviks, Nazis, Fascists, Sinn Fein, Mafia, and laundering drug money are fully documented in books, newspapers, police and court records.

From about the 6th century the Popes began to seek the aid of secular powers to suppress heresy. But in 1179 the Third Lateran Council declared open war on heretics. The Papacy persecuted Albigenses and Huguenots of France, Waldenses of Italy and Covenanters of Scotland. An estimated 50 million were slain and more tortured by the Pulley, Chafing Dish, Rack, Pendulum and Stake. This verse gives us the time of the vision. "Drunken" is past tense and retrospect whereas Revelation 13:7 gives a foreview of the future. This implies the time after the Reformation. Rome boasts she is "semper eadem" or "always the same." When a Roman priest is made Bishop, he takes an oath: "to persecute all heretics to the utmost of his power." The word "admiration" should be translated "astonishment." If the woman was heathen Rome, it would have caused him no surprise that she persecuted the saints. He himself was exiled to Patmos because of such persecution. What astonished him was that the woman

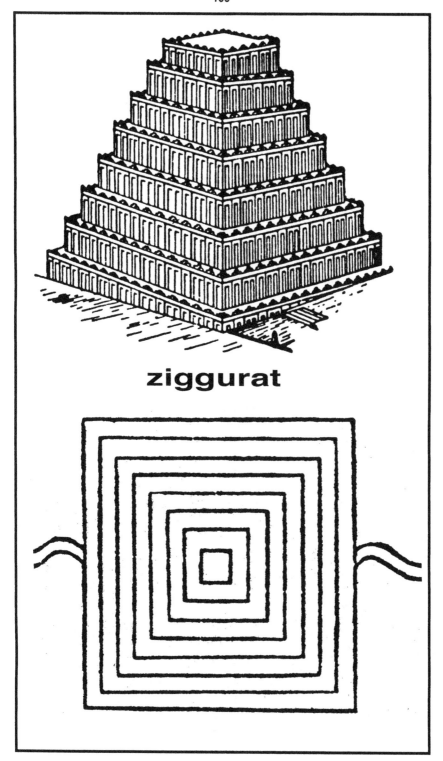

ziggurat

was a "Christian church" -- Papal Rome. "And the angel said unto me, Wherefore didst thou marvel? I will tell thee the mystery of the woman, and of the beast that carrieth her, which hath the seven heads and ten horns. The beast that thou sawest was, and is not; and shall ascend out of the bottomless pit, and go into perdition: and they that dwell on the earth shall wonder, whose names were not written in the book of life from the foundation of the world, when they behold the beast that was, and is not, and yet is" (Rev. 17:7-8).

Pagan Rome existed until 476 A.D. -- it "was." Then it was wounded to death by barbarians -- "is not." Then Papal Rome took the place of Pagan Rome in 554 A.D. -- "yet is." The Caesar was resurrected in the Pope. The beast came out of a "bottomless pit" (17:8). In the same way, the "man of sin" was to arise by means of "the working of Satan" (2 Th. 2:3,9). Satan gives the beast his "power, and his throne, and great authority" (Rev. 13:2). Therefore the "bottomless pit" must be where Satan works.

"And here is the mind which hath wisdom. The seven heads are seven mountains, on which the woman sitteth. And there are seven kings: five are fallen, and one is, and the other is not yet come; and when he cometh, he must continue a short space. And the beast that was, and is not, even he is the eighth, and is of the seven, and goeth into perdition"
(Rev. 17:9-11).

According to Herodotus 1:180-181, "Babylon being divided in the middle by the River Euphrates ... had on each side of the river an extraordinary structure. On one side of the river stood the royal palace ... on the other the temple of Jupiter Belus, existing yet in my time, and measuring in every direction 2 stadia (or 1250 feet) ... In the middle of this temple stood a massive tower 625 feet square at the base, and upon this another and another to the number of 8, and upon the last tower stood a great nave. And in the nave a great couch and a golden table; but no statue therein; and no man sleeps therein, say the Chaldean priests. Only some woman sleeps there whom the god may chance to like, for the god was said to come there in person." (cp. Dio. Sic. 2:7-8 & Plato's Republic) In other words, a harlot sat on a ziggurat of seven concentric man-made hills representing the seven planets -- counterfeits of the "seven stars" (Rev.1). Borsippa's Temple of the Seven Lights (Planets) dedicated to Nebo confirms this view. So do the seven pagodas stacked one on top of the other at Mahabalipur (lit. "Great Sun City"). The Eternal referred to Babylon's ziggurat as a "destroying mountain" (Jer. 51:25). The woman was Semiramis. The city of Rome is also situated on seven hills. Pliny mentions "the SEVEN HILLS" of Rome (Natural History 3:66). The Roman poets Virgil (Georg. 2:535) and Horace (Aen. 6:784; Carmen Saec.7) both call Rome the "SEVEN-HILLED" city. Martial calls them "SEVEN dominating MOUNTAINS" (Lib.4, Ep. 64, p.254). Propertius, the Latin poet, describes Rome as "The city high on SEVEN HILLS, That rules the boundless earth" (Lib.iii. Eleg. 9, p.721). They are called Palatinus, Quirinalis, Aventinus, Caelius, Viminalis, Esquilinus and Capitoline (or Janiculan). The old Roman imperial coins in John's day represented Rome as a woman seated on seven hills. The seven forms of government enumerated by Livy, Pliny and Tacitus were: 1. Kings (c.750-510 B.C.) 2. Consuls (510-498 B.C.) 3. Dictators (498-451 B.C.) 4. Decimvirs (451-443 B.C.) 5. Military Tribunes (443-27 B.C.) 6. Military Emperors (Imperial Caesars) (27 B.C.-284 A.D.) and 7. Despotic Emperors (284-313 A.D.), different from the preceding military Emperors because these last were absolute monarchs. This was the form "wounded to death" (Rev. 13:3) at the downfall of Pagan Rome (Edict of Toleration of Licinius). Christian Emperors beginning with Constantine, are not alluded to in this vision. Their seat was not at Rome, but at Constantinople for the Eastern Empire, and at Ravenna for the Western. It is not until the bishops and popes of Rome that a "head" again sits in Rome. The Papacy, therefore, is the "eighth" horn since the "little horn" uprooted three of the ten. It is the "eighth" head of Revelation 17:11. What eighth head? The woman's head, since the beast only had seven heads. Or if the "eighth" head took the place of the wounded seventh head, there would still just be seven heads on the beast. In John's day five systems had passed away -- were "fallen." Emperors (27 B.C.-284 A.D.) were ruling in John's day -- "one is." The form that had "not yet come" -- Despotic Emperors (284-313 A.D.) -- must continue a "short space" of barely thirty years, which truly was short compared to the eighth head -- the Papacy -- which was to continue 1260 years. "King" means "dynasty" since the four beasts are called four kings (Dan. 7:17) and Nebuchadnezzar and four successors reigned during the 70 years (Jer. 25:11). The Greek word "hora" translated "mountain" (Rev. 17:9) can also mean "continent" of which there are seven, rather than "seven mountains."

"And the ten horns which thou sawest are ten kings, which have received no kingdom as yet; but receive power as kings one hour with the beast. These have one mind, and shall give their power and strength unto the beast" (Rev. 17:12-13).

Ten states arose out of the old Roman Empire whose kings were crowned by the Pope and received authority from him and could not exercise it without him, thus acknowledging his overlordship. These are the "ten toes" of the statue of Daniel 2:42. Sir Isaac Newton said, "Seeing the body of the third beast is confined to the nations on this side of the Euphrates, and the body of the fourth beast is confined to the nations on this side of Greece, we are to look for all the four heads of the third beast among the nations on this side of the Euphrates, and for all the eleven horns of the fourth beast among the nations on this side of Greece. Therefore we do not reckon the Greek empire seated at Constantinople among the horns of the fourth beast, because it belongs to the body of the third."

"They have received no kingdom as yet" in 96 A.D. when John wrote. But after 476 A.D. "they receive power ... one hour" (Rev. 17:12). The twelfth part of a 360-day year is 30 days and since a day is a year (Num. 14:34; Ez. 4:6), the last "Holy Roman Empire" will last 30 years. The literal Greek is "mia hora" or "at one and the same time." These nations are all found in western Europe. Historically the ten horns were the Ostrogoths (Hungary & Yugoslavia), Visigoths (Spain), Vandals (N. Africa), Sueves (Portugal), Franks (France), Burgundians (Switzerland & S. Gaul), Heruli (Italy), Huns (Alemani), Lombards (Austria & Czechoslavakia) and Anglo-Saxons (England). Three separate authors all testify that these were the ten Gothic kingdoms

-- Gibbon, Procopius and Machiavelli (Hist. Floe. i). All ten horns must be confined to the western Roman Empire so that they are not considered part of the third or Greek (Byzantine) beast. Sometimes they have sunk to eight or nine, or have risen to eleven or twelve, but have averaged ten. They are Satan's counterfeit of the lost ten tribes of Israel, who were nine when Benjamin was lent to Judah and are thirteen if we separately count Manasseh or include Judah. The E.E.C. or "Common Market" was created January 1st, 1958. The original six were Italy, France, West Germany, Belgium, Holland and Luxembourg. Britain joined in January 1st of 1973, followed by Denmark, then Eire. Greece joined in 1981, followed by Spain and Portugal in 1986. When the Maastricht Treaty was signed in 1992, there were 25 members, but only ten permanent members. (Older German maps spell "Maastricht" as "Mastricht" which adds up to 666 when A=6, B=12, C=18 ...). The E.C. anthem is "Ode to Joy" with lyrics by Friedrich von Schiller set to music by Beethoven in his 9th Symphony, composed in honour of the Goddess of Liberty (Isis). Just as Britain historically dropped out of the ten-nation "Holy Roman Empire" in the fifteenth century, so she will "Come out" (Rev. 18:4) of this "Common Market" again in the end time. "And your covenant (treaty) with death shall be annulled, and your agreement with hell shall not stand" (Isa. 28:18). When the Russian bear destroys this "Babylon" (Roman Catholic Europe) by marching through the dried up riverbed of the Euphrates (Turkish Empire) just as the Medo-Persian bear marched anciently under Babylon's city wall through the riverbed, then Russia itself will be destroyed in Revelation 19:17-19.

"These shall make war with the Lamb, and the Lamb shall overcome them: for he is Lord of lords, and King of kings: and they that are with him are called, and chosen, and faithful" (Rev. 17:14).

The ten civil powers were compelled to carry out the edicts of the Papacy against heretics and against Britain-Israel. From the days of the Reformation onwards, both the true Church and the Protestant British Empire have "gotten the victory over the beast" of Catholic Europe.

"And he saith unto me, The waters which thou sawest, where the whore sitteth, are peoples, and multitudes, and nations, and tongues. And the ten horns which thou sawest upon the beast, these shall hate the whore, and shall make her desolate and naked, and shall eat her flesh, and burn her with fire. For God hath put in their hearts to fulfil his will, and to agree, and give their kingdom unto the beast, until the words of God shall be fulfilled" (Rev. 17:15-17).

Jesus also described these "waters" as "Sea and waves roaring" (Luke 21:25) as if "drunken" and at war. Stripping and turning out of doors was a common punishment for a woman convicted of adultery (See Tacitus Germ. 130; Ez. 16:39; 23:29). GERMANY began the Reformation in 1517 and was first to "burn her." BRITAIN was next in 1536 when thousands of monasteries and convents were destroyed. The NETHERLANDS and SWITZERLAND also threw off the Pope's supremacy in the sixteenth century. The Church possessed nearly a third of the lands of Europe before the French Revolution. Then FRANCE in 1789 with the French Revolution. France slew 2,000,000 people within five years. 24,000 priests were murdered and 40,000 churches turned into stables. The Roman Catholic religion was abolished in France. The Pope was forced to attend Napoleon's coronation in 1804 where Napoleon crowned himself, thereby putting the "beast" (or secular power) above the "woman" (Papacy) who was no longer carried by it (Rev. 17:7). The impact of the French Revolution spread to other Roman Catholic countries by means of the printing press and revolutionary agents. February 11th, 1798, Napoleon's general Berthier took Rome and established the Roman Republic February 15th 1798. Pope Pius VI was taken prisoner and he died in exile. The Vatican was plundered and stripped naked to its bare walls. The Roman Catholic Church was disestablished in France by law December 1905, thereby dissolving the alliance formed by Napoleon in 1801. A year later this law was made even stricter, with disastrous results for Rome. In 1907 France separated the Roman Catholic Church from the state, appropriated her estates, and expelled thousands of priests, monks and nuns from the country. ITALY next when Garibaldi overthrew the Papal States of Italy in stages: in October 1866 Venetia fell and in October 1870 Tuscany fell. In 1870 Italy dethroned the Pope and put an end to his temporal power. On 18th, February 1984, the Vatican was compelled to sign a new Concordat with the socialist Premiere of Italy. Almost all that had been granted by Mussolini in the Lateran Treaty of 1929 has been lost. Roman Catholicism ceases to be the state religion of Italy. Tax exempt status of the clergy is stripped away and power over the education system is broken. In 1910, PORTUGAL confiscated the estates of the Roman Catholic Church and drove the priests, monks and nuns from the country. Catholic schools were closed. The Church of Rome was disestablished. Since World War One, Mexico and South America also disestablished the Roman Catholic Church. SPAIN restricted its activities on proclamation of a Republic in April, 1931. The revolution in Spain, 1936-1938, came next. Communists carried out the identical atrocities on Roman Catholics which the Church of Rome had perpetrated on Protestants in those very same cities during the Spanish Inquisition. The wealth of the Church was confiscated. Her buildings were burned. Thousands of her clergy were killed. Communism on the fringe of Europe has already put to death or enslaved tens of thousands of Roman Catholic priests and nuns, destroyed thousands of churches and religious buildings, and confiscated vast amounts of "religious" property.

"And the woman which thou sawest is that great city, which reigneth over the kings of the earth" (Rev. 17:18).

Rome was the only city on seven hills reigning over kings in John's day. Rome is also the only city that has given its name to an ecclesiastical system.

158

Medals struck by King of France honoring Revocation of the Edict of Nantes, 1685 A.D. Huguenots were expelled for heresy -- not politics. "Heresies Extinguished" and "Religion Conqueror -- Calvn's Temple Overthrown."

Medal of Pope Paul II, showing the Bohemian Hussites being hunted as wild boars, A.D. 1469. The inscription on the reverse is: "The pious Shepherd wages war only against wild beasts."

Medal of Pope Gregory XIII, to commemorate the Massacre of St. Bartholemew, A.D. 1572. The inscription reads "Massacre of the Huguenots."

The Russian Invasion of Europe
(Chapter 18)
(near future)

The woman Babylon "is the great city which reigneth over the kings of the earth" (17:18). Therefore, chapter 18 describes the destruction of Roman Catholic Europe ("Latin-German" civilization). Babylon was briefly destroyed in Rev. 14:8 with the Protestant Reformation and sack of Rome; and then again in Rev. 16:19-21 as the judgment of the seventh vial of World War Two when Catholic nations were devastated. But Roman Catholic Europe will be completely destroyed by Russia (Rev. 18). The symbolism in Revelation 18 is all based on Old Testament prophecies of: 1. Isaiah concerning ancient Babylon which fell to the Medo-Persians in 539 B.C. and 2. Ezekiel concerning the fall of Tyre to Nebuchadnezzar in 572 B.C. Those historic events were types of the destruction of Roman Catholic Europe in the near future.

"And after these things I saw another angel come down from heaven, having great power; and the earth was lightened with his glory. And he cried mightily with a strong voice, saying, Babylon the great is fallen, is fallen, and is become the habitation of devils, and the hold of every foul spirit, and a cage of every unclean and hateful bird" (Rev. 18:1-2).

Who is this glorious ANGEL? Astronomically the angel with "great power" is Hercules (SAMSON). The "devils" are Drago, Serpens, Hydra and Cetus. The "unclean and hateful" birds are Corvus, Aquilla, Lyra and Cygnus. Also the Arab version of Eridanus portrays Ostriches and in Libra is an Owl. Historically, Paul defines Him as "the LORD (who) shall ... destroy with the brightness of his coming" the Man of Sin (2 Th. 2:8). Just as the "mighty ANGEL" of the Reformation (Rev. 10:1) was identified as CHRIST, so there will be a second Reformation which will "restore all things" (Matt. 17:11) more POWERFULLY by pulling down the Roman Catholic Philistine Temple in the British Empire and U.S. CHRIST will be preached by Reformers who don't "deny the POWER (OBEDIENCE -- Tit. 1:16) thereof" (2 Tim. 3:5). During the Third World War (or Russian phase of the 7th vial on "Babylon" in Rev. 18), Protestant Anglo-Saxondom will more fully OBEY God by means of the "latter rain" Holy Spirit (Joel 2:28-32; 3:1-2; James 5:7; Zech.10) which God gives "to those who OBEY him" (Acts 5:32).

Verse 2 is a summary of the numerous Old Testament prophecies of the Medo-Persian conquest of the ancient Babylon and of her ally Edom (Jer. 50:38-39; 51:8). The same historic destruction of Babylon and Edom was foretold by Isaiah who also linked them anti-typically with the "Day of the Lord" (Isa. 13:19-22; 34:9-15; Isa. 47:1-9). The totality of the desolation is indicated by the description of the land as a desert in which only evil spirits and unclean birds would dwell. "Is fallen, is fallen" refers to 539 B.C. and 1870 A.D. and the end-time. Verses 22 and 23 confirm the utter desolation of European civilization by comparing it to the cessation of all civil and social life in ancient Babylon (Isa. 24:8) and ancient Tyre (Ez. 26:13) and ancient Judea during the seventy years captivity (Jer. 25:9-11).

What would cause this kind of DESOLATION? A volcanic eruption maybe. There are ancient craters in and around Rome which could become active again. VESUVIUS is now active. NUCLEAR radiation and fall-out is also likely. They "Stand afar off for fear of her (radiation) torment" (18:10). It comes suddenly. "In one hour is thy judgment come" (18:10). There is fire and smoke.

Just as Babylon typified Roman Catholic Europe historically, so Babylon is today also represented by the United States. All were or are military SUPERPOWERS (Jer. 50:23; 51:20; Isa. 14:4-6) and two REPUBLICS. The United States is a leader in violence, drug-abuse, pornography and greed -- where homosexuality and abortion are allowed in public but the Bible is not allowed in the classroom. Just as Rome's false Papal religion was offered to the world to DRINK, so America's Hollywood "entertainment" industry, rock music and permissiveness have been DRUNK worldwide. Babylon is described as a lion with "EAGLE'S wings" (Dan. 7:4) and the SNAKE and the EAGLE have been symbols of both Rome and the U.S. Just as SEMIRAMIS invited the world's KINGS once a year to have ritual SEX with her on the New Year festival, and if they lived through the night, they were permitted to rule another year, so also the POPE invited KINGS to unite church and state in CONCORDATS with the Vatican and if they served her loyally they were not deposed. AMERICA also invites world LEADERS to visit "Lady Liberty" in New York for the U.N. If they are willing to follow corrupt American policies, they remain in power. Otherwise, they receive sanctions. She moved from Babylon to Rome to New York (Zech. 5:5-11). The LIBERTINE Semiramis became the goddess LIBERTAS worshipped at a temple on Aventine Hill in Rome, and later became the idolatrous "Statue of LIBERTY," facing east, standing in New York, inviting the world's multi-ethnic, multi-religious "wretched refuse" to integrate and intermarry and become "one" people just like at Babel (Gen. 11:6). The Italian Bertholdi was seeking a commission to construct a statue of the goddess Isis -- the Egyptian "queen of heaven" (Jer. 7:18; 44:16-19) -- to overlook the Suez Canal. Instead she was given to the U.S. The SEVEN spikes in her sunburst crown represent enlightenment of the sun god upon the seven continents and seven seas -- translated "seven hills." Staten Island even has seven hills. Isis or Ishtar was known in ancient Babylon as the "goddess of personal FREEDOM" and "mother of IMMIGRANTS." Instead of the ten commandments inscribed on her tablet, we find the date July 4, 1776 when she set men FREE from the laws of Britain-Israel's God. Her pedestal has TEN pyramid-like points plus one that is "stouter than his fellows" (Dan. 7:20). The statue has SEVEN concentric levels or floors in its foundation -- "SEVEN hills." The "golden CUP" is "full of abominations" just as the natural gas TORCH is smelly. It was painted gold in the 1980s. Just as God destroyed the tower of Babel, and allowed Moslems to destroy Constantinople, and barbarians to destroy Rome, so also the TWIN TOWERS were destroyed. "Is fallen, is fallen" is stated twice. The World Trade Center was destroyed in little over "ONE HOUR" and the whole world has seen "the SMOKE of her BURNING" on TV. There is a predominantly Jewish community of over

200,000 actually called "BABYLON" about 30 miles west of the World Trade Center site on Long Island, where ships must pass to enter the harbor, but right next to the Twin Towers the area around the Stock Exchange is known as "Little BABYLON." God tells his people to escape (Jer. 51:45; Zech. 2:7). The World Bank, Wall Street, United Nations, and Lady of Liberty all are in New York. Merchants mourn because nobody buys her products anymore after 9-11. "NEW YORK" actually adds up to 666 if A=6, B=12, C=18, etcetera. In a larger sense, the entire United States typifies Babylon because the statue of LIBERTAS, goddess of Rome, stands atop the U.S. Capitol building and MARS (Marduk) stands at its entrance. On the spring and fall equinox the main street of Washington D.C., Constitution Avenue, aligns to her home star SIRIUS. On June 21 the Washington Monument (Baal's PHALLUS) is in perfect alignment with the sun. The name of the sun god Utu's temple in Babylon was the "WHITE HOUSE." The Jefferson Memorial was modeled after the pagan Roman Pantheon and the Lincoln Memorial after the pagan Greek Parthenon. The significance of the United States typifying Babylon is that it will be overthrown "as Sodom and Gomorrah" (Isa. 13:19) and "be desolate forever" (Jer. 50:39-40; 51:62). Anciently when the Medes and Persians conquered Babylon, the city remained populated and barely a "shot" was "fired." It wasn't until 1400 A.D. that the water source ran out and the city was covered with sand. Jeremiah's prophecies have never been fulfilled. They sound like nuclear devastation from Medo-Persia (Russia) on a modern "Babylon." Just as the Israelites dwelt north of Babylon in MEDIA, so also the Israelites dwelt north of the Roman Empire in SCANDINAVIA-BRITAIN and the Israelites dwell north of the United States in CANADA. Mexicans believe the American southwest belongs to them and by 2050, 100 million immigrants will live there supported by the Catholic Church. They call it the "Reconquista." Just as Rome was symbolized by a DRAGON and an EAGLE, so is Mexico. The ten horns of this Mexican Catholic Union will be

Papal medal struck at Rome in 1825 shows Mother Rome (Ishtar) offering her cup of apostasy and transubstantiation to the world. "Ashtoreth" actually means "Turret Woman" or "Tower Woman" from TR in Hebrew. The "Statue of Liberty" tower was dedicated 28th October, 1886.

Texas, New Mexico, Arizona, California, Nevada, Utah, Colorado, Oklahoma, Arkansas and Louisiana with the Rockies and Mississippi being the dividing line from Moslems. Amazingly, both the European Union and Estados Unidos have E.U. as their abbreviation. Both are called "United States" (of Europe or of America).

"For all nations have drunk of the wine of the wrath of her fornication, and the kings of the earth have committed fornication with her, and the merchants of the earth are waxed rich through the abundance of her delicacies" (Rev. 18:3).

Anciently sacred temple prostitutes committed fornication with their followers who contributed offerings to the Temple -- all under the pretense of worshipping God. This gaudily dressed harlot made her clients drunk on false doctrines and idolatry which she poured into holy vessels stolen from God's Temple (cp. Dan. 5:3-4) and her clients gave her gifts. Hannah may have been referring to this practice when she said to Eli in the Temple, "I have drunk neither wine nor strong drink ... Count not thine handmaid for a daughter of Belial" (1 Sam. 1:15-16). This spiritual DRUNKENESS is the "COVERING cast over all people, and the VEIL that is spread over all nations" (Isa. 25:7) of blindness (2 Cor. 3:14-16). God's "feast of wines" in the kingdom (Isa. 25:6) will make people SOBER spiritually.

"And I heard another voice from heaven, saying, Come out of her, my people, that ye be not partakers of her sins, and that ye receive not of her plagues" (Rev. 18:4).

"Flee out of the midst of Babylon ... be not cut off in her iniquity" (Jer. 51:6,45). "Deliver thyself, O Zion, that dwellest with the daughter of Babylon" (Zech. 2:7; Micah 4:10). Physically and spiritually, in type and anti-type. Anciently the Jews had been in Babylonian captivity for a long time. Their restoration under Cyrus -- an "anointed" "shepherd" (Isa. 44:28; 45:1) -- a type of Christ -- was at hand as soon as Babylon was destroyed. "My people" refers to Israel (Ezekiel 38:16) or to anybody who obeys the Bible (Christians) (Lev. 26:12, Hos. 1:9-10; 2 Cor. 6:16-18). Jews fled from Babylon to Palestine. The Angles, Saxons, Jutes and Danes fled from the Roman Empire to Britain. Britain will come out of the E.E.C. "Common Market" since there is no "Common Market" under Communism. Americans will flee from the U.S. to British Columbia or Australia. "U.S. of America" adds up to 666 using A=6, B=12, C=18, etc.

The "voice from heaven" (Rev. 18:4) is "the coming of Elijah the prophet." God will raise up "Elijah the Prophet," and support him with signs and wonders to tell Anglo-Saxons the true Biblical doctrines and expose false Roman Catholic doctrines (Isaiah 52:7-8; Isaiah 40:1-10; Malachi 3:1; 4:5-6). The seventh vial of Revelation 16:17, and its details in Revelation 18, terminates in the "great and terrible day" of God's wrath. Malachi 4:5-6 foretells that just before this same "terrible day," God will send to Israel "Elijah the prophet" to turn our hearts back to Him in obedience. Anciently God used Elijah to humiliate and destroy Jezebel's prophets of Baal. God will again use "Elijah" to humiliate and destroy Roman Catholic clergy. Therefore the "voice from heaven" (Rev. 18:4) is "the coming of Elijah the prophet," and when the Roman

"Babylon" and American "Babylon" are in smoking ruins from the Communists, the voice of God's servant will be heralding forth the truth to the Anglo-Saxon nations. We will accept the doctrinal truths when "Elijah" comes to "restore all things" (Matt. 17:11) because his miracles will prove that God is working through him. Thus when God's vengeance is being poured out on the Roman Catholic Europe, and Roman Catholic America, His mercy will be poured out on Bible-obeying Britain and Canada and Australia (Jer. 50:15, 28; 51:11). Notice the pattern. The annihilation of Edom and Babylon in Isaiah 34 is followed by the "ransomed of the Lord returning to Zion" in Isaiah 35. The desolation of Babylon in Isaiah 13 is followed by the mercy of the Lord on Israel and their land in Isaiah 14. While Babylon is falling in Isaiah 48:20, the Lord redeems his servant Jacob (48:20). When God has judged Tyre in Ezekiel 26, 27, and 28, He is sanctified in Israel who then knows Him as her Lord and God in Ezekiel 28:25-26.

During the seventh and last vial on the air, the plague of the Russian "hail" or aerial invasions, the Exodus of the Protestant nations from Roman Catholic civilization will occur led by "Elijah." Then God will intervene and deliver his people from the Russian yoke by the second coming of Christ, the "anointed Shepherd."

"For her sins have reached unto heaven, and God hath remembered her iniquities. Reward her even as she rewarded you, and double unto her double according to her works: in the cup which she hath filled fill to her double. How much she hath glorified herself, and lived deliciously, so much torment and sorrow give her: for she saith in her heart, I sit a queen, and am no widow, and shall see no sorrow" (Rev. 18:5-7).

Like ancient Babylon toasting pagan gods with Israel's Temple utensils while the Medo-Persian armies surround its wall (Isa. 47:1,6-9); like the Church of Rome during the seventh vial refusing to repent of her claims to being the eternal spouse of her "Vicar-of-Christ" Pope while Russian armies invade Europe; so also Catholic America will refuse to repent of her unbiblical doctrines as bombs rain down from Communist China. Like ancient Babylon's tower that reached heaven (Gen. 11:4), so medieval and modern Europe's and America's "sins have reached unto heaven" (Rev.18:5). She repudiates any suggestion that these are judgments of God. She is the persecutor of God's servants from Abel onwards, whose Cain-like civilization has always brought wars and bloodshed to God's people. The Catholic Church glorifies its buildings at the expense of the poverty-stricken communities that surround it. No wonder the Italian and Spanish peasants vote for Communism which teaches "Religion is the opiate of the people." The Virgin daughter of Babylon says, "I shall be a lady forever ... the lady of kingdoms ... I shall not sit as a widow, neither shall I know the loss of children." She doesn't mourn over her lost husband, Jesus Christ, as the true church does. Her children broke away during the Protestant Reformation, and will be completely lost to her in the future. But God answers her and says, "Desolation shall come upon thee suddenly ... none shall save thee" (Isa. 47:7,5,11,15).

Why DOUBLE? "For all manner of trespass, whether it be for ox, for ass, for sheep, for raiment, or for any manner of lost thing, which another challenges to be his, the cause of both parties shall come before the judges; and whom the judges shall condemn, he shall pay DOUBLE unto his neighbor" (Ex. 22:9).

"Therefore shall her plagues come in one day, death, and mourning, and famine; and she shall be utterly burned with fire: for strong is the Lord God who judgeth her. And the kings of the earth, who have committed fornication and lived deliciously with her, shall bewail her, and lament for her, when they shall see the smoke of her burning" (Rev. 18:8-9).

Astronomically, the "smoke" is the Milky Way. Historically, Communist Russia's "kings of the east" will annihilate the civil, commercial Roman Catholic Europe in World War Three. Catholic America will be destroyed. It will occur quickly and violently, like a heavy millstone cast into the sea. "One day" refers to one year (Num. 14:34; Ez. 4:6). "Make bright the arrows, gather the shields; the Eternal hath raised up the spirit of the kings of the Medes, for his device is against Babylon, to destroy it, because it is the vengeance of the Eternal, the vengeance of his temple" (Jer. 51:11, 20-29) from where the golden cup was stolen. But the ten Latin-German nations of Europe make the religious Roman Catholic Church "desolate and naked." They will "eat her flesh, and burn her with fire." This suggests violent anti-Catholic Communist Revolutions throughout Europe such as occurred in Spain in 1936-1938. France, Italy, Portugal and Spain have the largest Communist parties today outside the Iron Curtain countries and are controlled by Socialism.

"Standing afar off for the fear of her torment, saying, Alas, alas, that great city Babylon, that mighty city! for in one hour is thy judgment come. And the merchants of the earth shall weep and mourn over her; for no man buyeth their merchandise any more: The merchandise of gold, and silver, and precious stones, and of pearls, and fine linen, and purple, and silk, and scarlet, and all thyine wood, and all manner vessels of ivory, and all manner vessels of most precious wood, and of brass, and iron, and marble" (Rev. 18:10-12).

To see a smoking city "afar off" is to see it on television. If there are twelve hours in a day (John 11:9) and a day is one year, "one hour" is 30 days. Rome and her empire will be destroyed in 30 days. Rome has priceless art treasures. The interior walls of St. Peter's are enriched with precious stones, offerings of devotees. The city is full of shrines at which similar offerings have been made. Catholics believe that costly gifts to the church of Rome purchase favor in heaven. That is why wealth is concentrated in Rome.

"And cinnamon, and odours, and ointments, and frankincense, and wine, and oil, and fine flour, and wheat, and beasts, and sheep, and horses, and chariots, and slaves, and souls of men. And the fruits that thy soul lusted after are departed from thee, and all things which were dainty and goodly are departed from thee, and thou shalt find them no more at all. The merchants of these things, which were made rich by her, shall stand afar off for the fear of her torment, weeping and wailing, And saying,

Alas, alas, that great city, that was clothed in fine linen, and purple, and scarlet, and decked with gold, and precious stones, and pearls! For in one hour so great riches is come to nought. And every shipmaster, and all the company in ships, and sailors, and as many as trade by sea, stood afar off, And cried when they saw the smoke of her burning, saying, What city is like unto this great city! And they cast dust on their heads, and cried, weeping and wailing, saying, Alas, alas, that great city, wherein were made rich all that had ships in the sea by reason of her costliness! for in one hour is she made desolate" (Rev. 18:13-19).

Astronomically, Argo the ship sees Cancer the great Cattlefold city. Several other constellations have alternate boat imagery. Orion and Ursa Major are both Canoes and Perseus is a celestial boat all watching Cancer burn. Historically, incense has a prominent place in Papal worship. When Rome charges a price to remove "souls of men" from purgatory, she is trading in "souls of men." Priests and monks are "merchants" who sell pardons for sin. Every sin can be committed by those who have the money to pay for the sin. If a nun enters a convent, she must give her money to the Church. Even her hair is cut off and sold. She is told she possesses nothing. But God gives us "without money and without price" (Isa. 55:1). Revelation 18:13-19 is quoted directly from the prophecies in Ezekiel 26: 27; and 28:27-36 of the fall of idolatrous Tyre fulfilled in 572 B.C. by Nebuchadnezzar. The anti-type is fulfilled in the Kings, Princes, Dukes, Counts and Bishops of the Roman Catholic Church, plus all who have gained a livlihood out of the Church of Rome -- the mainstay of the political, economic and social structure of European civilization and for that matter even United States' civilization.

Why aren't common people lamenting? They are fleeced and robbed by the Church. The common people will rob and spoil "Babylon's" treasures with Communism (Jer. 50:10,37). Revelation 18 repeats the prophecy in Isaiah 21 and 34 of the annihilation of Edom, the ally of Babylon on the "great and terrible day of the Lord." When Christ returns, he will complete the destruction of Roman Catholic Europe and Roman Catholic America. All Jewish commentators in past centuries, as well as some Protestant commentators, say that prophetic "Edom" represents the Roman Empire. The territories of the Latin-German nations will become an uninhabited wilderness, devoid of all human life. Same for the United States.

Although the Protestant nations gained the victory over the Latin-German nations in the 16th, 17th and 18th centuries, the Protestant Reformation has since been largely undone. Thousands of our churches and clergy are Roman Catholic. This is why God says, "Come out of her, my people, that ye be not partakers of her sins, and that ye receive not of her plagues" (Rev. 18:4). We also read, "Wherefore come out from among them, And be ye separate, saith the Lord and touch not the unclean thing; and I will receive you" (2 Cor. 6:17) and "Depart ye, depart, go out from thence, touch no unclean thing; go out of the midst of her; be ye clean, that bear the vessels of the Eternal" (Isa. 52:11). Andromeda (Israel) is in spiritual chains. "Let my people go" (Ex.5:1) from idolatrous, unclean Gentile worship. The national deliverance of the United States will depend on our obedience to the command to "Come out of Babylon." Any church denomination having totalitarian principles of government and an enforced creed with suppression of human liberties, denial of freedom of conscience, and freedom of expression, is in Babylon no matter how "biblical" its beliefs are.

"Rejoice over her, thou heaven, and ye holy apostles and prophets; for God hath avenged you on her. And a mighty angel took up a stone like a great millstone, and cast it into the sea, saying, Thus with violence shall that great city Babylon be thrown down, and shall be found no more at all. And the voice of harpers, and musicians, and of pipers, and trumpeters, shall be heard no more at all in thee; and no craftsman, of whatsoever craft he be, shall be found any more in thee; and the sound of a millstone shall be heard no more at all in thee; And the light of a candle shall shine no more at all in thee; and the voice of the bridegroom and of the bride shall be heard no more at all in thee: for thy merchants were the great men of the earth; for by thy sorceries were all nations deceived. And in her was found the blood of prophets, and of saints, and of all that were slain upon the earth" (Rev. 18:20-24).

Astronomically, Orion is the "mighty angel" and his club is the pestle (used with a mortar) or "millstone" that he "casts into the sea" of Eridanus. Historically "Jeremiah wrote in a book all the evil that should come upon Babylon (ch. 51) ... when thou hast finished reading this book ... thou shalt bind a stone to it, and cast it into the midst of the Euphrates ... Thus shall Babylon sink" (Jer. 51:60-64). The Catholic Church's habit of placing candles before an image or picture of the Madonna at prayer-time believing that this useless practice would aid the ascent of their prayers may be described in verse 23. The European Papal Roman earth is the historic meaning of "earth" in verse 24, while the entire globe may be the meaning in the end time.

The power behind all European wars has been Rome. For instance the War of 1870 was a failed Jesuit attempt to overthrow Lutheran Prussia. The Boer War of 1901 was caused by agitation of two Irish Fenians sent by Jesuits to create discontent in Transvaal. Gladstone's surrender at Majuba Hill was a Jesuit betrayal. Before the First World War, the Pope told the Kaiser that "Germany must become the sword of the Catholic Church" to restore the Holy Roman Empire. Then Pope Pius X issued a "Concordat" against Serbia, namely a document stating that Serbia, a Greek Orthodox country, was henceforth politically and religiously under authority of Papal Rome. Austrian Archduke Ferdinand went to Rome and offered to use Austria to enforce this "Concordat" by war if necessary. That is why he was murdered in 1914. This murder was then used as a pretext to declare war on Serbia. During the war, the Vatican remained silent in not condemning proven German atrocities but blessed the Irish Easter uprising in Dublin, 1916. Furthermore, Vatican pacifist propaganda was responsible for the disastrous retreat of the Italian army at Caporetto in 1917. Thus the Pope was barred by Treaty of London from attending the Peace Conference in 1919 because of his conspiracy with defeated Germany and Austria. The 2nd World War was also a religious war. Papal Europe against Protestant Britain, the U.S. and European Jews. Jesuits for many centuries battled Judaism, Freemasonry and Protestantism because these are the three chief advocates of tolerance for other religions (than Catholicism) and they teach that other men have rights (not just Catholics). The ideas of the rights of man, of freedom of conscience, freedom of speech and freedom of press are heresies to Catholics. They think Papal Rome exclusively has all truth and all rights. But "where the Spirit of the Lord is, there is liberty" (2 Cor. 3:17). Catholicism is not the true religion. Protestants and Jews believe that in an atmosphere of the free exchange of contradictory ideas, where there is no coercion or intimidation, the truth will prevail against lies (pp.3-11, Behind the Dictators by Lehmann).

The Protocols of the Learned Elders of Zion published in 1903 originated in France and date from the Dreyfus affair, instigated by Jesuits to overthrow the "Judaic-Masonic" French Republic and thus nullify the French Revolution of 1789. The Protocols were forgeries by Jesuits intended to instill hatred of Jews and Freemasons and discredit Protestant democracies. Once again the Jesuits followed their slogan: "Be suave

Fascism,
Catholicism
and Nazism

(diplomatic) in manner, aggressive in act." They contributed greatly to Nazi-Fascist victories (pp. 12-19, 45 of ibid.).

The Pope wasn't neutral. Pope Pius XI congratulated Mussolini and distributed sacred amulets to the Italian troops going to Ethiopia in 1935. He sent Francisco Franco his blessing in the Spanish Civil War against democracy and liberty (falsely called Communism) and presented Franco's soldiers with victory medals in 1936. Why? Because the Spanish Republic, after discovering dead baby bodies buried under the convents, had dared abolish Catholic tax exemption for the vast domains of the Pope and had taken schools out of the hands of the Catholic Church and told the Jesuits to leave. German and Italian bombers retaliated against the Spanish Republic thereby supporting Franco. In 1942 the Pope welcomed the Japanese ambassador to the Vatican. In 1943 Pope Pius XII's New Year's message was anti-Communist, thus supporting the Axis against the Soviet Union (p.50, 96-97 of ibid.)

Hitler's Mein Kampf was written by Jesuit Father Staempfle. In it Hitler says he imbibed his hatred of Jews and Masonry from the Catholics (p.70). An ethnic Jew cannot even be admitted to the Jesuit Order. The Catholic crusades of the Middle Ages began with persecution of Jews. By accusing the Jews of inventing Communism, Hitler generated hatred for Jews while also fighting atheistic Communism -- both enemies of the Papacy. Actually Marx and Engels, who wrote the Communist Manifesto in the 1800s, were coached and directed by Jesuit priests who invented Communism to destroy Russia's royal family who protected the Orthodox Church -- another enemy of Rome. The Pope payed for this revolution in gold which passed through Germany into Russia in 1917 with Lenin. It was estimated to be worth 666 million dollars (Leon Trotsky by Carmichael, p.171; The Sealed Train by Pearson, p.290). Hitler approved of the indisputability of Catholic dogmas (p.293), of intolerant Catholic education (p.385), of the necessity of blind Catholic faith (p.417), of the infallibility of the Pope (p.507) and of required celibacy of the Catholic clergy (p.513). Hitler disapproved of Protestants protecting Jews (p.123) (Behind the Dictators by Lehmann, pp. 33-34). "Adolf Hitler, son of the Catholic Church, died while defending Christianity (Roman Catholicism) ... with the palm of the martyr, God gives Hitler the Laurels of Victory" -- General Franco, 3rd May, 1945. Hitler's name "Schicklgruber" actually adds up to 667: S=100, C=3, H=8, I=9, C=3, K=20, L=30, G=7, R=90, U=300, B=2, E=5, R=90.

Hitler and Mussolini adopted Nazi-Fascism to destroy the enemies of Pope Pius XI's Roman Catholicism. Cardinal Stepinac declared, "Adolf Hitler is the envoy of God." As soon as Mussolini came to power, he purged Italy of Communists. The Lateran Treaty occurred in 1929 revealing his hidden sponsor. This treaty gave the Catholic Church 750 million Lire in cash, one billion Lire in government stock, Vatican City, and the exclusive right to teach Italians. Pope Pius XI made a concordat with Hitler's Germany in 1933. Franz von Papen, a Papal Knight and Hitler's most successful henchman, declared in Der Volkischer Beobachter of January 14th 1934: "The Third Reich is the first world power which not only recognizes, but which puts into practice the high principles of the Papacy." Hitler,

Goebbels, Himmler, Doenitz, von Pappen and most of the highest officials in the Third Reich were Catholics by birth and education. The German Secret Service, or Gestapo, had been constituted by Heinrich Himmler, according to the principles of the Jesuit Order (The Psychopathic God Adolf Hitler by Waite, p.32). Hitler told his friends, "I can see Himmler as our Ignatius of Loyola." Many Roman Catholic priests wore the black Gestapo uniform and proceeded to persecute Jews and Protestants. Nazi attacks against Catholics were purges against liberal elements within the Church. Nothing more.

As Adolf Hitler said, "I reject that book ...It was written by a Protestant. It is not a party book ... as a Catholic I never feel comfortable in the evangelical church or its structures ... as for the Jews, I am just carrying on with the same policy which the Catholic Church has adopted for fifteen hundred years, when it has regarded the Jews as dangerous and pushed them into ghettos, etc., because it knew what the Jews were like. I don't put race above religion, but I do see the danger in the representatives of this race for church and state, and perhaps I am doing Christianity a great service" (The Nazi Persecution of the Churches by Conway, pp. 25-26, 162).

Greek art portrayed ancient Phrygians wearing a soft, conical cap. This cap has been associated, since the late 18th and early 19th centuries, with the red "liberty cap." Ancient Phrygia (Galatia) became modern France (Gaul) because the Greeks put an "n" before a "gg" as in Phraggoi. The red caps looked like a plague of "sores" (Rev. 16:2) on the European populace.

170

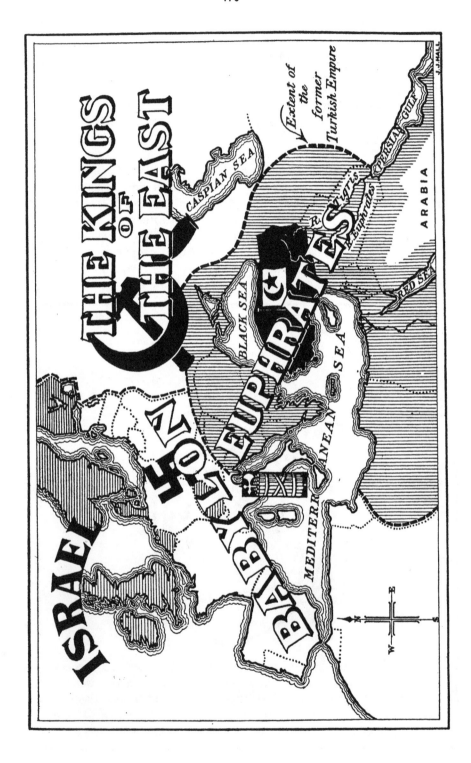

China & Russia Defeated at Messiah's Coming
Chapter 19
(near future)

W e read, "And after these things I heard a great voice of much people in heaven, saying, Alleluia; Salvation, and glory, and honour, and power, unto the Lord our God: For true and righteous are his judgments: for he hath judged the great whore, which did corrupt the earth with her fornication, and hath avenged the blood of his servants at her hand. And again they said, Alleluia. And her smoke rose up for ever and ever. And the four and twenty elders and the four beasts fell down and worshipped God that sat on the throne, saying, Amen; Alleluia. And a voice came out of the throne, saying, Praise our God, all ye his servants, and ye that fear him, both small and great. And I heard as it were the voice of a great multitude, and as the voice of many waters, and as the voice of mighty thunderings, saying, Alleluia: for the Lord God omnipotent reigneth" (Rev. 19:1-6).

The "voice of much people in heaven" (19:1,6) is probably the dead in Christ resurrected, who with living Christians, receive their reward. The Papacy has been punished for its cruelty to Protestants and Jews and it's attacks on Israel-Britain.

"Alleluia" is Hebrew for "Praise ye Yah." The name "Yah" was first used in Moses' Song in Exodus 15:2. This shows that Revelation 19:1-6 is the celebration of another "Red Sea" deliverance from the spiritual Egypt of Catholic Europe and Catholic America. The name "Yah" also occurs twice in Psalm 68:4,18 which looks back to the first Exodus and then forward to the second Exodus. This Psalm is therefore prophetic of Armageddon as its details show. We read in 1 Corinthians 10:1-4,11 "that all our fathers were under the cloud, and all passed through the sea; And were all baptized unto Moses in the cloud and in the sea; And did all eat the same spiritual meat; And did all drink the same spiritual drink: for they drank of that spiritual Rock that followed them: and that Rock was Christ (anointed) .... Now all these things happened unto them for ensamples: and they are written for our admonition, upon whom the ends of the world are come."

Just as ISRAEL left Egyptian IDOLATRIES and slavery, and was then "BAPTISED into Moses" under the cloud of God's presence and in the Red Sea, and became GOD'S KINGDOM at Sinai through Moses, so also in the seventh vial (cup), the ANGLO-SAXON peoples (Israel) will come out of the Roman Catholic IDOLATRIES of Nazi-Fascist Europe (called "Egypt") and will be "BAPTISED into Christ" under the cloud of the outpouring of the second Pentecost -- from NORMANDY France (where the French harlot "Statue of Liberty" beckons people to come) to London's

VICTORIA Station in the SE corner of the BRITISH Isles across the English Channel (Red Sea) and become GOD'S KINGDOM at Christ's return. (From Napoleon to Hitler, Britain was Europe's only safe haven.) Then the British Empire will rule the world (be exalted to the political "heaven") as she becomes the model for the rest of the world. William III, Prince of Orange, came from the SEVEN United Provinces (Elijah's 7000) to deliver Britain and defeat Popery on the banks of the River Boyne in July 1690 thereby preserving the Protestant character of the Royal Throne by requiring a Coronation oath to be a "faithful Protestant." If we take this parallel to the other side of the world, perhaps ANGLO-SAXONS will come out of Roman Catholic IDOLATRIES of a new Nazi-Fascist United States dominated in the west by Mexican Catholics for three-and-a-half years which will represent "Babylon" or "Egypt" or "Jericho" and Jewish Christians will evacuate to VICTORIA, BRITISH Columbia in the SE corner of Vancouver ISLAND from NORMANDY Park, Washington (which also has a harlot statue of Liberty) being baptised in the Puget Sound (Red Sea). Another "Prince of Orange" or Elijah-like church of 7000 Protesters in Washington State may have supernatural signs and wonders as their credentials to convince Americans to flee from this new Mexican Catholicism to Vancouver Island. In the eastern U.S., there will be a Nebuchadnezzar-Darius-Alexander-Caesar succession of tyrants for three-and-a-half years and then a Moslem sultan for the next three-and-a-half years with Washington D.C. being "Constantinople" in anti-type. Each half will parallel Europe's 1260-year history which sets the precedent. The Rocky Mountains are a natural dividing line between the two camps that will take shape in America just as the Adriatic Sea divided the two camps in Europe. Perhaps Vancouver Island will be the safest haven in North America in the troubles to come. Further, Australia's VICTORIA Province in the SE corner of Australia (another British Isle) represents another safe haven after baptism in the Pacific Ocean for fleeing Americans. Just as pure Christianity originated in Galilee and the first-century true Christians fled from Palestine in the eastern Roman Empire to Britain in the west because the Roman dragon tried to devour them, and later some sailed for the new world as Pilgrims from Holland, so also in the anti-type, pure Christianity developed in Plymouth, Massachusetts but many true Christians on the eastern coast of the U.S. will also flee west to BRITISH Columbia because the U.S. dragon will try to devour them and later some will sail for Australia from Washington State. Just as CONSTANTINE came from BRITAIN and conquered pagan ROME using a Chi-Rho SIGN in heaven and then ruled the Roman world from the eastern capital of CONSTANTINOPLE, so also CHRIST may touch down first on Vancouver Island, BRITISH Columbia and charge southeast and conquer the western capital of the U.S. -- let's say PHOENIX, Arizona -- when his "SIGN of the son of man appear in heaven" (Matt. 24:30). From there we know the prophecies that he will land on the Mount of Olives in JERUSALEM and rule from this eastern capital. Just as NAPOLEON imprisoned the Pope, so MESSIAH will take the "false prophet" of Phoenix and cast him into a lake of fire (Rev. 19:20) and then imprison Satan. Just as Queen ELIZABETH used Drake"s FIRE SHIPS against the Spanish Armada which was also blown by an east WIND, so also "the LORD will come with FIRE, and with his CHARIOTS like a WHIRLWIND" (Isa. 66:15) when Vancouver Island is attacked by a Mexican-Catholic navy. Are these parallels just coincidence, or a deliberate design from God to warn all parts of the Anglo-Saxon globe of where they should flee and where they should fight? "The thing that hath been, it is that which shall be; and that which is done, is that which shall be done" (Eccl. 1:9).

If true British Jewish-Christianity can be compared to Olympic champions in a foot race (1 Cor. 9:24; Gal. 2:2; 5:7; Philip 2:16; 3:14; Heb. 12:1), then they must print and broadcast the Moses-Elijah message of "Let my people go" (Ex. 5:1) and "How long will you straddle the fence between the Eternal and Baal?" (cp. 1 Ki. 18:21) to Roman Catholic Nazi-Fascist FROGS (Phrygians or Fraggoi of France) in the E.U. and U.S. to win the GOLD medal (1 Cor. 3:12) and the BLUE ribbon (Nu. 15:38). Sports stadiums and colosseums in America, just as in ancient Rome, may become places of martyrdom for Christians in the near future. These "Elijahs" are likened to "CHARIOTS of fire" (2 Ki. 2:11-12). "For, behold, the Eternal will come with fire, and with his CHARIOTS like the whirlwind, to render his anger with fury, and his rebuke with flames of fire" (Isa. 66:15) -- Auriga with the star Capella -- the Charioteer with his CHARIOT superimposed. Anciently, Leo, Ursa Major and Ursa Minor were all given the CHARIOT symbol as well. Astronomically, Perseus has wings on his heels as he turns stoney hearts to flesh.

Revelation 19:4 is the last notice we have in Revelation of the "24 elders and four cherubims." This shows that at this point their symbolism passes into fulfillment. Israel will from then onward enter upon her destiny as an holy nation of kings and priests ruling with God. From Revelation 20 onward, we read only of the "Holy Jerusalem," "New Jerusalem" and the "Temple" of twelve-tribed Israel in which God dwells.

"Let us be glad and rejoice, and give honour to him: for the marriage of the Lamb is come, and his wife hath made herself ready. And to her was granted that she should be arrayed in fine linen, clean and white: for the fine linen is the righteousness of saints. And he saith unto me, Write, Blessed are they which are called unto the marriage supper of the Lamb. And he saith unto me, These are the true sayings of God" (Rev. 19:7-9).

Two of Christ's parables have their fulfillment at this time. The parable of the king who made a wedding for his son (Matt. 22:1-14) and the parable of the ten virgins who went forth to meet the bridegroom (Matt. 25:1-13). The ten virgins are the ten lost tribes of Israel. A race -- not just a church -- is the meaning (Isaiah 54:5-8, 62:4-5, Hosea 2:16, Jeremiah 3:14). In this seventh vial (cup), the harlot Roman-Latin church, wife of Antichrist, may have deceived the five foolish Anglo-Saxon Israelite virgins who must wait for his "return from the wedding" (Luke 12:35-36). Their Catholic religion "slew" the king's servants (Matt. 22:6) while the pure Protestant Anglo-Saxon Israelite church may be the five wise virgins who marry Christ immediately. It is also a contrast of two cities -- Babylon (Rome and New York burnt -- 19:3 & Matt. 22:7) and Jerusalem (London and Victoria married -- 21:2). The difference between the two groups is that Babylon is not wearing "wedding garments" (Matt. 22:11-14) which is "righteousness" (Rev. 19:8). Who does God give his Holy Spirit to? "The Holy Spirit, whom God hath given to them that OBEY him" (Acts 5:32). Regarding Protestant Jewish Israel, "He shall change their vile bodies, that they may be fashioned like unto his glorious body" (Phil. 3:21). She will now be spirit of his spirit rather than bone of his bone and flesh of his flesh -- "not having spot or wrinkle" (Eph. 5:27).

"And I fell at his feet to worship him. And he said unto me, See thou do it not: I am thy fellowservant, and of thy brethren that have the testimony of Jesus: worship God: for the testimony of Jesus is the spirit of prophecy. And I saw heaven opened, and behold a white horse; and he that sat upon him was called Faithful and True, and in righteousness he doth judge and make war. His eyes were as a flame of fire, and on his head were many crowns; and he had a name written, that no man knew, but he himself. And he was clothed with a vesture dipped in blood: and his name is called The Word of God. And the armies which were in heaven followed him upon white horses, clothed in fine linen, white and clean. And out of his mouth goeth a sharp sword, that with it he should smite the nations: and he shall rule them with a rod of iron: and he treadeth the winepress of the fierceness and wrath of Almighty God. And he hath on his vesture and on his thigh a name written, KING OF KINGS, AND LORD OF LORDS" (19:10-16)

Astronomically, John saw the sun in the eyes ("eyes like a flame of fire") of "Centaur" -- a man riding a "white HORSE." Symbolically, who is the HORSE? God led his "house of ISRAEL ... like a HORSE" (Isa. 63:7,13). The "house of JUDAH ... his goodly HORSE in the battle" (Zech 10:3). Historically, "This same Jesus ... shall so come in like manner as ye have seen him go" (Acts 1:11). He went up in "a cloud" (Acts 1:9) and he will return "with clouds" (Rev. 1:7). He ascended from Mount Olivet (Acts 1:12) and "His feet shall stand in that day upon the Mount of Olives" (Zech. 14:4). His first coming had two stages: at birth and at age 30. The Second Coming has two stages just as Jacob married Leah and then Rachel. Remember that "all these things happened unto them for ensamples: and they are written for our admonition, upon whom the ends of the world are come" (1 Cor. 10:11). First he comes for his Leah people on Feast of Trumpets. Then he returns with his Leah people seven years later (seven Days of Awe) for Rachel (Gen. 29:21-28) on Day of Atonement . Leah represents the resurrection of pre-tribulation Philadelphia saints whom Christ takes to heaven to his father's house for a seven-year honeymoon (Matt. 25:10; 23:39; Ps. 47:5-8; Dan. 12:2; Isa. 26:20; Rev. 3:10; 1 Th. 4:13-5:9; 1 Cor. 15:50-52). Rachel represents tribulation Laodicea saints resurrected at his return from the wedding and honeymoon (Luke 12:36; Zech. 14:1-7; Jude 14; Isa. 27:13; Matt. 24:30-31; Rev. 3:18; Isa. 66:8; Rev. 6:9-11; 7:14). The armies upon white horses are the resurrected Leah saints. "Behold the Lord cometh with ten thousands of his saints, to execute judgment ... upon the ungodly sinners" (Jude 14-15; cp. 2 Thess. 1:7-10). Those that remain on earth and suffer for seven years of tribulation are Rachel, "like men that wait for their lord, when he will return from the wedding" (Luke 12:36). See Psalm 45:3-6.

"Old NICK" refers to "the evil one" (Noah Webster's 1828 Dictionary 2:22). SANTA was a name for Nimrod used throughout Asia Minor (p.37, Langer's Encyclopedia of World History). SANTA CLAUS adds up to 666 if A=6, B=12, C=18, etcetera.

More importantly, SANTA is SATAN, with the letters merely rearranged, who counterfeits Christ returning from the NORTH POLE (Isa. 14:13; Ps. 48:2; 75:6). He flies throughthe air wearing a RED garment and WHITE BEARD -- just like the returning Christ (Rev.19:13; 1:14). Yes, SATAN sees you when you're sleeping and knows when you're awake just like Christ (Pr. 5:21). He knows if you've been bad or good just like Christ (Pr. 15:3). SATAN has counterfeited all these traits. Truly, SATAN is "the god of this world" (2 Cor. 4:4; Isa. 14:14) and has a sinister, uncontrollable laugh -- "Ho, Ho, Ho." SATAN says, "I will ascend above the heights of the clouds (as he is pulled by reindeer in his sleigh); I will be like the Most High" (Isa. 14:14). Doesn't SANTA usurp God's glory and God's praise and actually take the place of God every winter solstice in the minds and hearts of millions of children?

The climax of the "Armageddon" of Revelation 16:14-16 now takes place. The three demon-inspired ideologies of Nazism, Fascism and Roman Catholicism have finally been defeated in World War Three. The Russian Medo-Persian bear will have defeated Roman Catholic Europe. We believe Anglo-Saxon Protestants and Jews at this time will have also been defeated and enslaved. The British Lion and American Eagle absorbed by Babylon -- a Lion with Eagle's wings. But Christ returns and destroys what is left of Europe's armies as well as the Russian and Chinese ("kings of the east") armies. Revelation 19 is the detailed version of the same event as Revelation 11:15-19 summarizes by the seventh trumpet. The sword is the word of God (Eph. 6:17) and God is a "man of war" (Ex. 15:3). God says, "Those mine enemies, who would not that I should reign over them, bring them hither (to Jerusalem) and slay them before me" (Luke 19:27). Christ may wear the crowns of Constantine, Napoleon and Queen Elizabeth -- all who typified his work.

The figure of speech, in Rev. 19:13,15, of one treading the winepress of wrath refers back to Isaiah 63:1-6 describing God's destruction of "Edom" on the same "day of vengeance." Since we have just read of the destruction of "the great whore" of Rev. 19:2 (Babylon), Babylon must be Edom. Many biblical commentators have stated that "Edom" represents the Roman Empire, Pagan and Papal (Babylon). "The name 'Edom' is used by the Talmudists for the Roman Empire, and they applied to Rome every passage of the Bible referring to Edom or to Esau ... the symbolic name 'Seir' was used by the poets of the Middle Ages, not only for Rome, but also for Christianity" (The Jewish Encyclopedia 5:41 under "Edom") meaning Roman Catholic "Christianity." "Whatever the prophets have spoken of the destruction of Edom in the last times, they have spoken concerning Rome. When Rome shall be laid desolate, then shall be redemption to Israel." -- David Kimchi, A.D. 1160-1225, Hebrew Grammarian and commentator who exercised great influence in the translation of the Bible.

Isaiah mentions that God treads the winepress of Edom-Babylon "alone" and there will be "none to help" and "none to uphold" (Isa. 63:3,5). In World War Two when the British and Americans defeated Nazi-Fascist Babylon, they "helped" God. But in World War Three apparently there is no human help or hope of withstanding the European or Russian conquests of the world. Why not? What happened to

Britain and America? "The house of Israel went into captivity for their iniquity; because they trespassed against me, therefore hid I my face from them, and gave them into the hand of their enemies; so fell they all by the sword" (Ez. 39:23). The British LION and the American EAGLE have both been absorbed by Babylon which is portrayed as a LION with EAGLE'S wings (Dan. 7:4). Our Lord will stand alone. Rev. 19:15 takes us back to Psalm 2 which is a prophecy of World War Three because it mentions our Lord's "rod of iron" breaking unbiblical nations.

"And I saw an angel standing in the sun; and he cried with a loud voice, saying to all the fowls that fly in the midst of heaven, Come and gather yourselves together unto the supper of the great God; That ye may eat the flesh of kings, and the flesh of captains, and the flesh of mighty men, and the flesh of horses, and of them that sit on them, and the flesh of all men, both free and bond, both small and great. And I saw the beast, and the kings of the earth, and their armies, gathered together to make war against him that sat on the horse, and against his army. And the beast was taken, and with him the false prophet that wrought miracles before him, with which he deceived them that had received the mark of the beast, and them that worshipped his image. These both were cast alive into a lake of fire burning with brimstone. And the remnant were slain with the sword of him that sat upon the horse, which sword proceeded out of his mouth: and all the fowls were filled with their flesh" (Rev. 19:17-21).

Who are the FOWLS? Astronomically, Corvus the Raven devours the Hydra (Pr. 30:17; 1 Sam. 17:46). Historically, Ezekiel 39:17 gives the complete sentence. "Speak unto every feathered FOWL, and to every BEAST of the FIELD ... eat flesh and drink blood" (Ez. 39:17). BEASTS with BIRD wings are KINGDOMS (Dan.7:17,23) and the FIELD "is the WORLD" (Matt. 13:38). Therefore the world's nations launch nuclear-tipped missiles at eachother using planes. The Russians and Chinese attack European armies and Europe attacks Russia and China. These FOWLS devour eachother's flesh. "I will gather all nations against Jerusalem to battle; and the city shall be taken, and the houses rifled, and the women ravished; and half of the city shall go forth into captivity ... And this shall be the plague with which the Eternal will smite all the peoples that have fought against Jerusalem: their flesh shall consume away while they stand upon their feet, and their eyes shall consume away in their holes, and their tongue shall consume away in their mouth" (Zech. 14:2,12). This describes nuclear warfare. But this "supper" is a marriage feast for Anglo-Saxons (Israelites) and Jews. Daniel says, "I beheld even till the beast was slain, and his body destroyed, and given to the burning flame" (Dan. 7:11).

The feast for FOWLS is foretold in the prophecy of Ezekiel 39:17-21 (see also Joel 3 & Zech 14 & Matt. 24:28). There the slaughter is revealed of the Communist armies of Russia and China ("Gog [Geougen or Tartars] ... Magog [Mongols; Moguls] ... Rosh [Russia] ... Meshech [Moscow] and Tubal [Tobolsk; Tblisi]" -- Ez. 38:2) which will have invaded Palestine since "I will gather all nations against Jerusalem to battle" (Zech. 14:2). They set foot "upon the mountains of Israel" (Ez. 39:17,23-24) and God gives the command to "Put in the (Communist) SICKLE" to harvest (Joel 3:13). God says "I will rain upon him ... great hailstones, fire, and brimstone" (Ez. 38:22). I am against thee, O GOG, prince of ROSH, MESHECH and TUBAL ... I will give thee unto the ravenous BIRDS of every sort ... I will send a fire on MAGOG ... I will give unto GOG a place there of graves in Israel" (Ez. 39:1,4, 11,17-21)

Revelation 19:19 completes the process started in Rev. 16:13-15, the gathering of the whole world by the forces of Nazism, Fascism and Roman Catholicism to the day of wrath. At the point reached in Rev. 19:19, Russian and Chinese armies (Medo-Persian "kings of the east") will have destroyed Catholic Europe (Babylon) and Catholic United States of America (Babylon). They will be encamped in "the Valley of Jehoshaphat" (Kidron) (Joel 3:2) where they will be annihilated.

Just as CYRUS of Persia RELEASED God's people from the 70 YEARS captivity in BABYLON (609-539 B.C. -- Jer. 25:11; Ezra 1:3), so CHRIST will RELEASE his Anglo-Saxon British Empire from a 7-YEAR captivity in a worldwide BABYLON. Cyrus ("ANOINTED" -- Isa. 45:1) is described as "a BIRD of prey" (Isa. 46:10-11) because "the Persians bore an EAGLE fixed to the end of a lance" (Encyc. Brit. 10:454). In the same way, Messiah ("ANOINTED") is described as "an EAGLE" (Deut. 32:11-12) and has an army composed of ravenous BIRDS who are resurrected saints. If the "marriage SUPPER of the Lamb" is eaten by Messiah's "WIFE" (Rev. 19:8-9), and the "SUPPER of the great God" is eaten by "BIRDS" in heaven (Rev. 19:17-18, RSV), then the "BIRDS" correspond to the "WIFE" -- resurrected saints -- his army. Although Anglo-Saxon Israel will have been defeated in war (Ez. 39:22-29), Protestant and Jewish martyrs will be in the first resurrection as Christ's "army" of EAGLES (Rev. 19:19).

But first, China may drain the U.S. economy (Euphrates -- Isa. 44:27; Jer. 50:38; Her. 1:191-192) and march through a dried up riverbed of runaway inflation and drop a "great plague of hail" "into the air" (Rev. 16:17-21) -- a sudden nuclear attack to obliterate U.S. population centers. Isaiah 26:20 tells us to "enter thou into thy chambers (bomb shelters), and shut thy doors about thee; hide thyself ... until the indignation be past." Just as "the day that Noah entered into the ark the flood came" and just as the "day Lot went out of Sodom, it rained fire and brimstone," so also "when the Son of man is revealed," don't return to your house to get your possessions. "Remember Lot's wife." "Whosoever shall seek to save his life shall lose it" (Luke 17:26-33). Highways will be immediately clogged and vehicles will be useless. "Their quiver (missile silo) is like an open sepulcher" (Jer. 5:16) and their "horses (missiles) are swifter than eagles. Woe unto us! For we are spoiled" (Jer. 4:13).

Readers of Revelation have noticed at least four "2nd comings" so far (Rev. 2:5,16; 6:16; 11:17). These are punishments of God or visitations such as the conversion of Constantine (6:16) or the Protestant Reformation (11:17). But here in the 19th chapter we have the actual 2nd coming. Judgments of God on individuals and nations are called visitations (Isa. 13:6,9; 19:1; 30:27-30; Jer. 5:9,29; Jer. 9:9; Jer. 11:23; Ps. 89:32; Matt. 10:23; John 21:22).

Top Left: The EU flag contains twelve gold stars in a circle on blue. Unveiled 11th December, 1955 -- date of the Feast of Immaculate Conception of Mary -- it symbolizes "Blue the colour of our lady (Mary), and gold the papal colour" (<u>Pope John Paul II</u> by St. John-Stevas, p. 21) (cp. Rev. 12:1). Top Right: Tower of Louise Weiss Building, part of European Parliament in Strasbourg, France, looks unfinished. It was designed to resemble the Tower of Babel as depicted in Flemish Pieter Bruegel's 1563 painting. Bottom Left: Poster produced by the EU depicts twelve stars of EU flag overseeing rebuilding the Tower of Babel and the motto: "Europe: Many Tongues, One Voice." Stars are inverted pentagrams -- an occult symbol for Satan. Pyramids of Egypt in background and "block-head robot" slave builders in foreground. Bottom Right: British postage stamp commemorates a woman Europa of Tyre (Papacy) on seven hills of water (Rome) beckoning a child (Protestant Britain) to join her as she rides Zeus the bull (EU beast) who rapes her (cp. Rev. 17:16).

The Millenium Rest
Chapter 20
(near future)

John wrote, "And I saw an angel come down from heaven, having the key of the bottomless pit and a great chain in his hand. And he laid hold on the dragon, that old serpent, which is the Devil, and Satan, and bound him a thousand years, And cast him into the bottomless pit, and shut him up, and set a seal upon him, that he should deceive the nations no more, till the thousand years should be fulfilled: and after that he must be loosed a little season" (Rev. 20:1-3).

Who is this "ANGEL"? Astronomically, Ophiuchus grabs hold of Serpens which is a "great chain" and binds Scorpio which is alternately the "serpent" and locks him in Crater, the "bottomless pit," using Cassiopeia which is alternately the "key." Historically, in Malachi, the Messiah is called the "ANGEL" or "MESSENGER of the Covenant" (Mal. 3:1) and in Revelation 1:18 we read that Jesus Christ has "the keys of the grave and of death." Therefore, Christ binds Satan just as the live GOAT is bound and carried "by the hand of a FIT MAN into the wilderness ... unto a land not inhabited" (Lev. 16:20-22; cp. Isa. 24:21-22) which is the bottomless pit (abyss). Yes, "Satan ... deceiveth the whole world" (Rev. 12:9).

Sunday is the first day of the week. Saturday is the seventh day of the week. To be consistent with this Millennial rest, Christians need to rest on Saturday rather than Sunday. Bible chronology indicates Adam and Even were created approximately 4000 B.C. Man has been given the first 6000 YEARS to do what he pleases. But the seventh period of 1000 YEARS is God's MILLENIUM. This teaching can be found in the Slavic version of the Book of Enoch 33:1-2 ; Talmud Sanhedrin 97a; Avodah Zarah 9a; Epistle of Barnabas 13:4 as well as Psalm 90:4, 2 Peter 3:8, Revelation 20:1-7 and Hebrews 4:1-11. The first SIX MONTHS of the sacred calendar contain only THREE holy days. But in the SEVENTH MONTH the remaining FOUR holy days all come together. This tells us that MAJOR EVENTS CRESCENDO in the MILLENIUM. SOLOMON, the prince of peace, in his wisdom, wealth and glory was a shadow of the MESSIAH to come. SIX STEPS (six thousand years) led to his THRONE (the millenium) (2 Chr.9:17-19). Both Solomon and Christ are wise, wealthy KINGS and SONS of DAVID who build a wonderful TEMPLE and create an era of PEACE. Solomon had 1000 wives from around the WORLD which typifies the true church, composed of Jewish Christians from around the WORLD, married to Christ. Jesus went to the WEDDING in Cana on the seventh day SABBATH. The first four days are found in John 1:19, 29, 35 and 43. On the fourth day he TAKES a TRIP, and is not seen again until the seventh day in chapter 2 (John 2:3). Yes, after 4000 YEARS, Christ TOOK A TRIP to earth, but we won't see him again till the end of 6000 YEARS when he has his WEDDING. Noah was 600 YEARS old when the FLOOD came (Gen.7:6). Then "in the 601st year, in the first month, the first day of the month, the waters were dried up ... and Noah removed the covering of the ark" (Gen.8:13). Christ said "There are some standing here, who shall not taste of death, till they see the Son of man coming in his kingdom" (Matt.16:28). Then, "AFTER SIX DAYS Jesus taketh Peter, James, and John, his brother, and bringeth them up into an high MOUNTAIN (kingdom -- Dan.2:35,44-45) privately, and was TRANSFIGURED before them; and his face did shine like the sun, and his raiment was as white as the light. And, behold, there appeared unto them Moses and Elijah talking with him" (Matt.17:1-3). Again, we read about JOASH the HEIR to the throne of Judah being "hidden in the house of the Eternal SIX YEARS ... And the SEVENTH YEAR Jehoiada sent and fetched the rulers over hundreds, with the captains and the guard, and brought them to him into the house of the Eternal, and made a covenant with them ... And he brought forth the king's son, and put the crown upon him" (2 Kings 11:3,4,12). Even with all this evidence, some have suggested that the Millenium is not literal but symbolic. However, the scale of a day for a year (Nu. 14:34; Ez. 4:6) only applies to the "seven times" in which it operates. With the close of that era, the necessity for concealment by use of a cypher disappears. This is a literal 1000-year Sabbath. Not forever in heaven playing harps. But 1000 years on earth (rev. 5:10) administering church and state affairs.

"And I saw thrones, and they sat upon them, and judgment was given unto them: and I saw the souls of them that were beheaded for the witness of Jesus, and for the word of God, and which had not worshipped the beast, neither his image, neither had received his mark upon their foreheads, or in their hands; and they lived and reigned with Christ a thousand years. But the rest of the dead lived not again until the thousand years were finished. This is the first resurrection. Blessed and holy is he that hath part in the first resurrection: on such the second death hath no power, but they shall be priests of God and of Christ, and shall reign with him a thousand years" (Rev. 20:4-6).

God said to Israel, "If ye will obey my voice ... ye shall be unto me a kingdom of priests" (Ex. 19:5-6). The "saints shall judge the world" (1 Cor.6:2). Saints will be "kings and priests" and "reign on the earth" (Rev. 5:10). These saints are "a royal priesthood" (1 Pet. 2:9) The twelve apostles will sit on twelve thrones (Matt. 19:28). Here we see that "he that loseth his life for my sake shall find it" (Matt. 10:39). "If we suffer, we shall also reign with him" (2 Tim. 2:12). Verse 5 should have parentheses around it from "But" to "finished."

There are two resurrections. Those who qualify will be resurrected to immortal life at the end of this 6000 YEARS (1 Cor.15:23). This is "a better resurrection" (Heb. 11:35) -- "the resurrection of the just" (Luke 14:14). "For the time is come that judgment must begin at the house of God" (1 Pet.4:17; Rom.8:14). Then the "saints shall judge the world" for 1000 years (1 Cor.6:2). ALL THE REST of humanity who have lived and died without ever knowing the plan of salvation (Matt.10:14-15; 11:21-25; 12:41-42) will be resurrected back to physical life (Ez.37:1-14) AFTER the Millenium (Rev.20:5; Isa. 65:20). They will also be "JUDGED every man according to their works" (Rev.20:13) and then resurrected or destroyed (Rev.20:15). As Christ said, "the hour is coming, in which all that are in the graves shall hear his voice, And shall come forth: they that have done good, unto THE RESURRECTION of LIFE (the first resurrection to immortality); and they that have done evil, unto THE RESURRECTION of DAMNATION (lit. "judgment") (the resurrection to mortality)" (John 5:28-29). In Revelation 20:4-6 we read that John "saw the souls of them that were beheaded for the witness of Jesus, and for the word of God, and who had not worshipped the beast ... and they lived and reigned with Christ a thousand years. (But the REST OF THE DEAD lived not again until the THOUSAND YEARS WERE FINISHED.) This is the FIRST RESURRECTION. Blessed and holy is he that hath part in the FIRST RESURRECTION; on such the second death hath no power." Again we see TWO RESURRECTIONS one thousand years apart. The first to IMMORTALITY and the second to MORTALITY. "And many of those who sleep in the dust of the earth shall awake, some to EVERLASTING LIFE (first resurrection after 6000 years) and some to shame and EVERLASTING CONTEMPT" (second resurrection after 7000 years)" (Dan.12:2). Yes, "in Christ shall all be made alive; But every man in his own order: Christ the first fruits; afterward they that are Christ's at his coming (FIRST RESURRECTION to IMMORTALITY). Then cometh the end, when he shall have delivered up the kingdom of God, even the Father, when he shall have put down all rule and all authority and power (RESURRECTION to MORTALITY). For he must reign, till he hath put all enemies under his feet. The last enemy that shall be destroyed is death" (1 Cor.15:22-26). Jesus the Messiah "shall judge the quick (living) and the dead at his appearing (FIRST RESURRECTION to IMMORTALITY) and his kingdom" (SECOND RESURRECTION to MORTALITY) (2 Tim.4:1). "For we must all appear before the judgment seat of Christ, that everyone may receive the things done in his body, according to that he hath done, whether it be good or bad."

In the Millenium, humans will live out a full life of "an hundred years" before dying (Isa.65:20). War will end (Isa. 2:4). "All shall know the Lord, from the least even to the greatest" (Jer. 31:34). Carnivorous and poisonous animals (as well as men) will become vegetarians and harmless (Isa. 11:6-9; 65:25) just as originally at creation (Gen. 1:29-31) and before the flood (Gen. 9:3). Whenever men "turn to the right hand" or "turn to the left" they will "hear a word behind" them saying "This is the way, walk ye in it" (Isa. 30:21).

"And when the thousand years are expired, Satan shall be loosed out of his prison, And shall go out to deceive the nations which are in the four quarters of the earth, Gog and Magog, to gather them together to battle: the number of whom is as the sand of the sea. And they went up on the breadth of the earth, and compassed the camp of the saints about, and the beloved city: and fire came down from God out of heaven, and devoured them. And the devil that deceived them was cast into the lake of fire and brimstone, where the beast and the false prophet are (were cast), and shall be tormented day and night for ever and ever. And I saw a great white throne, and him that sat on it, from whose face the earth and the heaven fled away; and there was found no place for them. And I saw the dead, small and great, stand before God;

and the books were opened: and another book was opened, which is the book of life: and the dead were judged out of those things which were written in the books, according to their works. And the sea gave up the dead which were in it; and death and hell delivered up the dead which were in them: and they were judged every man according to their works. And death and hell were cast into the lake of fire. This is the second death. And whosoever was not found written in the book of life was cast into the lake of fire" (Rev. 20:7-15).

Verse 10 should be translated "were cast" not "are" since this is now 1000 years later. Astronomically, the "lake of fire" is Ara (the altar).

Who sits on the "WHITE THRONE"? God has "appointed a day, in which he will judge the world in righteousness by that man (Jesus Christ) whom he hath ordained" (Acts 17:31). "In the day when God shall judge the secrets of men by Jesus Christ" (Rom. 2:16). "The Father judgeth no man, but hath committed all judgment unto the Son" (John 5:22). Therefore, Jesus the Son, not God the Father, sits in that "white throne."

Which "BOOKS" are opened? The "books" are opened to people's understanding (Isa. 25:7). They are "the Book of the Law" (John 5:45), the book of the Bible (John 12:48), the "Book of Remembrance" in which are written the deeds of the good and the wicked (Isa. 65:6; Ps. 56:3; Mal. 3:16), and the "Book of Life" (Ex. 32:32-33; Dan. 12:1; Luke 10:20). "He that rejecteth me, and receiveth not my words, hath one that judgeth him; the word that I have spoken, the same shall judge him in the last day" (John 12:48). True Christians do not come before this throne. They already have eternal life. With immortality, the dying process is stopped (v.14). "Hell" in verse 14 is Greek "hades" referring to the grave. "The last enemy that shall be destroyed is death" (1 Cor. 15:26).

New Jerusalem -- A Huge Green Pyramid
Chapter 21
(about 1000 years from now)

Then John wrote, "And I saw a new heaven and a new earth: for the first heaven and the first earth were passed away; and there was no more sea. And I John saw the holy city, new Jerusalem, coming down from God out of heaven, prepared as a bride adorned for her husband. And I heard a great voice out of heaven saying, Behold, the tabernacle of God is with men, and he will dwell with them, and they shall be his people, and God himself shall be with them, and be their God. And God shall wipe away all tears from their eyes; and there shall be no more death, neither sorrow, nor crying, neither shall there be any more pain: for the former things are passed away" (Rev. 21:1-4).

After the Millenium, the "heavens shall pass away with a great noise, and the elements shall melt with fervent heat; the earth also, and the works that are in it, shall be burned up" (2 Pet. 3:10). Then "we ... look for new heavens and a new earth, wherein dwelleth righteousness" (2 Pet. 3:13). "New heaven" figuratively means "new government." "New earth" figuratively means "new society" (cp. Isa. 65:17; 66:22-24). In addition to the literal meaning, "no more SEA" means no more "PEOPLES, and multitudes, and NATIONS and tongues" (Rev. 17:15) because they have all either been resurrected or destroyed. That is why there is "no more death" (verse 4). "Many PEOPLE ... make a noise like ... the SEAS ... The NATIONS shall rush like ... many WATERS" (Isa. 17:12-13). But not any more. Ezekiel 37:27 says, "My tabernacle also shall be with them (Israel), yea, I will be their God, and they (Israel) shall be my people." Verse 4 restates Isaiah 51:11.

"And he that sat upon the throne said, Behold, I make all things new. And he said unto me, Write: for these words are true and faithful. And he said unto me, It is done. I am Alpha and Omega, the beginning and the end. I will give unto him that is athirst of the fountain of the water of life freely. He that overcometh shall inherit all things; and I will be his God, and he shall be my son. But the fearful, and unbelieving, and the abominable, and murderers, and whoremongers, and sorcerers, and idolaters, and all liars, shall have their part in the lake which burneth with fire and brimstone: which is the second death" (Rev. 21:5-8).

"To him that overcometh will I give ... a white stone" (Rev. 2:17) which is defined further on as a PEARL. But since the PEARL is the gate of the city, it is really "all things." "But the fearful (afraid of what their Catholic friends might think), and unbelieving (many Catholics don't believe the Bible), and the abominable (those who eat bacon, pork, clam chowder and shrimp) and murderers (abortionists; Catholics who execute "heretic" Protestants and Jews) and whoremongers (Nuns and Priests who fornicate because forbidden to marry) and sorcerers (drug pushers) and idolaters (Catholic priests) and all liars (Jesuits who lie to betray Protestant governments) shall have their part in the lake which burneth with fire" (Rev. 21:8). "Whosoever shall deny me before men (out of fear?), him will I also deny before my Father which is in heaven" (Matt. 10:33).

"And there came unto me one of the seven angels which had the seven vials full of the seven last plagues, and talked with me, saying, Come hither, I will shew thee the bride, the Lamb's wife. And he carried me away in the spirit to a great and high mountain, and shewed me that great city, the holy Jerusalem, descending out of heaven from God, Having the glory of God: and her light was like unto a stone most precious, even like a jasper stone, clear as crystal; And had a wall great and high, and had twelve gates, and at the gates twelve angels, and names written thereon, which are the names of the twelve tribes of the children of Israel: On the east three gates; on the north three gates; on the south three gates; and on the west three gates. And the wall of the city had twelve foundations, and in them the names of the twelve apostles of the Lamb. And he that talked with me had a golden reed to measure the city, and the gates thereof, and the wall thereof. And the city lieth foursquare, and the length is as large as the breadth: and he measured the city with the reed, twelve thousand furlongs. The length and the breadth and the height of it are equal. And he measured the wall thereof, an hundred and forty and four cubits, according to the measure of a man, that is, of the angel. And the building of the wall of it was of jasper: and the city was pure gold, like unto clear glass. And the foundations of the wall of the city were garnished with all manner of precious stones. The first foundation was jasper; the second, sapphire; the third, a chalcedony; the fourth, an emerald; the fifth, sardonyx; the sixth, sardius; the seventh, chrysolite; the eighth, beryl; the ninth, a topaz; the tenth, a chrysoprasus; the eleventh, a jacinth; the twelfth, an amethyst. And the twelve gates were twelve pearls; every several gate was of one pearl: and the street of the city was pure gold, as it were transparent glass" (Rev. 21:9-21).

Revelation 21:9-21 should come between verses 3 and 4 of Revelation 20. It is out of place here (see An Attempt to Recover the Original Order of the Text of Revelation 20:4 - 22 by Canon Charles D.D.). The fact that it was one of the seven vial angels (Rev. 21:9; 17:1) which revealed the vision of the "Lamb's wife" to John, shows that this vision is in contrast with that of the rival harlot "Babylon" (Rev. 19:7) and should appear in the same context of the seven vials -- Rev. 15 to Rev. 20:3 -- not after the Millenial and post-Millenial reigns of Christ shown in Rev. 20:4-15 and Rev. 21:1-8.

What is the "HIGH MOUNTAIN"? Astronomically, Cancer is the Sheepfold or New Jerusalem. The "golden reed" is Orion's Belt. Historically, the "great and high mountain" is the kingdom of Israel since Daniel 2:35,44-45 describe Israel as a "stone" growing into "a great mountain." Yes, "In the last days the mountain of the Lord's house shall be established in the top of the (Gentile) mountains" (Isa. 2:2-3). Hebrews 12:22-24 says "MOUNT Zion" is "the city of the Living God" and "the heavenly Jerusalem." "New Jerusalem" is a PYRAMID rather than a cube because in addition to having a "foundation of the apostles and prophets" it has Jesus Christ as the "chief corner stone" (Eph. 2:20-22). The only type of building which has one chief cornerstone is a

PYRAMID. Babylon's four ancient walls were 120 stadia long each (Herod. 1:178). In the midst of Babylon was a PYRAMIDAL tower one furlong square rising tier above tier to the temple at the top which contained only the throne of Bel and the bride of Bel (Her.1:181). Each tier was a different color dedicated to a different planet. Ecbatana was built on the scheme of the planets also, with seven concentric tiers colored white, black, purple, blue, red, silver and gold to correspond to the Moon, Sun, Mercury, Venus, Saturn, Jupiter and Mars (Her. 1:98). The Euphrates flowed through the midst of it. New Jerusalem is 100 times as great -- equal dimensions of 12,000 stadia (1500 miles) in length, width and height. If set down in Europe, its four corners would cover Gibraltar, Greece, St. Petersburg and the Hebrides and it would soar 100 times higher than the Himalayas -- unless the 12,000 stadia are the circumference in which case we divide by four. The throne of God and the Lamb is at the summit so the river of life can flow down from it. The Bride of the Lamb lives there. Jesus said he would "prepare a place" for us (John 14:2) -- "a city which hath foundations, whose builder and maker is God" (Heb. 11:10). Christians are "living stones" (1 Pet. 2:5). Worthy saints are compared to "gold, silver, and precious stones" (1 Cor. 3:12).

What do the "PEARLY GATES" symbolize? The twelve gates made of PEARLS show that entrance to this city requires forsaking all to buy the "PEARL of great price" (Matt. 13:46). Jesus was the merchant who sold all he had (was crucified) to buy the field (world) with a hidden PEARL representing ISRAEL. Jesus told us to not "cast your PEARLS before swine" (Matt. 7:6). Therefore, Christians shouldn't give the keys to the PEARLY GATES to swine and dogs who are not allowed to enter. "Thou shalt call thy walls Salvation, and thy gates Praise" (Isa. 60:18).

Why is the number TWELVE repeated so often? Because TWELVE represents perfect government. For example, the sun which "rules" the day, and the moon and stars which rule the night, pass through TWELVE Zodiac signs. From Seth to Noah were TWELVE patriarchs. From Shem to Jacob were TWELVE. There were TWELVE sons of Jacob and TWELVE tribes of Israel. There were TWELVE judges or deliverers. TWELVE apostles. Our Lord said there were TWELVE legions of angels (Matt. 26:53).

Foundation stones represent the apostles (21:14): "jasper (dark green) ... sapphire (celestial blue) ... chalcedony (deep red) ... emerald (green) ... sardonyx (pale pink) ... sardius (flesh color) ... chrysolite (gold) ... beryl (sea green) ... topaz (yellow) ... chrysoprasus (purple) ... jacinth (orange) ... and amethyst (violet)" (Rev. 21:19-20). New Jerusalem is not founded on the twelve tribes of literal Israel anymore, but on the twelve apostles because "On this rock I will build my church" (not tribes) -- membership is now based on righteous behavior rather than physical heredity.

Why "PRECIOUS STONES"? Christ's promise in Matthew 6:33 was that if Israel were to seek first God's kingdom and his righteousness, all these material things would be added. God promised divorced Israel, "I will lay thy stones with fair colors, and lay thy foundations with sapphires. And I will make thy windows of agates, and thy gates of carbuncles, and all thy borders of pleasant stones. And all thy children shall be taught of the Eternal ... In righteousness shalt thou be established ... No weapon that is formed against thee shall prosper" (Isa.54:11-17). The street of pure gold refers back to the floor of the Holy of Holies in Solomon's Temple as being overlaid with gold (1 Ki. 6:30).

"And I saw no temple therein: for the Lord God Almighty and the Lamb are the temple of it. And the city had no need of the sun, neither of the moon, to shine in it: for the glory of God did lighten it, and the Lamb is the light thereof. And the nations (of them which are saved) shall walk in the light of it: and the kings of the earth do bring their glory and honour into it. And the gates of it shall not be shut at all by day: for there shall be no night there. And they shall bring the glory and honour of the nations into it. And there shall in no wise enter into it any thing that defileth, neither whatsoever worketh abomination, or maketh a lie: but they which are written in the Lamb's book of life" (Rev. 21:22-27).

In verse 23, the "Shekinah Glory" of the Lord filled the tabernacle of Moses in the wilderness (Ex. 40:34-35). This glory also filled the Temple of Solomon (1 Ki. 8:10-11). "The moon shall be confounded, and the sun ashamed, when the Lord of Hosts shall reign in Zion, and in Jerusalem, before his ancients gloriously" (Isa. 24:23). "Thy gates shall be open continually; they shall not be shut day nor night, that men may bring unto thee the forces (wealth) of the Gentiles, and that their kings may be brought.... The sun shall be no more thy light by day; neither for brightness shall the moon give light unto thee: But the Lord shall be unto thee an everlasting light, and thy God thy glory. Thy sun shall no more go down; neither shall thy moon withdraw itself: for the Lord shall be thine everlasting light, and the days of thy mourning shall be ended" (Isa. 60:11,19-20). Now the whole kingdom of Israel (after the Millenium) -- just as the elect church (before the Millenium) -- is "builded together (as an immortal structure) for an habitation of God through the Spirit" (Eph. 2:22). The clause "of them which are saved" is spurious and has no textual authority in verse 24. But this makes little difference in light of Micah 4:2 which says, "Many nations shall come, and say, Come, and let us go up to the mountain of the Eternal, and to the house of the God of Jacob; and he will teach us of his ways, and we will walk in his paths; for the law shall go forth from Zion, and the word of the Lord from Jerusalem." "Lift up thine eyes round about, and behold; all these (Gentiles?) gather themselves together, and come to thee. As I live, saith the Eternal, thou shalt surely clothe thee with them all, as with an ornament, and bind them on thee, as a bride doeth" (Isa. 49:18). Gentiles can become Israelites because "If ye be Christ's, then are ye Abraham's seed" (Gal. 3:29). This is how God will "make a full end of all nations" (Jer. 30:11) except Israel. Otherwise Gentiles "have no hope and are without God in the world" (Eph. 2:12).

Why is New Jerusalem composed mainly of JASPER? Rev. 4:3 says GOD is "to look upon like a JASPER." New Jerusalem is "perfect through MY comliness which I had put upon thee, saith the Lord God" (Ez. 16:14). Furthermore, BENJAMIN was given spiritual understanding described as "LIGHT" (1 Ki. 11:13, 32,36). This tribe's stone was JASPER according to birth order and the stones on the breastplate (Ex. 28:15-21). This New Jerusalem is composed mainly of JASPER which emphasizes the fact that

Godly wisdom, knowledge and understanding will be the governing and controlling factor throughout the life of this CITY. All the disciples of Jesus were from the tribe of BENJAMIN except Judas Iscariot. This tribe was given to the Kingdom of Judah "that David my servant may have a LIGHT always before me in JERUSALEM" (2 Ki. 11:13,32,36; 15:4; 1 Ki. 8:19; 2 Chr. 21:7). Jesus told his disciples "ye are the LIGHT of the world" and "a CITY that is set on a hill cannot be hid" (Matt. 5:14-16). The apostle Paul said he was of the tribe of BENJAMIN (Philip. 3:5). BENJAMIN'S mission was "say ye, The Lord hath redeemed his servant Jacob" (Isa. 48:20). Therefore it is easy to see why JASPER is the color of New Jerusalem.

The gates of the cities in ancient times had to be shut at night to keep out evildoers. In God's kingdom there will be no "darkness" behind which fear or evil can hide. The light of the truth will destroy all darkness of error.

Revelation 21:22-27 are taken from Isaiah 60:11,19,20 and demonstrate again that God's servant nation will be Israel until the goal of the creation of an immortal human race is reached.

The Universal Product Code bar code containing 666 -- sometimes with an "F" and "H" below standing for "Forehead" and "Hand." The "okay" hand signal displaying 666. The RFID microchip injected "in" the hand or forehead (Rev. 13:16) and a dancing Satyr (Satan) whose name adds up to 666.

Monks and priests cut bald <u>TONSURES</u> upon their heads. But God says, "They shall not make <u>BALDNESS</u> upon their head" (Lev. 21:5). Men "shave the hair of their heads as, they say, Dionysius, shaved the hair of his. That is, they cut their hair in <u>CIRCULAR</u> shape and shave the temples" (Herodotus' <u>Histories</u> 3:8). Juvenal 6:530 says, the image of Isis was "escorted by the <u>TONSURED</u> surpliced train." "Ye shall not <u>ROUND</u> the corners of your head" (Lev. 19:27). Also Zephaniah 1:4 mentions "Chemarim" from the Hebrew root "kamar" meaning to "be <u>BLACK</u>" because Baal-worshippers wore <u>BLACK</u> robes.

New Jerusalem
Chapter 22
(continued)

Finally we read, "And he shewed me a pure river of water of life, clear as crystal, proceeding out of the throne of God and of the Lamb. In the midst of the street of it, and on either side of the river, was there the tree of life, which bare twelve manner of fruits, and yielded her fruit every month: and the leaves of the tree were for the healing of the nations. And there shall be no more curse: but the throne of God and of the Lamb shall be in it; and his servants shall serve him: And they shall see his face; and his name shall be in their foreheads. And there shall be no night there; and they need no candle, neither light of the sun; for the Lord God giveth them light: and they shall reign for ever and ever" (Rev. 22:1-5).

Astronomically, the Milky Way River flows from the throne of Cepheus. Canis Minor is alternately the Mulberry Tree with white, red and then black fruit. It represents the Tree of Life.

Notice the contrasting parallels between Genesis and Revelation. These parallels prove that Revelation is the final book of the Bible. Earth created (1:1). Earth passes away (21:1). Sun made visible (1:16). No need of the sun (21:23). Darkness called night (1:5). "No night there" (21:25; 22:5). Waters called seas (1:10). "No more sea" (21:1). Sin enters (3:4-7). End of sin (21:4,8; 22:14-15). Curse pronounced (3:14-18). "No more curse" (22:3). Death entered (3:19). "No more death" (21:4). Tree of life forbidden (3:24). "Right to tree of life" (22:14). Sorrow and suffering enter (3:17-19). "No more sorrow or crying" (21:4). Marriage of first Adam to a physical woman built by God (2:18-24). Marriage of last Adam to a spiritual woman built by God (19:1-9). Nimrod builds Babylon (10:8-9). "Babylon ... is fallen" (18:2). The Euphrates River (of Eden) ran through the middle of ancient Babylon. The river of the Water of Life runs through the middle of New Jerusalem (22:1). Ancient Babylon had a multi-colored, 7-tiered, astrological tower in the shape of a pyramid zigguret where the wife of Bel dwelt in a throne room (Her. 1:98,178,181). New Jerusalem will have a multi-colored, 12-tiered, astronomical pyramid where the Lamb's wife will dwell in his throne room (21). Two angels visit Sodom (19). Two witnesses visit Babylon (spiritual Sodom) (11:1-12). Lot comes out of Sodom to escape plagues (19:15-17). Saints "come out of" Babylon to escape plagues (18:4). Etcetera.

These changes all become possible when we "put on immortality" (1 Cor. 15:53-54 taken from Isaiah 25:6-9 talking about Israel). Then "O death, where is thy sting" (1 Cor. 15:55 taken from Hosea 13:14 talking about Israel). By means of phylacteries, the Jews put the name Shaddai on their foreheads when they pray.

"And he said unto me, These sayings are faithful and true: and the Lord God of the holy prophets sent his angel to shew unto his servants the things which must shortly be done. Behold, I come quickly: blessed is he that keepeth the sayings of the prophecy of this book. And I John saw these things, and heard them. And when I had heard and seen, I fell down to worship before the feet of the angel which shewed me these things. Then saith he unto me, See thou do it not: for I am thy fellowservant, and of thy brethren the prophets, and of them which keep the sayings of this book: worship God. And he saith unto me, Seal not the sayings of the prophecy of this book: for the time is at hand. He that is unjust, let him be unjust still: and he which is filthy, let him be filthy still: and he that is righteous, let him be righteous still: and he that is holy, let him be holy still" (Rev. 22:6-11).

Daniel was told to "Shut up the words, and seal the book, even to the time of the end" (Dan. 12:4). John was told the opposite -- "Seal not." In other words, Explain it since the time of the end is here. But just as Daniel was told that "the wicked shall do wickedly: and none of the wicked shall understand" (Dan. 12:10), so also John is told to let the unjust remain that way. "Give not that which is holy unto the dogs, neither cast your pearls before swine, lest they trample them under their feet, and turn again and rend you" (Matt. 7:6). There comes a time in the life of men and nations when their fate is fixed. Ways become set and habits callously harden. We eventually become what our actions over time and habits make us. Punishment is then the only remedy.

"And, behold, I come quickly; and my reward is with me, to give every man according as his work shall be. I am Alpha and Omega, the beginning and the end, the first and the last. Blessed are they that do his commandments, that they may have right to the tree of life, and may enter in through the gates into the city. For without are dogs, and sorcerers, and whoremongers, and murderers, and idolaters, and whosoever loveth and maketh a lie" (Rev. 22:12-15).

We are saved by grace, but rewarded according to our works. Verse 13 is taken from Isaiah 44:6 which says, "Thus saith the Eternal, the king of Israel, and his Redeemer the Eternal of hosts; I am the first, and I am the last; and beside Me there is no God." (cp. Isaiah 41:4) Some translators claim that the original text of verse 14 reads "Blessed are they who wash their robes ..." similar to Rev. 7:14. But Eternal life requires more than merely accepting Christ as Savior. The very next verse prohibits four of the ten commandments -- murder, lying, idolatry and fornication -- showing that commandment-keeping is required to get into the city. "Dogs" is an Eastern term given for all unclean persons. In fact, the list in Rev. 21:8 has "abominable" while the list in Rev. 22:15 has "dogs" instead showing that the two are interchangeable. The other five terms are the same in both lists. Astronomically, Canis Major (Big Dog) and Canis Minor (Small Dog), as well as the alternate image of Leo as a Great Dog and Bootes' Canes Venatici (Hunting Dogs) are all outside "Cancer" (the Cattlefold) -- New Jerusalem.

"I Jesus have sent mine angel to testify unto you these things in the churches. I am the root and the offspring of David, and the bright and morning star" (Rev. 22:16).

Jesus has sent his faithful angel or messenger John to pass on the details of the whole wonderful vision. What is the "Morning Star"? In Chaldean astrology, the constellation Cassiopeia, also known as "Eratu -- "the woman with child" -- brought forth every 315 years a bright new star, her child. It makes an appearance for about 16 months and then disappears again. She was known as "the Queen of Joppa" the chief city of Palestine indicating to the Magi (Matt. 2:2) that the Jews had brought forth an heir to the throne.

"And the Spirit and the bride say, Come. And let him that heareth say, Come. And let him that is athirst come. And whosoever will, let him take the water of life freely. For I testify unto every man that heareth the words of the prophecy of this book, If any man shall add unto these things, God shall add unto him the plagues that are written in this book: And if any man shall take away from the words of the book of this prophecy, God shall take away his part out of the book of life, and out of the holy city, and from the things which are written in this book. He which testifieth these things saith, Surely I come quickly. Amen. Even so, come, Lord Jesus. The grace of our Lord Jesus Christ be with you all. Amen" (Rev. 22:17-21).

In Deuteronomy 4:2 and 12:32 God commanded Israel not to add to or diminish from the word he had spoken. Here in verse 19 is the same warning. Yet "Bulls" from the pope, the "Koran" by Mohammed, "the Book of Mormon," by Joseph Smith, "the Great Controversy" by Ellen G. White, "Science and Health" by Mary Baker Eddy and "Dianetics" by L. Ron Hubbard are just a few of the additions. We can agree with John who answered Jesus by saying "Even so, come, Lord Jesus."

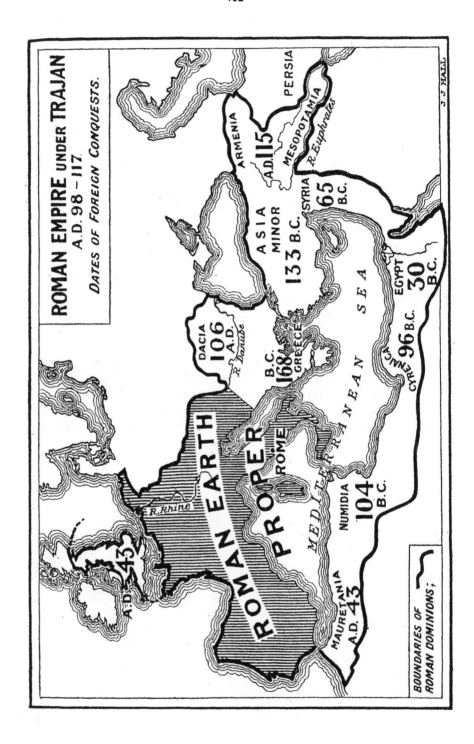

World History Foretold

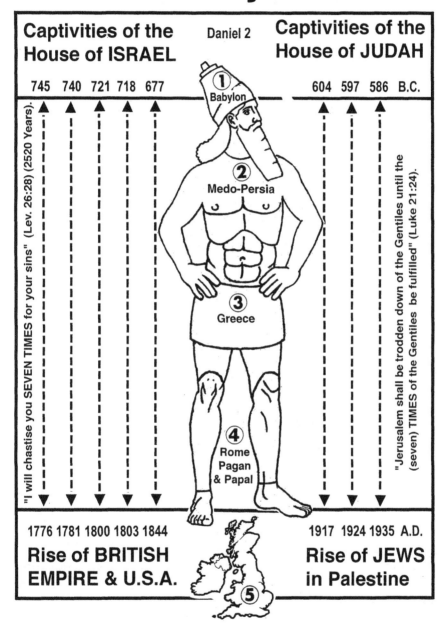

Captivities of the House of ISRAEL

Daniel 2

Captivities of the House of JUDAH

745   740   721 718   677

604   597   586   B.C.

"I will chastise you SEVEN TIMES for your sins" (Lev. 26:28) (2520 Years).

"Jerusalem shall be trodden down of the Gentiles until the (seven) TIMES of the Gentiles be fulfilled" (Luke 21:24).

① Babylon

② Medo-Persia

③ Greece

④ Rome Pagan & Papal

⑤

1776 1781 1800 1803 1844
Rise of BRITISH EMPIRE & U.S.A.

1917 1924 1935 A.D.
Rise of JEWS in Palestine

"A stone was cut out (of Europe) without hands, which smote the image upon its feet ... and the stone became a great mountain (kingdom -- Isa. 2:2), and filled the whole earth" (Dan. 2:34-35). This is the British Empire and the United States.

APPENDIX

Revelation 2: Read about the 10 persecutions by pagan Rome in Fox's Book of Martyrs, pp. 13-31." ¶ Pergamos fulfilled the "falling away" at the time the antichrist was revealed (2 Th. 2:3-7). ¶ God would "kill her children with DEATH" (2:23). This was the PLAGUE of the BLACK DEATH beginning in 1347. Pope Clement VI at Avignon estimated that over 23 million people died of the BLACK PLAGUE (see Deut. 28:21-22).

Revelation 3: Verse 17 illustrates that Laodiceans are "supposing that gain is godliness. From such withdraw thyself" (1 Tim. 6:5)

Revelation 4: The "SEA of GLASS" refers to the BRAZEN SEA before the throne of God in the temple. In this sea the priests were to wash themselves (Ex. 30:18-19) and victims (1 Ki. 7:23). ¶ Ezekiel saw 25 men serving in the Temple: representatives of the 24 courses of the priesthood plus the High Priest (Ez. 8:16).

Revelation 6: Gibbon 1:95 says, "If a man was called upon to fix the period in the history of the world, during which the condition of the human race was most PROSPEROUS and HAPPY, he would without hesitation name that which elapsed from the death of Domitian to the accession of Commodus" (96 to 180 A.D. -- the WHITE horse -- Pax Romana). Sismondi's Fall of the Roman Empire 1:36 describes 192 to 284 A.D. as "Ninety-two years of almost incessant civil warfare" (RED horse). A BLACK horse typifies famine because "Our skin was BLACK like an oven, because of the terrible FAMINE" (Lam. 5:10). People in a FAMINE "eat bread by weight and with care" (Ez. 4:16) -- hence WEIGH SCALES. Before the famine, a person could buy 15 to 20 measures for one penny. Now he could only get one measure for a penny. ¶ A medal of this fifth seal of martyrdom period (303 to 313 A.D.) portrays Maximian as Hercules destroying the seven-headed Hydra of Christianity.

Revelation 8: The historian Claudian compared the invasions by the Goths to a "HAILSTORM." Regarding the Goths, Gibbon says, "Blood and conflagration and the BURNING of TREES and HERBAGE mark their path." ¶ Gibbon relates that Attila was "king of the (Mongol) Huns" (3:391), hence a STAR. ¶ Gibbon says that ALL of Attila the Hun's major battles were fought on RIVERS. His strategy was to lure Roman armies into crossing the RIVERS after he had feigned a retreat. While the armies were crossing the RIVERS he ordered his troops to attack. Gibbon describes the time when Attila's horse bloodied its foot and upon retracing its steps, he found the point of a sword sticking out of the ground. Digging the sword out he declared it the Sword of MARS having been CAST DOWN from HEAVEN. He then claimed to be the Son of MARS. This fits the symbol of a STAR FALLING from HEAVEN into the rivers and making them bitter by turning them to blood. Romans knew nothing of the Hungarian nation before 440 A.D. About that time a warrior appeared suddenly, like a METEOR, upon the banks of the Danube RIVER, with 800,000 fighting men. They came from central Asia, marched north of the Euxine Sea through Russia, and crossed the RIVER Danube -- the boundary of the Roman Empire. They rushed west, crossed the RIVER Rhine, and on the RIVER Marne met Rome's forces in battle. Blood of the slaughtered made the river run red (from 150 to 300 thousand bodies lay dead). Then they desolated the RIVER Rhine to its mouth. Turning southward, on the banks of the RIVER Rhone, the armies met again in fury. Then on the banks of the RIVER Po, contending for Italy. Victorius, Attila marched south to seize the Imperial prize. Unable to contend longer, Rome sent a priestly deputation to ask him to depart. By rich bribes and by work on his superstition they succeeded, and he retired, made Buda, on the RIVER Danube, his capital, and founded the Hungarian nation. When he died, his followers turned the waters of the Danube from its course, buried him in its bed, and then let them return to flow over the grave of the hero. Beneath the RIVER Danube still lie the bones of the star called Wormwood, that fell upon the RIVERS. ¶ The fall of Rome in 476 A.D. caused the education, road-building, culture and commerce to fall into chaos for over a thousand years in the West. The "DARK AGES" got their name directly from Revelation 8:12 which describes the western third of the sun, moon and stars "DARKENED." ¶ The first four trumpets by the barbarians are covered in just six verses suggesting a SHORT time period. But the 5th and 6th trumpets occupy 21 verses indicating a much LONGER time period. ¶ The Roman world was divided into THREE PARTS for about 1000 years: "From the age of Charlemagne to that of the Crusades, the world was occupied and disputed by the THREE great EMPIRES, or nations of the Greeks, Saracens, and the Franks" (Gibbon, ch.53). "The THREE great NATIONS of the world, the

Greeks, the Saracens, and the Franks, encountered eachother on the plains of Italy" (ch. 56). "THREE CLASSES of men are conspicuous, the Saracens or Arabians, the Latins or Franks, inhabitants of Western Europe, and the Byzantine Greeks" (Phil. Inquiries, part III).

Revelation 9: 606 A.D. -- Mohammed formulated his religious doctrines in a cave. The leader of the Moslems was Abaddon (HEBREW) and Apollyon (GREEK) because he was the destroyer of both the Jews (HEBREWS) and Christians (GREEK ORTHODOX). Mohammed was literally a FALLEN STAR (ruler). He was a PRINCE by birth of the house of Koreish, the HEIR of the RULERS of Mecca who possessed the "keys of Caaba" symbolic of their rulership. But his grandfather and father dying while he was young, he was PUSHED ASIDE and became a SERVANT. ¶ Pliny's Natural History 7:28 speaks of "the turbaned Arabs with their UNCUT HAIR." ¶ Men who have rebelled against God are compared to "SCORPIONS" (Ez. 2:6). ¶ Muslim oppression of Christians whom they called "dogs" included prohibition of building new churches or ringing church bells, or the use of arms; an annual "life-redemption" tax, distinctive dress, the obligation to stand deferentially in presence of any Muslim and to admit any insulting Muslim to any church. Muslims offered strong inducement to apostasy with death penalty for return to Christianity. Christian women were also terribly abused. This is the SCORPION STING. But in 762 A.D., "War was no longer the passion of the Saracens" (Gibbon) and the Abaside Caliph began to construct a new capital east of the Euphrates called Baghdad. ¶ Rev. 9:7 "horses" are native to Arabia. ¶ The span of the truce granted to Richard "the Lion-Hearted" by Saladin (1187 A.D.) was for "three hours, three days, three weeks, three months, three years" all added together (Elliott 1:528-530). ¶ FOUR BRASS HORNS of the altar (Rev. 9) correspond to FOUR HORNS of the shaggy goat (Dan. 8) and the belly and thighs of BRASS (Dan.2). ¶ The prince commissioned by the Caliph to attack the GREEK Empire was named Togrul, but dying, his son, Alp Arslan, led the Turks across the Euphrates, and when he was slain in battle, he was succeeded by Malek Shah. Volume 5, page 532 of Gibbon says that Malek Shah's empire was divided into FOUR principalities, under his FOUR sons, which are described by the historian under the names of Persia, Kerman or India, Syria, and Roum or Asia Minor, extending from the shores of the Indian Ocean to the Mediterranean. These were the "FOUR angels." ¶ Gibbon mentions, "the MYRIADS of the Turkish horse overspreading the GREEK frontier" and "both men and horses, proudly compute by MILLIONS" (7:287, p.351). ¶ The Sultan Mahomet possessed 67 cannons. ¶ Muslim Turkish armies continued to enlarge their empire until the decisive sea battle of Lepanto in 1571.

Revelation 10: "The law of the Lord is ... sweeter also than honey" (Ps. 19:7-10).

Revelation 11: Pagan Romans besieged Jewish Jerusalem between 66.5 and 70 A.D. which was 1260 days. These gentiles treaded down the holy city for 42 months. The true church fled into the wilderness of Judea (Pella) from the face of the serpent (Titus) before 70 A.D. ¶ From the "Edict of Stephen," (254 A.D.) which asserted that the bishop of Rome was the Supreme Pontiff, to the "5th Laterine Council" of 1514 where the papacy proclaimed doctrtinal victory: "Jam nemo reclamat, nullus obsistit!" is 1260 years. ¶ Rome was anciently known as "the great city" (Rev. 11:8) according to Manilius, Lib iv (2.434, n.2) and is so called in six other passages (16:19; 17:18; 18:10,16,18,19,21) -- but Jerusalem also qualifies. ¶ In the Council of Tours (A.D. 1163), Pope Alexander III forbade giving refuge to the Albigensian "heretics," forbidding BUYING or SELLING, or otherwise communicating with them. In the 3rd Lateran Council A.D. 1179 Christian BURIAL was denied heretics and "no man should EXERCISE TRAFFIC with them." The same in the 4th Lateran Council A.D. 1215, and the Papal Decree of Gregory IX in 1227 A.D. and in Pope Martin's decree immediately after the Council of Constance in 1422 A.D., which Council ordered that Wycliff's body should be EXHUMED, and the ashes of Huss, INSTEAD OF BURIAL, be cast into Lake Constance. Savonarola's ashes were similarly cast into the Arno in 1498 A.D. In the first bull entrusted to the Cardinal Cajetan, against Luther, as well as that afterwards, one of the penalties was that both Luther and his partisans should be deprived of Christian BURIAL. ¶ "Seven THOUSANDS" should be translated "seven PROVINCES" because although originally it meant a NUMBER (Ex. 18:21,25), upon settlement in Canaan, it came to refer to the TERRITORY where each THOUSAND originally settled (Judges 6:15; 1 Sam. 10:19; Micah 5:2) irrespective of the population increase. ¶ Also, after the proclamation of the First French Republic in September 22, 1792, a new calendar was introduced. The day of the proclamation of the Republic was declared to be day one of the first month of the year one. November 24, 1793, all Christian churches in Paris were forcibly closed down, and the Christian religion was banned. The Christian

God was replaced by the goddess of "Reason" and later by a "Supreme Being." The hatred toward Christianity eventually died down, and in February 21, 1795, which was the beginning of the sixth month of the third Revolutionary Year, freedom of religion was restored by law. This was THREE-AND-A-HALF years the Old and New TESTAMENTS were "DEAD." Also, laws banning the Bible and religious exercise were passed by the Convention on November 24, 1793 under penalty of DEATH. Religious freedom came back early in 1797 when THREE-AND-A-HALF years after the official laws were passed against all religion, the revolutionary laws were abolished (Victor Duray, A Short History of France, E.P. Dutton, London, 1918, p.364). In the summer of 1797 Napoleon wrote, "Society cannot exist ... without religion. The people have to have a religion; this religion must be in the control of the government" (p.69, John McManners, ibid.) -- not controlled by the Papacy. Also in 1797 he wrote, "Our religious revolution is a failure" (John McManners; Lectures in European History, 1789-1914; Oxford, 1977, p.64). He decided not to export even the anti-clericalism, much less the atheism of the revolution to the nations he intended to reorganize. Napoleon was cynical about religion, but he saw the political necessity of supporting religion and the futility of suppressing it. ¶ The Older and Newer TESTAMENTS are the two WITNESSES because "TESTAMENT" means "to bear WITNESS." To TESTIFY. Also, Moses and Aaron in Egypt, Elijah and Elishah in Israel (2 Ki. 1:10; 1 Ki. 17:1; Ex. 7:17) "smite the earth with plagues" when in answer to their prayers vengeance comes (Luke 18:7-8).

Revelation 12: Actually 11:19 "opened in heaven" belongs in chapter 12 just as 4:1 "opened in heaven" began the first scroll. ¶ "CLOTHED with the SUN" means Christianity was "PRO-TECTED by the chief RULER." ¶ "He (the Lord) subdued nations under us, peoples UNDER OUR FEET" (Ps. 47:3). ¶ The red dragon waiting to devour the woman's son has several fulfillments: Egypt's PHARAOH is called a "dragon" (Ez. 29:8; Isa. 51:9) and tried to devour Israelite male children -- specifically MOSES (Ex. 1:16). But they were caught up to heaven (Exodus to PROMISED LAND). Rome is called a dragon and Rome's puppet-king was HEROD who slew all the children of Bethlehem. But the CHRIST CHILD was caught up to heaven (EGYPT). Again PILATE tried to kill CHRIST but he was caught up to heaven (resurrected to HEAVEN). MAXENTIUS tried to kill Constantine but he was caught up to heaven (ruler of Rome). ¶ In 312 Constantine left Britain and marched his armies through Gaul into Italy. Maxentius, a pagan Italian emperor was defeated in three great battles and in the last was slain and Constantine became ruler of Rome. In the East, another emperor, Licinius, a pagan and a persecutor, still held the reins of power. Wars, truces and battles followed, until in 324 A.D. he was crushed and put to death. In this sixteen-year conflict, six emperors in all strove for the pre-eminence, of whom Constantine remained the sole survivor. In 319 A.D., before his final triumph, he decreed that his mother's religion should be tolerated as an acknowledged faith of the empire. In 321 A.D. he decreed that Sunday, the sacred day of Christianity, should be observed in all the cities by cessation of trade and labor. In 325 A.D. he abolished the bloody gladiator combats, where men killed eachother to amuse the popu-lace, a Roman institution that had existed for a thousand years. In 331 A.D. he decreed that the pagan religion should no longer exist, and that all the heathen temples should be leveled, or converted into churches. Old Roman laws were remodeled according to Christianity also. In 324 A.D. he removed the capital from Italy (where the crown had been worn for eleven cen-turies) to a new city upon the banks of the hellespont -- called Constantinople after himself. The western mountain was "moved out of" its place (Rev. 12:6). ¶ The birth pains "as travail upon a woman with child" (1 Th. 5:3) begin the LABOR contractions which may be persecu-tion (Matt. 24:8; Isa. 13:8). "These things are the beginning of travail" (Matt. 24:7-8) until "born again" (John 3:3), composed of spirit this time (John 3:6). Jesus was the "firstborn among many brethren" (Rom. 8:29). From Daniel's "Seventy-Weeks Prophecy" ending in 34 A.D., we add a nine-month PREGNANCY (270 years) to come to the "BIRTH PANGS" of 303-313 A.D. when Diocletian persecuted Christians or 280 years to the "man child" Constantine himself. -- a type of the plan just before the real second coming of Christ. ¶ "When the enemy shall come in like a flood" (Isa. 59:19), the earth helped the woman (12:16). The Hussites protected themselves under Zisca by force of arms; the German princes protected Luther; the Edict of Nantes gave French Protestants a rest.

Revelation 13: The Roman Empire occupied the territory of Babylon (lion), Medo-Persia (bear), Greece (leopard) and new territory of its own (dragon). ¶ The religious image of the beast is more specifically the Pope. The Roman clergy, the cardinals, create the Pope; and in their own ceremonial and language -- quem creant, adorant -- "whom they create, they adore" like all other idolaters. Thus the Pope becomes the "man of sin, sitting in the temple of God, showing himself that he is God" (2 Th. 2:4). The Pope is the most perfect image of the Roman Emperor; claiming the same universal dominion, the same titles and prerogatives, in the same city. ¶ Jerusalem (Old and New) was/will be rebuilt after Babylon (and Rome) was/will be destroyed. ¶ When a man burned his pinch of incense to Caesar, he was given a certificate to say he had done so. The mark of the beast could have been this certificate of worship which a Christian obtained by denying his faith. ¶ "George Bush" has two Hes (ה=5) and two Ayins (ע=70) to equal 666. ¶ "We hold the place of Almighty God on earth" (Apostolic Letter of Pope Leo XIII, June 20, 1894). "I am the Way, the Truth, and the Life" (from a speech of Pope Pius IX, as attributed to himself and reported by Lord Acton in his Quirinus--Letters on the Council, p.285). "You know that I am the Holy Father, the representative of God on the earth, the Vicar of Christ, which means that I am God on the earth (Pope Pius XI in the Vatican throne room, April 30, 1922, as reported in The Bulwark [October, 1922] 104).

Revelation 16: Napoleon dismembered the Holy Roman Empire. Of the more than 380 states with direct allegiance to the Papacy only 30 survived after Napoleon and they had no further dependence on Papal authority. ¶ The infant American fleet by the close of 1800 had captured or sunk ninety French vessels, carrying more than 700 guns; and a great number of American vessels were retaken (from Emerson's Nineteenth Century Year by Year). Lord Bridgeport defeated the French and Dutch fleets at Cape Good Hope in 1795. See Revelation 16:3. ¶ Rev.16:14 is the first mention of "whole world" (entire globe) rather than just the Roman earth. The European wars have now become "WORLD" wars. Chinese Communism may be the "RED DRAGON" in a future fulfillment of the three frogs.¶ Feb. 15, 1798 the Pope was arrested, his ring signifying his office as husband of the Church removed from his finger, and he was carried off as a prisoner to France. ¶ For the first time in 1867, the kings of Europe were not invited by the Vatican to attend the Vatican I Council. ¶ It is noteworthy that while Danton was a young boy, he sucked on a cow's udder and was attacked by a bull whose horn curled his lip and disfigured his face permanently. Later his face was trampled by a herd of pigs. Still later he contracted smallpox. All of these experiences disfigured his face and he said, "My ugliness is my strength."

Revelation 17: The first six forms of Roman government are mentioned by both Livy in his History, book 1:60; 3:33; 4:7 and 6:1 (59 B.C. till 17 A.D.) and Tacitus Annals 1:1 (56 A.D.-118 A.D.). Neither lived to see the seventh (Despotic Emperors) or eighth (Papacy). ¶ The "cup" alludes to the practice of harlots giving love-potions to their paramours, very expressive of the indulgences, absolutions, preferments, etcetera by which Catholicism attracts disciples to her idolatry. This harlot is finally burnt because Leviticus 21:9 says the daughter of a priest who plays the harlot should be burned with fire. ¶ "Your eminence" means "Mountain" and was a title of princes which agrees with the symbolism of mountains.¶ From 538 (Justinian's law enforced) to 1798 A.D. (Napoleon had the Pope arrested and put in jail) is 1260 years; from 610 (death of Emperor Phocas) to 1870 A.D. (Papal France overthrown by Prussia -- Sept. 19) (rise of United Italy Oct. 1870; rise of Protestant Germany Jan. 28, 1871) is 1260 years.

Revelation 19: Modern COMMUNISM actually began with the French Revolution and "Jacobinism." From 607 A.D. till 1848 A.D. when Marx wrote the COMMUNIST Manifesto and the resulting European Revolutions that same year was 1260 prophetic years (1241.88 solar). This is when Babylon's "Euphrates" began to "dry up" or the riches and commodities became less plentiful, preparing the way for COMMUNISM of the "kings of the East" to conquer Catholic Europe (Babylon). Perhaps this is why the dragon is "RED." The European Common Market is SOCIALIST and hostile to the Vatican that rides it. ¶ Who is the "false prophet"? Perhaps MOHAMMED is the "false prophet." The PAPACY used the advance of ISLAM for centuries to DECEPTIVELY maintain the need for gathering armies to fight the Crusades. After the Fall of Constantinople in 1453, the PAPACY continued using Turkish ISLAM for at least 200 years more as the reason for maintaining PAPAL lands, armies and allies. Thus "the false prophet with which he (the beast) DECEIVED them" makes sense (Rev. 19:20). Also in 16:13 we find that the beast and false prophet are ALLIES. This occurred in World War One when Turkey (MOSLEM) and Germany (CATHOLIC) fought on the same side. ¶ "He shall smite the earth with the rod of his mouth, and with the breath of His lips shall he slay the wicked" (Isa. 11:4).

Amazing Bible Research Available

1.) <u>Are The FOOD LAWS Scientific</u>? A 42-page booklet explaining from the Bible which plants are edible; why blood and fat are forbidden; why cloven-hooved ruminants and fish with fins and scales are edible; the rule for birds and fowl; all about grasshoppers and much more. Illustrated...$4.00

2.) <u>Were The FEAST DAYS Abolished</u>? A 55-page booklet proving that Jesus and Paul celebrated the feasts. Were the festivals commanded "forever"? Sinai-Pentecost proven. Counterfeit festivals exposed. Proof that every major event in the Old Testament occurred on a festival. Is Rosh HaShanah the day when Christians are resurrected and judged? Is Yom Kippur when Messiah will return? Illustrated...$5.00

3.) <u>Should Christians TITHE</u>? A 30-page booklet proving three separate tithes from biblical and secular sources; the cycle of Sabbatical years; the "carnal commandment," and proof that both Christ and Paul tithed. Illustrated....... $3.00

4.) <u>What Does It Mean To "TURN THE OTHER CHEEK"</u>? A 14-page booklet revealing the Bible's own interpretation of Christ's words. Is "an eye for an eye" really abolished? Is self-defense biblical? $2.00

5.) <u>Which Day Is The SABBATH</u>? A 74-page booklet addressing many of the issues facing Sabbath-keepers. What is the mark of the beast? What does it mean to ride on the high places of the earth? Do humans have a weekly rhythm? Is it wrong to burn wood on the Sabbath (Ex.35:3)? Nehemiah said don't "carry forth a burden" but Jesus said do "carry thy bed"? Are we allowed to take a bath or prepare food? Should there be a torah-reading or sermon preaching? Illustrated...$4.00

6.) <u>What's Wrong With SEX</u>? A 136-page booklet discussing such topics as why Abraham and Jacob practiced polygamy; the scientific reason for being circumcised the eighth day, and whether Lot offered his daughters to homosexuals or not. Is abortion murder? What precautions did Moses take against venereal disease? Why avoid sexual intercourse during menstruation? Is the presence of a hymen proof of virginity? Under what conditions did Christ allow divorce? Illustrated.. $5.00

7.) <u>What's Wrong With The CALENDAR</u>? A 71-page booklet defining the biblical day on the north or south pole. Isn't the International Date Line in the wrong place? Did Joshua's long day destroy the weekly cycle? Was there ever a Saturn-like ring around the earth? When did the four seasons begin? Should we use the visible crescent or the lunar conjunction; local sightings or Jerusalem? How do we calculate the monthly date line? Should we use "green ears" or the equinox; how do we calculate festivals from scratch using the almanac? Illustrated...$4.00

8.) <u>The United States and the British Empire FORETOLD in the Bible</u>? A 113-page booklet. Did the Saxons come from Isaac's sons? Are the Jutes descendants of Judah? Were the Danes members of the tribe of Dan? Is Hibernia the home of Hebrews? Proof from language, history, archaeology, geneology, heraldry and prophecy. Did Jesus visit Britain? Was the American Revolution of 1776 predicted long ago? Is the Panama Canal mentioned in the Bible? Illustrated..$4.00

9.) Do The PURITY LAWS Prevent Sickness? A 35-page booklet asking such questions as "Is the germ theory found in the Bible? Was circumcision abolished (Gal 5:2)? Why forbid sexual intercourse during menstruation (Lev. 18:19)? Did Quarantine come from the Bible (Lev. 13:46)? Is toxic mold the leprosy of the house (Lev. 14:34)? What precautions did Moses take against venereal disease? Why immerse in a pool of water after contact with a leper, menstruant, corpse, idol, manure, childbirth or pig? Illustrated..$3.00

10.) Was Jesus a HILLELITE Pharisee? A 21-page booklet refuting the claim that the New Testament is anti-Semitic. Why did Jesus call the Pharisees "snakes, murderers and hypocrites" (Matt.23)? Why did he call the Jews "children of the Devil" (John 8:44) and label their gathering places "synagogues of Satan" (Rev. 2:9; 3:9)? Why did Paul say they "killed the Lord Jesus and their own prophets and have persecuted us; and they please not God, and are contrary to all men" (1 Th.2:15)? Could it be that both Jesus and Paul were Hillel Pharisees in the midst of Shammai Pharisees?.. $2.00

12.) The Feasts of the Bible A 107-page booklet answering such questions as: Why do Jews use a shankbone at Passover when the Bible commands lamb? Should we use wine or grape juice at the seder? Is Passover the 14th or 15th of Abib? What is the definition of leaven? Is Pentecost Sivan 6 or Sunday? Why celebrate two days of Rosh HaShanah when the Bible says only one? Should we blow a ram's horn if we can't see the crescent? What does "afflict your souls" mean on Yom Kippur? Should we wave the palm branches or build sukkahs with them? Why take down the sukkah on the eighth day? What does it all mean? Illustrated. $7.00

13.) The Amazing HISTORY of the World's RACES A 140-page booklet by Henry Anderson including many illustrations, charts and a world map. Where did Noah's grandsons migrate (Gen. 10)? What did they look like? Who are they today? Did CUSH settle in India? PUT in Africa? Did GOMER give his name to the Khmer Empire of Cambodia? Did MAGOG become Mongolia? MADAI the Medes in the Ukraine? JAVAN Japan? TUBAL Tobolsk? MESHECH Moscow? TIRAS the "red" Thracians and Etruscans (American Indians)? ELAM the Persians in Yugoslavia and Prussians in Poland? ASSHUR Assyria or Austria and Germany? LUD Albania? ARAM America and Kurdistan? Is ARPACHSHAD the Chaldeans in Italy (Rev.17:5)? Is ISHMAEL the Arabs? LABAN the Lebanese? EDOM the Ottoman Empire? Is KETURAH the Brahmins (Abraham's) and northern Germans? Are ISAAC'S SONS the Saxons? Much more also...$9.00

14.) What's Wrong With CHRISTMAS? A 16-page booklet. Why decorate evergreen trees on the winter solstice? Why kiss under mistletoe? Where did "jolly old Saint Nick" come from and why should we lie to our children about him? Isn't it idolatry to sing "O Tannenbaum" and give presents to a tree? Are halos and wreathes merely images of sun-worship? Is Santa just another name for Satan? When was Jesus born? Who is the "Fool King" or "Lord of Misrule"? Did the Babylon Mystery Religion worship a "mother & child"? Illustrated.. $3.00

15.) What's Wrong With EASTER? A 15-page booklet. What do Colored EASTER EGGS have to do with the resurrection? What do bunny RABBITS have to do with the cru- cifixion? Where did the custom of eating HOT CROSS BUNS come from? Why attend an EASTER SUNRISE service? Why observe 40 days of abstinence called LENT? What's so "good" about "GOOD FRIDAY"? How do we get "three days" between "GOOD FRIDAY" and "EASTER SUNDAY"? Did early Christians celebrate Easter or Passover? Illustrated..$3.00

16.) What's Wrong With The ROMAN CATHOLIC Church? A 32-page booklet. Why pray to Mary and to dead saints (Deut. 18:10-12) when the Bible teaches us to pray to God (Matt. 6:9; Luke 18:1-7)? Why confess our sins to a priest when scripture teaches that we can confess our sins to God for forgiveness (1 John 1:9) and to one another (James 5:16)? Is Mary the "queen of heaven" or a "perpetual virgin" or the "co-redemptress" or "another mediator" between God and man (Acts 4:12; 1 Tim. 2:5)? Do the bread and wine actually change into Christ's body and blood at the Eucharist or was he sacrificed only "once" (Heb. 9:25-28)? Do Papal decrees nullify scripture? Do Catholics worship "graven images" (Ex. 20:4)? Should the priesthood be celibate or married (1 Cor. 9:5; 1 Tim. 4:3)? Is "freedom of religion" merely "liberty to err" as the Pope says? What does the number 666 mean? Who is the anti-Christ? Who is the "Little Horn" of Daniel? Who is the "Scarlet Harlot of Babylon"? Who is the Two-Horned Lamb Dragon? Illustrated... $4.00

17.) EUROPEAN HISTORY Foretold (volumes 1 & 2). A total of 187-pages in two volumes. This is a historical commentary on the Book of Revelation demonstrat- ing the amazing accuracy of John's ancient prophecies. Many illustrations and diagrams. Who are the two witnesses? What is the mark of the beast? What does the number 666 refer to? Does the Apocalypse mention Constantine's conversion to Christ? Attila the Hun? Mohammed and Islam's rise? Martin Luther's Reformation? Queen Elizabeth and the Spanish Armada? Napoleon Bonaparte and the French Revolution? Adolf Hitler and World War Two? What do the seals, trumpets, and cups mean? Who is the woman who sits on seven hills? Who are the three frogs? Who is the beast with seven heads and ten horns? Did God predict the rise of the United States? Illustrated...$19.00

Circle the books or items you want and return this price list along with a check or money order payable to "Harold Hemenway." Make sure to include your complete name and address below. Add 10% postage and handling for any size order. Write to: Harold Hemenway, Box 88401, Tukwila, Washington, 98138, U.S.A. Quantity discounts on all booklets. For 10 or more of any combination of booklets, de- duct 10% from the total before shipping. For 50 or more of any combination of booklets, deduct 20% from the total before shipping. For 100 or more, deduct 30%. Visit our web site at www.british-israel.us for many rare, hard-to-find books.

CPSIA information can be obtained
at www.ICGtesting.com
Printed in the USA
BVHW080109280620
582384BV00002B/275

9 781602 667969